Disappear

Talitha Stevenson

virago

VIRAGO

First published in Great Britain in 2010 by Virago Press
Copyright © 2010 Talitha Stevenson

A CIP catalogue record for this book
is available from the British Library.

ISBN 978-1-84408-266-7

Typeset in Bembo
by Palimpsest Book Production Limited,
Grangemouth, Stirlingshire

Printed and bound in Great Britain by Clays Ltd, St Ives plc

Papers used by Virago are natural, renewable and recyclable
products sourced from well-managed forests and certified
in accordance with the rules of the Forest Stewardship Council.

Mixed Sources
Product group from well-managed
forests and other controlled sources
www.fsc.org Cert no. SGS-COC-004081
© 1996 Forest Stewardship Council
FSC

Virago Press
An imprint of
Little, Brown Book Group
100 Victoria Embankment
London EC4Y 0DY

An Hachette UK Company
www.hachette.co.uk

www.virago.co.uk

For my big sisters, Cara and Heni

Perfect love means to love the one through whom one became unhappy.
Søren Kierkegaard

Sometimes with one I love, I fill myself with rage, for fear I effuse un-return'd love;
But now I think there is no unreturn'd love — the pay is certain, one way or another.
(I loved a certain person ardently and my love was not return'd,
Yet out of that, I have written these songs.)
Walt Whitman

Chapter 1

Outside in the street Leila heard the taxi move off, then the front door closed and then in came Charlie with his case. She had known she was pregnant for a week and a half and had not yet told him.

'Surprise,' he said, tossing a newspaper across the kitchen.

She caught it and smoothed out the page.

'It's you!' She did him a big smile. 'Why didn't you tell me?'

When she looked up he was humming, cigarette in mouth, opening a bottle of gin. Beside him was a stack of boxes and he reached into one of them for a glass. It was covered in dust and he wiped it off roughly on the arm of his shirt leaving a large smudge.

'If you want to know what I really look forward to,' he went on, 'it's seeing how the Old Bastard avoids mentioning this one. Don't you think?' Leila flipped a long brown plait on to her shoulder and examined the end. 'I mean it's his fucking daily. It gets dropped on the man's doormat every morning.'

She watched him slice the lemon and pour in the tonic. The ice dropped in with a loud fizz. He tasted it, closing his eyes. Then he squeezed in a little more lemon.

None of his friends would have guessed how meticulous Charlie could be in private. To them he would always be wild, aged seventeen, radiant with his expulsion from school.

'Well you ought to be very pleased with yourself,' Leila told him, flattening her hand on the paper. 'It says here "Bell–Sanders is one of the most promising new hedge funds in the country." It's *wonderful*, Charlie.'

'Mmm? Oh, it's pretty embarrassing, really.'

She smiled, knowing him.

'Yes, but in a nice way.'

At Charlie's feet was a suitcase. After squinting at it for a few seconds he gave it a kick. It had been a boring week of meetings in Geneva. It was all right when his business partner Hugo was there, because they overate in grand style together, they talked strategy, they bitched about their rivals over drinks. But Hugo had gone back on Tuesday and there had been three days alone.

Normally he would have gone back himself and left Hugo to deal with it all, but they were trying to raise more funds. As usual, they were trying to raise a large amount in a short space of time. An audacious amount, as his father would probably say. So on this occasion it had been best for Charlie himself to sit it out in front of the blank, tax-haven faces, the glum front-men for the various 'high net worth individuals' they were trying to squeeze for cash.

Geneva, Charlie thought. What was there to say? There was a lake. There were people on bicycles. And Swiss inter-trust directors were not the most exciting prospect either. He blew out a long jet of smoke.

All in all it had been the least enjoyable trip so far, which was crazy when in many ways it was the one all the others had led up to. Banks – big banks – were prepared to gamble on him. It was exciting; they believed him, they took him seriously. It was what he'd always wanted.

Even so, he thought, it was good to be back in London.

He levered himself up on to the kitchen sideboard and began to stretch. First he rotated his shoulders, then he tilted his neck from side to side and lastly he raised his broad arms over his head and lengthened them all the way out. It was a little routine his old tennis coach had taught him at school and it never failed to make him feel better. He gave a large yawn.

From the opposite corner of the kitchen, Leila observed him. Just then he looked almost aggressively healthy: white-toothed, olive-skinned, bright-eyed. He swung his legs and took a drag on his cigarette.

Then he put down his glass.

'Hang on,' he said, drawing his eyebrows together. 'Have I gone mad? Is this room completely different? Or . . . or am I remembering somewhere else?' For a moment his face was childlike and she found this oddly disturbing. She flinched at the sight of it. Then his expression changed to one of accusation and her hands shot up to her mouth.

Was it possible, she thought? In the chaos of the past week or so, had it really slipped her mind to tell him the whole kitchen was being redone? But even as she asked herself this she knew that it had. It had been a relief to absorb herself in practical details, in painting cupboard doors and choosing door handles. But not to mention it to him was downright crazy. He would be furious. He was furious. She bit her lip, unable to meet his eyes again.

The sight of his confusion was all too familiar anyway. They had made full use of the housing boom in London. All in all, they had moved house seven times in five years and there were regularly such flashes, when they forgot where they were. Just for a second or two. They chucked their keys at a hall table, only to see them whiz through a doorway instead. It was a kind of primal fear.

'I thought I was being clever getting it finished while you were away,' she said.

She could feel him staring at her, thinking she had been even more absent-minded than usual, that there was obviously something wrong.

She would have to say it now, she thought. Now. But when finally she willed herself to meet his eyes, the dread vanished. Her mind became curiously light and in one vivid moment, half of which was taken up by thought and half by a pulse of energy in her limbs, it struck her that she could always just run out into the street. She could always run away. People did – all the time. Her heart began to beat faster. She repressed a strange desire to laugh. Her hand went into her pocket: a ten-pound note, maybe a twenty. She pinched it between her fingers. A cab might pass, she thought. He would be a figure in the rear window, on the steps. Five years of marriage reduced to a snapshot.

'Seriously,' said Charlie, 'I don't get you sometimes, Leila. I mean we spoke every day – sometimes twice. Wasn't the drilling a bit of a reminder? The hammering? You could have bloody mentioned it.'

But it was no good – she couldn't move. Sometimes it was as if she had no will of her own; as if she was nothing more than an idea in Charlie's mind. Her fingers let go of the money. Her head hung.

'I thought I had mentioned it,' she said.

He frowned and took a deep breath. She seemed appalled, he noticed – terrified even. He felt sorry for her.

'Oh, never mind, never mind. We won't argue.'

'No.'

His feet began to swing to and fro, tapping against the cupboard again and it occurred to her that they wouldn't argue because they never ever did.

In a different frame of mind already, Charlie ran his fingers over the new glass-covered sideboard, appreciating it. He liked the way the sunshine fell in a rectangle across the floor and how everywhere you turned, the glass panels gave off a reflection of the world outside the windows. Such effects were Leila's trademark: she found space; she found light out of nowhere.

'Well, you've done a good job with the design,' he said. 'It's twice the size. We'll get that twat in from Tenterton Blake obviously,' he went on, 'but I can tell for myself you've added value. Be rather interesting to see how much.' He rubbed his hands together and laughed, then he stopped himself abruptly – 'I mean . . . not that we're certain we bought to sell.'

He noticed the dust on his sleeve. They hadn't yet talked about selling this place. All the others had been investments – all part of the frenzy of the setting-up days when they'd done anything to raise cash for his fund. But they didn't need the extra money any more. In truth they hadn't needed it for a while and the last two moves had been unnecessary. Maybe even the last three.

Charlie undid his cufflinks. Then he rolled up his sleeves.

'So,' he said brightly, 'was it only design this time or were you hauling and hammering too?' He grinned at her but their eye contact was brief. They both knew he had always been uncomfortable with her working alongside their builders – being friends with them. John had bought her a set of overalls for her birthday. It was true that in the early days they'd never have got the flats redone so fast if she hadn't done the decorating and been there to keep an eye on everyone – but it wasn't exactly something he told his friends now.

'Bit of painting,' she said, 'and the tiles.' She made an awkward hand gesture.

But he did not really hear her anyway. He nodded and poured himself some more gin. The large street-facing window was open and it was just possible to hear the traffic on the high street. The evenings were getting warmer and the air would soon have the fumey thickness of a city in midsummer. He listened: cars passed; buses passed. Just beneath the window a series of bikes ran over a loose paving stone. One, two, three, four, he counted. He pictured them: boys – gangly secrets beneath their hoods, hunched over tiny BMX's. They were everywhere these days: weaving through the

4

traffic, jumping the lights, a new species; cartoon characters who couldn't die.

Glancing into the hallway, he picked out the scrawl on a cardboard box: *Side table + assorted bits.* Did they own a side table? It seemed unlikely. Assorted bits had a ring of truth to it.

Leila studied him, her long fingers turning her rings.

'So, what time are we invited to Hugo's for?' she said at last.

Charlie wrinkled his nose.

'I doubt he'll be handing round the hors d'oeuvres. This is Hugo we're talking about – he'll be wrecked. Doubly so on his birthday. Let's go now-ish though, before he's incoherent. Also I want to see Gavin.'

'Gavin? Is Gavin back?' Her face brightened. 'I'll run upstairs and get Hugo's present then.'

'His present? I was planning on grabbing him some booze on the way – couple of bottles of that filthy single malt he likes or something. But you've got him a present.' Why was it that even her kindness could irritate him sometimes? 'Great, we won't have to stop. I shall sit back and have another fag.'

The thought of whatever she had got for Hugo appeared to have brought Leila back to life. She clapped her hands and rushed out of the room. 'I hope you like it – it's highly original!'

'I'd expect nothing less,' he called back.

Soon her footsteps creaked on the floor above. It was not, strictly speaking, a flat. It was a maisonette. But there was only a bedroom and a bathroom upstairs. The bedroom had a double mattress on the floor.

Charlie clicked the joints of his fingers. Then he hopped down off the sideboard and went over to the newspaper. 'Young British Whiz-Kids' was the title. He swirled his ice and took a swig. It *was* almost embarrassing, really – the Bell-Sanders hedge fund was at least ten times bigger than any of the other businesses. There were two girls who imported hats, for fuck's sake.

The photo took up most of the left-hand page. It was a close-up: a large window with a view of skyscrapers and Charlie in front of it in his blue shirt. None of the others were pictured. Not even Hugo. Would he be pissed off? No, Charlie thought, he was used to it. And anyway, who could mistake the fact that Hugo, of all people, was only in it for the money?

There was creaking on the floor above, then hurried footsteps on

the stairs and then Leila came back in. She had unplaited her hair
and it fell in loose brown waves around her face. Her eyes, which
could vary in colour, were just then a piercing light grey against the
whiteness of her skin. She was slightly out of breath. For the first time
since coming in he noticed her appearance. She was wearing a very
plain white cotton dress.

Couldn't she ever be just a little more glamorous? he thought. His
mother, Daria, often mentioned this and he saw what she meant. Even
those dreadful boots – and no jewellery. Nothing. Why did she insist
on ignoring the stuff his parents had given her? There were the pearls,
the gold bracelets, and that beautiful necklace with the sapphires or
whatever they were. It was jewellery Leila ought to have been proud
to wear – just as his mother had been proud to wear it. Why was she
not proud to wear it?

At last, feeling thoroughly annoyed again, his eyes rested on the
object in her arms.

'Fuck me,' he said, 'what the hell is that?'

It was a large glass box with a paper cover sitting over it. With a
lot of rustling she heaved it on to the sideboard.

'Ready?'

'Come *on*, Leila. *Yes*.' With a magician's flourish she drew off the
cover. 'Oh,' he said. 'It's a pot plant.'

'What? It's not! It isn't a *pot plant*. It's a bonsai; it's a Flowering
Quince Tree – exactly like a real one, only miniature. They trim the
branches back for years and years to make them grow like this; it's
like a living sculpture. There's a whole art form. It's amazing when
you hear about it.'

'I'm sure.'

'Well, it is. But you have to hear about it from someone who knows
– not just me.'

Charlie couldn't help giggling at her expression. Leila got worked
up about the weirdest things.

'Babe, if you don't mind me asking, what exactly is Hugo Sanders
supposed to do with a bonsai peach tree? He's been known to sleep
in his suit. He gets ketchup on his tie. He eats takeaway curry for
breakfast.'

She felt a great surge of indignation, which made her blush deeply
and turn her back. Almost immediately this gave way to embarrassment
and then to fear. Charlie was right: it was a crazy present to have chosen
for Hugo.

6

As if the very existence of the tree was now in question she ran her fingers over the leaves. 'I'm an idiot,' she said. She had paid too much for it, too.

She shoved the pot away a little, scared she was about to cry.

Behind her, Charlie locked the window. He was humming again. He walked over and stood in the doorway to check the other windows were shut. Briefly it struck him that he was used to Leila making supernatural guesses about what people wanted as presents. She was the only person who could perform the miracle of choosing something to please his mother. Still, he thought, it couldn't have mattered less about Hugo.

All the windows were safely locked and Charlie inhaled contentedly. Geneva was over and done with, there was a good party to go to that night and it was not so bad to think that his friends would all have seen an article about him in the paper. Perhaps even Gavin would have seen it, he thought.

During the last few minutes, late evening sunshine had filled the room. The last memories of the business trip now left Charlie's mind. He thought of something his father had once said. In one of their bigger showdowns, Gideon had told him that recklessness sprang from an inability to see how lucky one was. Charlie could not have disagreed more strongly, then or now. At school he had hurled himself at the ball, scaled walls, seduced the cleaning girls, smoked joints behind the science labs, precisely *because* he knew his own luck. He had always gloried in it.

And it was in just the same spirit that over the past three years he had risked more than anyone knew – his father, Leila, even Hugo – and now here he was, winning. Just because his father's way had been dogged will and conservatism had never meant it ought to be his. He took risks and the world responded.

Not bad for a no-good waster, he thought. Not bad for a shameless drop-out.

Just then he would have liked to shout into the sunny room, so large was the sensation of life in his arms and legs. The world was too still sometimes for Charlie, too like the placid surface of a lake just begging him to skip a stone across it.

He flicked off the light.

'Come on then, dreamboat,' he said. 'We'll stop for that booze on the way.'

7

Chapter 2

Hugo's flat was on the top floor of a glassy conversion near the Albert Bridge. By the time Charlie and Leila arrived the party was going strong. The door to the flat itself had been left swinging open on to the corridor and they went straight in. The place was unrecognisable. There must have been over a hundred balloons, all in different shades of green, in various sizes. Some were filled with air, some with helium so that they bobbed along the floor or drifted about at eye level, trailing their shiny strings. Pine-scented candles burnt along the bookshelves and garlands of leaves and fairy lights looped on the walls.

Charlie laughed with delight.

'It's insane,' he said. 'Who the hell's done all this?'

He ducked to avoid an oncoming balloon. The air was full of them, their mute presence making the room seem even more crowded than it was. Half object, half person, they bounced up like old friends or insinuated themselves with obscure purpose. Every so often one of them met with a spiked heel or a lit cigarette and there was a bang followed by screams of laughter.

'It was Zoë,' said Leila.

'Zoë. The one with the laugh? I thought they just split up.'

'They have. She'd been working it all out with a party designer for weeks. It was meant to be his birthday present: "A Midsummer Night's Dream". It was all paid for I suppose, so they just came and did it without her.'

The music was very loud. Making his way towards them through the crowd was a tall, thin man. Charlie raised his arm. They smiled at each other.

'Hello, you two,' said Gavin. He kissed Leila warmly, then hugged Charlie.

With his way of gently towering and surveying, Gavin always reminded Leila of a heron on a riverbank. He was not broad like Charlie, but except for a slightly pigeon chest, which had been the main reason he was bullied at school, he was well built. He had brown eyes and fine blondish hair, which was now in its usual mess.

Behind him came a slim young man in his mid-twenties carrying two bottles of beer. No one could ever believe it, but this was Hugo's younger brother, Sam.

Sam nodded hello to the others. Then he handed Gavin a beer and in a sort of half whisper, he said, 'Yes, but for the record, that's what I was actually saying, Gavin, OK? What we need is an alternative to theatre like that.'

But there was no response. Of course not, Sam thought, he's seen Charlie. He lit a cigarette.

'So . . . *Young British Whiz-Kid?*' said Gavin, relishing the phrase and turning it into one of his half questions. 'Did you know Hugo's got your mugshot stuck on his fridge? *Very* regal these days, aren't we? I've just finished doing you a nice bushy moustache.'

Charlie laughed. Leila always loved seeing them together. Most people found it hard to imagine how they'd become friends at school: the sporty, rebellious Charlie Bell, and Gavin Blackdale, head scholar, prized for his translations of Ovid.

He put his hand on Leila's shoulder.

'Are you well too, gorgeous lady?'

'Nothing like as well as you.'

'The heroic tan? I'm afraid a lot of it is really filth. It was flog all the way from Heathrow to my grotty bit of London to change – or come straight here for a drink. I thought since we're all old friends . . .'

Leila squeezed his fingers.

'You *promised* you were only going for two weeks.'

'It was only a month. Have you been bored? Hasn't *any*thing happened since I left?'

'Nothing at all.'

'Except him and Hugo making even more money, of course.'

'Except that.' She smiled. 'So how was it? How was *Ephesus?*'

His face transformed.

'Leila, it was archaeology paradise; it was digging in sandpits *heaven*.

9

It was such a blast I was furious I had to sleep or eat or look up when someone asked me a question.'

'Bits of old crockery again, was it?'

'Yes, Charlie,' sighed Gavin. 'Only we didn't only find bits of old crockery this time. This time we found a bit of *mosaic*.'

Leila pressed her hands against her cheeks. 'You didn't!'

'Fragment – only a fragment, but yup, there it was. A woman's face. I mean, eyes almost as beautiful as yours, Leila, thousands of years old . . . and yet there they are. *Bang*: a human identity, exploding out of the past. I don't know why,' he glanced down for a second, 'but it's enough to make me believe in God. Oh, briefly anyway, then it's lunch or something.'

Sam gave a low whistle.

'Crikey,' he said, 'you want to watch it, Gav. Perhaps it really is in the genes. You might be about to *un-lapse*.'

Gavin did mock horror, then he laughed and took a gulp of beer.

'Oh, Sam. I don't know. But then I don't know anything.' He inhaled deeply, expanding his chest. 'But archaeologists can be as uncertain as they like. Playwrights, too. Not exactly an immediate danger to anyone, is it? Now, Charlie on the other hand – he's the one out to make things happen round here; he's the one with his fingers in the *futures and options*, whatever those electrifying words actually mean. Scary, really: it genuinely matters what his principles are.'

Sam felt his face going red. Charlie reached out for Gavin's beer and took a long swig.

There was a DJ in charge of the music now. Something came on that got a few cheers and a group began to dance by the bookshelves. Then quite suddenly a girl in a gold dress burst two balloons at once and a small dog came scampering and barking across the floor.

'Christ. What is that?' said Charlie.

'Boo-Boo,' said Sam. He straightened up. 'It belongs to Hugo's ex-girlfriend. I'm looking after it till Tuesday.'

Gavin faced him in surprise.

'"Ex"? Oh no, why? I liked Zoë.'

'You about to un-lapse?' said Charlie.

Sam looked away.

'No,' Gavin laughed. 'It had nothing whatsoever to do with her enormous bosoms; though you'll appreciate I did notice them. No,

I liked Zoë because . . . because she thought everything was funny, I suppose – which of course it is. But Hugo liked her too, didn't he? I don't understand.'

'Yes, he did like her,' said Sam, 'but that's his problem. He's tortured, agonised, always thinks he's got better options waiting out there in the bushes. *Futures and options,*' he said bitterly, pleased with this formulation. 'It's a cultural pathology, of course, but my brother's really made it his own.'

Charlie raised his eyebrows.

'Remind me, Sam,' he said, 'how long has Hugo been putting you up for?'

'As I think I've told you before,' Sam replied, 'it's just while I finish my play.'

Gavin brought his hands together in a loud clap.

'Right. Well, I reckon it's time to drag the young whiz-kid off in search of a drink. His *own* drink.'

'Good idea,' said Leila, returning his look.

'Not coming?'

'No. I'll say hello to a few people. And you don't want girls anyway, you know you don't.'

They wandered away together in the direction of the roof terrace, already absorbed in their world of old stories. Leila stood still, her fingers twisting her rings, her face pale and tense.

It had been years since she had made a decision. She was beginning to doubt she had ever made one at all. When she looked back at her life it seemed to be a long fall, with the occasional snagging branch on the way. Everything seemed to have happened by chance. She saw herself and Charlie at the altar, still tipsy from the night before, trying not to catch each other's eye in case they laughed. She saw the church crammed with Daria's flowers, with Gideon's business associates. They had barely known anyone there.

Her head was spinning. She needed to sit down.

'Leila? Are you all right?'

'Oh! Yes – yes, I'm sorry, Sam.'

'Forgot I was here.'

'Of *course* not. Don't be silly. No, I'm just . . . just feeling a bit dizzy. Late night. Hangover. I might go out to the stairs.'

None of the other girls could have worn a dress that simple, he thought.

'The stairs? Don't sit on the stairs. Look, if you some want peace and quiet, there won't be anyone in my room. I lock it. The key's above the doorframe.'

She smiled at him.

'Sam, that's really — thanks. Thank you.'

'My pleasure.'

She bit her lip.

'But you . . . you won't say anything to anyone though, will you? There's nothing wrong with me, it's just a hangover and I don't want anyone worrying. You know how it is.'

'I won't say anything.'

He was close enough for her to be able to smell his aftershave — and yet he didn't have the first idea what was going on in her mind. Nobody, she thought, not one person, knows the truth about anyone else. The world was full of strangers. It was a huge, chaotic crowd of strangers who collided now and then and were lost to each other.

She smiled again.

'OK. Just for five minutes.'

'As long as you want, Leila.'

Her voice was so quiet these days, he thought. He watched her walk away, moving slowly through the obstacle course of wine glasses and bowls of olives, and for a moment he remembered her as he had first seen her: in rolled-up jeans and sandals and a red T-shirt; the most vivid person on earth, already wearing Charlie's leather jacket, already laughing at each of his jokes, plainly captivated by him as he was by her.

And yet for all that, there she had been, like a miracle at their breakfast table, poised for a few more hours in safety: unkissed, unclaimed.

But it had been obvious he would take her.

Out on the roof terrace were dozens of red paper lanterns on strings overhead. More huge scented candles burned at intervals along the wall. It had not been long before the candles were peppered with cigarette butts, but their lemonish perfume still filled the air and the glow of the lanterns stood out exotically against the sky.

The others had all gone in for cake or to dance and Charlie and Hugo were alone. They leant against the rail sharing a bottle of wine. Beneath them, boats moved up and down the river now and then, and a little way along cars crossed the bridge between Chelsea and Battersea.

'More?' said Hugo, filling their glasses. 'Very decent Merlot. Not that you ever know what you're drinking.'

Hugo had been enjoying birthday rounds since four o'clock that afternoon and his face was bright pink. In the warmth of the evening, his light blonde hair stuck to his head, his eyes were bloodshot and his belly strained the buttons on his shirt. He was unquestionably overweight and unhealthy – facts that couldn't have bothered him less – and yet his face was still handsome. Even though it was plump, its proportions were unusually even and his lips, like Sam's, were elegantly curved and full.

He fished around in his jacket pocket.

'They're stogies,' he said. 'Lucas gave them to me. You can have one if you're very good.'

'I'm a saint,' said Charlie. 'Patron saint of short straws. D'you have any idea how boring it was out there this week?'

Hugo missed a swipe at his breast pocket and rebalanced himself on the wall. He frowned.

'Boring? What's the matter with you these days? This was another fucking Bell-Sanders victory. Tell me I'm wrong. We've blown the fucking heads off everyone's expectations this year – including mine. And what you did out there this week . . . I mean, did you spike them? These fuckers are *chucking* money at us. This isn't appetite for risk, this is gorging!'

'Yes, I do know that, Hugo,' said Charlie. 'That's why I did it.'

'And that's why I love you,' said Hugo, raising his glass.

Charlie glanced out at the river. A party boat with a dance floor on it went past on its slow circuit. People danced on the deck beneath all the lights and the water sparkled around it. But as beautiful as it looked, once you got on, it must be impossible to get off, he thought. You were trapped. He shuddered slightly at the idea of this.

'I wonder where Leila is,' he said.

Hugo had been eyeing him unsteadily.

'Fuck me,' he said, 'don't you do a number on me now, matey.'

Charlie faced him.

'What d'you mean a number?'

'I don't know. Get antsy. Freak out or something. So there's been a little increase in volatility. We've all seen a few paranoid articles here and there. So what? We're cool – we can handle it. This is the beauty of hedge funds. And anyway, we've always been risk junkies, you and

I. Haven't we? Hey? Ever since school. We've known each other since we were *thirteen*. D'you know that?'

'Yes, Hugo, I know that. What is this?'

'Nothing. Nothing.' He took a swig of wine. 'Just . . . don't do a number on me, that's all I'm saying. I haven't got an old bastard to inherit off, remember. We're a different species, you and me.'

This was the only thing they had ever rowed about.

Thankfully Hugo now found the cigars.

'Shifty fuckers,' he said, pulling them out of a pocket he was sure he had already searched. He waved them and Charlie took one and bit off the end.

Hugo made more of a mess of his. He swore and picked lumps of tobacco off his lip.

'So why'd Leila bugger off so early then?' he said. 'No birthday kiss. Bit unlike her.'

'What are you on about? She hasn't gone anywhere.'

Hugo struck a match and worked vigorously on his cigar.

'I think,' he said between puffs, 'I think you'll find you're mistaken. Uh-oh. Didn't you know? Dear oh dear. You must be in the doghouse too. Join me, my friend. I find it's simpler to set up home here.'

Charlie flung off the comradely arm.

'Hugo, she hasn't gone bloody anywhere. She's inside, chatting to people.' Hugo shook his head and then continued to puff on the cigar, unable to get it started and, taken aback by the violence of his re-action, Charlie was so irritated by the delay he had to stop himself from snatching it out of Hugo's mouth. 'She's *inside*,' he repeated.

With a smacking sound, Hugo came up for air.

'Nope,' he said, 'no one's seen her all evening.'

'Listen. People are *drunk*. They all are. They don't know what they're on about. Leila would never just fucking leave without telling me. Never has, never would. *Never*.'

'Bow-wow,' Hugo said. 'Welcome.'

'OK, you wanker, I'll go and fucking get her then and prove it to you. Catch,' said Charlie, chucking back the unlit cigar, almost hitting Hugo in the face with it.

Unable to think why he was quite so furious, why his face was hot and his mouth had gone dry, he strode back in through the balcony doors and out into the centre of the room. She was not on any of the sofas. She wasn't dancing by the bookshelves or standing by the drinks table in the corner. What had she been wearing? Jeans, probably. No, no, that white dress, he thought. Where was she? Where the hell was she?

He pushed his way over to the kitchen where the inevitable joint rollers were clustered round a table littered with plates of half-eaten cake. She was not there either, but then this was hardly her scene. He went off more hopefully towards Hugo's room where the mirrored table was always laid out for coke.

He nudged open the door. Two blonde girls were cutting lines at either end. He did not recognise either of them. Increasingly worked up he went back out into the corridor and walked straight into Sam.

'Watch it.'

'Sorry,' said Sam. Charlie began to move past. 'Charlie, I . . . I saw you walking about. I thought you might be looking for Leila.' Charlie stopped. It was such a strong face, Sam thought: a Coriolanus even.

Yes, you go ahead and cast him, he told himself. Try hitting him and he will put you in hospital. Such is the essential information in life.

'She – she wasn't feeling great,' he explained, deepening his voice a bit. 'She wanted to get out of the noise so I, well, I suggested she go in there about an hour ago.' He gestured vaguely at a door behind him.

'Right. What's in there?'

It struck Sam that Charlie seemed almost frightened, or nervous at any rate. But he must be imagining it. It would be mockery of some kind.

'There's nothing in there. It's my bedroom, that's all. Look, she didn't want me to get you or I would have, OK? I would have come and got you.'

Charlie went in and closed the door behind him.

It was dark and perfumey in there, like a girl's room. He felt for the light switch, but there was no bulb. This seemed somehow predictable.

'Leila, you in here?' As his eyes adjusted he made her out just ahead of him in a chair and right away he felt a flood of relief. 'I knew you wouldn't go,' he said. She didn't respond. 'What are you doing lurking in Sam's stinky old cave?'

There was a lamp beside her and he switched it on. The sight of her caused him to gasp.

'Jesus, Leila. What the fuck's going on?' Her eyes were swollen and pink with crying.

15

She sat up straight and put her feet on the floor. The past week and half had been the most frightening of her life and now that their moment of crisis had come, fear was replaced by a sense of release. Simply the act of telling him would make her feel better – it would make her body feel better, like putting down a heavy bag. She experienced a jolt of desperate, irrational excitement: maybe all she needed was to be free of it – just to be free of a secret she had no right to keep. Perhaps as soon as she said it out loud its power would go and it would all be over and she could go on living as normal, as if it had never happened.

'I'm pregnant,' she said, 'and I don't want us to be married any more.'

Charlie's eyes narrowed slightly. Then he touched his right temple with his fingertips. An overwhelming sensation of something physically breaking in his brain was coupled with a certainty that he had not locked the car.

Chapter 3

The receiver clicked back into place and Charlie's mother, Daria, stubbed out her cigarette. Conversations with her sister were exasperating. Pilar was so stubborn, so completely unchanged since the days when they had argued fiercely as children. There flashed into her mind a fight over a red swimsuit – a hairbrush flung in rage, a chipped tooth. Whose tooth had it been? Her fingers went halfway to her mouth, then she tutted, picturing the appalling Rodrigo, her brother-in-law. Why did these girls want to sleep with that old baldy anyway?

God, Barcelona must be looking dazzling by now, she thought.

Overhead, Gideon closed his study door. She wrinkled up her nose at the ceiling.

The English summer whispered irritatingly at the window, tapping a branch, and as if making a point to a negligent hostess Daria sat up and pulled her little cashmere cardigan around her. Then she took off her earrings and chucked them on to the coffee table. She massaged her neck a bit and as she did so her eye was caught by the enamelled boxes on the stand to her left. She had begun collecting them a few years ago with her friend Grette; you searched little auctions for them, you snapped up the treasure – it was fun! She reached out for one, a tiny red oval one made by Gormiere. Her favourite. On the top was a garland of blue flowers and within its confines a tiny little man bowed to a tiny little woman and offered her a rose.

Her tongue began to tingle for another drink and she put the box back. Another bit of something with ice, she thought to herself, casually picking up her glass. As she went over to the drinks cupboard, she half danced a couple of steps and in a mini-drama of indecision her fingers trailed over the decanters.

But she already knew. Whisky, as she always said, gave a lovely burn in the throat.

She slugged in a double and topped it up with soda. Then she carried it over to the bay window to admire the view.

No matter what, she thought, it was a stunning crescent – everything she had wanted a London street to look like when she had first arrived. It was everything her plump twenty-year-old self with its starchy collar and its crucifix and its ungovernable trembly kneed lust had wanted her home to be.

Just then it was silent out there and as if the stage curtain had just gone up, a cloud shifted and the moon illuminated the leaves of the enormous plane trees. Daria smiled. Curving to the left and the right the giant houses of Hampstead towered like an enchanted forest sparkling with chandeliers and drawing-room mirrors and cash.

Sometimes she liked to pretend she was all alone in a tower. It was something she had done since she was a little girl.

The noise of a car engine burst rudely into the dream and she tutted irritably, but as it slowed and pulled up outside the house she could see that driving it was her son, Charlie. She stepped back a little, out of the light. She squinted. Was it really him?

It was!

With his hands in his pockets he crunched up the drive. He paused to see if Gideon's light was on, then he disappeared and the bell rang. Almost breathless with excitement, Daria deposited her glass on the desk and hurried out to the front door.

She flung it open.

'Carlos! My darling!' she said, pressing her hand to her chest. Too *thin*, she thought, too thin! Not eating properly! But so tall, so *handsome* – so like Papa!

'Hiya, Mum,' he said. He always forgot how strong her accent was. She gazed at him. 'You going to let me in then or what?'

Daria laughed. 'Oh my goodness – *silly* Mummy!'

She kissed him on both cheeks then she turned around ahead of him, leading the way. He watched her little shoes slap-slap against her bare feet as she went – off past the coats, past an enormous vase of lilies and then left into the drawing room.

As she went in she leant down for her drink. She arched an eyebrow at him and jiggled the glass.

'Big one,' he replied. 'Whatever you're having.'

Daria clicked her tongue in delight. She loved it when they drank together.

Charlie rested his hand on the back of the sofa. It felt large and solid. It had been a good few months since he had last been home. He took it all in almost as if he were breathing it – all its familiar rich textures, the velvet curtains, the silk cushions, the heavily patterned walls. It was all typical of his mother; everything had been added to somehow – brocaded, embroidered, betasselled. Each shiny surface was loaded with treasures: jade or enamel boxes, silver birds and ornate photograph frames featuring himself and the tanned members of what his father had used to call the Spanish contingent. His own image grinned at him from assorted points around the room. There he was aged six on skis, aged twelve kissing the National Schools tennis trophy; there beside him he was a grinning fourteen with his cousin Jaime. Charlie leant over and picked up the frame. Two lean boys on a diving board, arms round each other in eternal friendship. In the background a table was laid for lunch. He hadn't spoken to Jaime in years.

He inhaled deeply. It felt better, calmer to be at home. Leila would be asleep by now – at least he could be sure of that. He had never seen her so exhausted – he had almost had to help her up the stairs to their flat. There had been no choice but for them to wait to talk in the morning. But he was glad of that – just as he was glad to be here, with his mother.

He returned the frame. 'I thought you might be having a dinner party,' he said casually. 'I thought I might get here and find a bunch of ravenous English people still waiting to be fed.' Shoving a tower of little cushions aside he sat down on the window seat. 'I thought I was about to get stuck with someone – Cynthia Bartlett or someone, asking me what a hedge fund is. *Is it a bit laike leeyandscape gardening?*' he mimicked.

'Ouuf,' Daria agreed, doing Cynthia's buck teeth as she sloshed out the whisky. 'No, tonight we were out. Tonight was dinner with Michael and Laura. Let me tell you, Charlie: number one prize of most boring couple in the world.' She grimaced and rolled her eyes.

Charlie smiled. His mother the character; with her irrepressible Spanish accent. It drove his father mad, which was always good value,

19

but then you had to see his point: it was impossible to believe she had lived in England for over thirty years. Her grammatical errors seemed to be acts of will – of violence, occasionally.

She handed him the drink.

'Chin-chin,' she said, implausibly, having long known it amused.

'Why so boring then – your dinner?'

She flapped her hand,

'Oh, just Daddy.'

'What, arguing?'

Daria blinked for yes as she took another gulp.

'What about?'

'My God – so *rude*, Charlie,' she said. 'About what? Pouf – I don't know. Some silly thing.' She slid a pile of magazines off the end of the sofa and threw herself down full length. 'Debt something. Debt is terrible – debt is wonderful. I don't know. Just Daddy. But let me tell you, the food was *fabulous* like always. *Bacalao a la Rotena!*' she kissed her bunched fingertips.

'Not Galicia *again*? You always go there.'

Daria sat up. 'OK then, Carlos, please tell me where else can I eat in London? Mmm? Tell me another *real, true Spanish restaurant* – not this Rincon or La Boquerdia which is like an *Italian* almost, my *God*. Tell me another restaurant and I will also go there.'

'You're bonkers.'

'Bonkers nothing! I don't want this *French*, this' – she screwed up her face – 'this *Japanese* like Adrian and Anna took us to. Please – what is this sushi? Huge lump, you stuff it in, you swallow, you get in the car? *No*.' She smoothed her cream trouser leg pensively. 'And anyway Javier is at Galicia.'

Charlie rolled his eyes.

'Javier the waiter,' he said. 'Javier the waiter who wants to get in your knickers.'

'*Por Dios*, Carlos. What rubbish. He's a gentleman. A Spanish gentleman.' She tutted. 'Knickers nothing.'

'What planet do you live on, Mum? He never leaves you alone! *"Aqui tiene Senorita Bell. Crema Catalana: dulce como su piel."*'

Feigning impatience with this subject, Daria stood up. She loved to hear Charlie speak Spanish – and she loved even more to hear his touching jealousy over the waiter. It was an old and favourite routine. So as to conceal her pleasure in it she went over to the drinks table under the pretext of needing an extra piece of ice.

Charlie dug the heel of his shoe into the carpet. How could she be such an innocent? But he never pushed the point far.

'This temper, this fire, Charlie. *Calma te*,' said Daria.

'All right, all right,' he said.

He coughed and cleared his throat. In his chest was a mounting pressure, like a fist pinning him against a wall. He coughed again, but the effect was minimal. Daria arrived beside him and ran a hand through his hair. 'Hmm?'

'So how's the shop?' he asked, out of nowhere.

She narrowed her brown eyes at him. They were his brown eyes.

'What shop? This little gallery? For the scarves and the pots and so on?' she whistled. 'Charlie, this finished *two thousand years ago*. You know this.'

'Oh, shit, of course I do. Sorry. I meant the tulips. Aren't you importing silk tulips?' He had a vague memory that she and Grette had started another of their ventures. It was so hard to keep track – all the sparkly openings and the quiet little closings a few months later on.

Daria held up her hand and averted her face. 'OK,' she said. 'OK, let me tell you about *silk tulips*. If I could, Carlos, I will *kill* these bastards. I said to Daddy – I say to him: these Dutch, they are absolutely *bas*tards! Please tell me how could we know? Yes, yes, *OK* we do a *cardinal sin*, we give all the money *in advance of the order* – but please God, I ask you, I mean it's *flowers*, OK? This is silk bloody tulips, it's not *cocaine*.'

Charlie was unable to conceal his amusement and Daria smacked his leg.

'Sounds awful. Seriously. How much did they nick?'

'No,' she said, 'I don't tell you.'

'Oh, go on, spoilsport.'

'*Everything*.'

'Shit. So what did Dad say?'

She lengthened her face to represent pomposity and did her English voice: '"*Welcome to the real world, Daria.*"' She continued the impression, hooking her thumbs into an imaginary waistcoat and doing a funny walk. It was quite unlike Gideon in any physical sense, in fact it bore more relation to the portrait of Edward Bell, Charlie's grandfather, which hung in the hall, but there was truth in it of some kind. They laughed together like children.

They had always ganged up against Gideon like this. Sometimes when he held forth over supper on one of his pet subjects they trembled together helplessly. It was enough only to catch one another's eye and all was lost.

'*Enough, enough,*' said Daria, catching her breath. 'Come on now. Come on – what can you tell me? How is this terrible Hugo and how is the *fund*?'

It was only then it occurred to Charlie that she had not seen the article about him in the paper. It wasn't such an important event in the reality of his career, but it was something she would have understood. She would never have seen it herself, given she only read *El Pais* – but she might have been shown it, he thought with a spasm of anger, his father might have fucking shown it to her.

'Hugo?' he said lightly. 'Still terrible. No great change there.'

'And he has become engaged yet?'

'Hmm? No. No – not yet.'

Daria shook her head.

'And the fund,' said Charlie, not wanting to discuss Hugo or his love life, 'the fund's doing wonderfully, thanks. We're fully invested. I've just been out in Switzerland closing a deal.'

He studied her warily. It was always a mixed pleasure to tell Daria about his work. As much as he wanted her to know, he couldn't help being sure she didn't understand the terms he used and so wasn't fully appreciating what he was saying, or worse still that she was building up a false impression which would then be relayed vibrantly to friends over cappuccino.

She beamed at him ecstatically. 'My darling – you are *so* clever!' And he frowned at the carpet, torn between deep pride and an uneasy sense that she was only congratulating him in some motherly way that didn't really count.

'Oh, well, look,' he said touchily, 'the climate's basically been great for hedge funds, so – so you know.'

'I know, darling. I know.'

'Yes, but not that it isn't a success, though, OK? It's not inevitable or anything. Nothing is in the financial world.' He took a deep breath, realizing how worked up he was getting and how far he had veered from what he needed to say. How on earth had he not actually said it yet? Tell her, he urged himself, but his mouth went dry at the thought. 'Essentially it's all great,' he said quietly.

Daria stroked his hair again and walked away. He was being a prickly pear – as he so often was about his work. She could say nothing right, so it was best not to say much at all.

In her precise, almost balletic manner she took a cigarette from the box on the table, then she lay down on the sofa, resting her tanned little feet on a cushion. She lit a match.

In the soft light it struck Charlie that his mother was still very pretty – she might have been in her early forties. *Why*, he thought with unexpected anger, *why couldn't she just let herself get old like a normal mother?*

She blew smoke above her head. 'It's "*all great*",' she repeated. 'OK then, Charlie, please can you explain me one thing? Why darling, when "it's all great" you are sitting with your mother on a Saturday night? Mmm? Where is Leila? Why you are not in a party together? In a club – I don't know.'

Charlie flicked the tassel on the Roman blind. It swung in a series of wild circles and batted the glass.

'What is it, darling? What's the matter?' said Daria, suddenly frightened.

He rested his forehead on the windowpane.

'It's Leila,' he said, 'she's pregnant.'

And for what was only the second time in her life, Daria was speechless. The first time had been shortly before her own wedding. She and her mother had gone out for a rare lunch together and as they waited for the bill her mother was amused to learn that Daria had no idea her father had cheated from the day they were married.

She gazed desperately at her son – at her little boy with his pudgy arms who came to her bed in the morning and listened to her whispers. What he liked most was when you kissed his tummy and blew on it to make a loud noise. 'Rasby,' he said '*Otra vez*! Rasby!' and he rolled around on your lap.

Daria leant forward, 'Carlos . . . *is it yours?*' she said fiercely.

He jumped. '*What?* Mum, are you serious?'

She covered her mouth.

'No. *No!* I'm not thinking, Charlie. Forgive me, *cariño*. It's the . . . the surprise. Just the surprise, darling.' In a huge effort to regain control of herself she swung her legs round and felt for her shoes. She clipped on her earrings. 'Darling, it's *fantastic*. A baby!' she shouted.

He flicked the tassel again.

'It isn't fantastic,' he told her. 'She wants to split up. She told me everything this evening.'

Daria blinked incredulously, her mind slapped dumb once again. The ash towered on her cigarette.

No, this is too much, she thought. *Divorce?* She had no clear sense of where the insult was directed – only that it was all-encompassing, that this somehow was an absolute defilement of all that was sacred in the world.

'But *Charlie*, how can she . . . *Why* would she . . . ? Does she not know how many girls would . . . Does she not know how lucky . . . That *girl*!' Daria brought her hands down on to her knees with a smack, showering the carpet with ash. 'I *knew* it. I *knew* it, Carlos, the second when I saw these men's clothes, this hair with all the knots in it, these terrible nails. "*Mummy, this is Leila. We know each other forty-five minutes: I love her.*" Terrible!' She implored him, she willed him, '*Crazy*, Charlie – *mad*!'

But even as she spoke, even as she hated Leila, a deep part of her knew she was being unfair. The truth was that she couldn't help liking her daughter-in-law for all the reasons she said she disliked her. When, on one of their first meetings, Leila had knocked a glass of wine on to the tablecloth and plunged in her own sleeve to mop it up, Daria had looked on and thought: I was once like that myself. It would have been hard for her to say when exactly this was, but she was certain it was true.

At last the cigarette end began to burn her fingers and she crushed it out. She noticed the ash on the carpet now and was glad to busy herself with picking it up and laboriously blowing and rubbing until the mark was gone.

As she did this she felt a surge of self-hatred. What was the matter with her? Why did she not go over to her son – to her poor son who had so sweetly come for her advice? Was she a mother or not?

Reluctantly she raised her head – and then, in spite of herself, she flinched at the sight of him. With his legs stretched out he balanced the heel of one shoe on the toe of the other and squinted as if he was making sure they were straight. Incredibly, this was something Gideon did – something he did all the time. In the early days of their marriage it had made her frantic, this strange balancing act full of mysterious precision the very moment she was upset. Once she had simply pulled the damned shoes off and chucked them into her bubble bath. There they were the next day, bloated and sinister.

A sound in the hallway gave her a start. With his usual hopeless timing, there were Gideon's feet on the stairs.

'Daria, you in there?' he called. 'You and Leonie have been hiding things again. I can't find my yellow file anywhere.' He pushed open

24

the door. 'What are your thoughts? Oh,' he said, noticing Charlie, 'I didn't know you were here.' He frowned and fiddled with his glasses, apparently testing their flexibility under strain.

'Still working?' said Charlie.

'Trying to. But people keep going into my study and moving things about. It's an elaborate form of mental torture.'

Daria tutted, bored by this age-old complaint.

'We hide *nothing*, Gideon,' she sighed. 'Leonie *cleans* in there. My God.'

Returned to normality for a moment, her face slackened. Your husband, she thought: his reading glasses, his greying hair, his cashmere vest with its little paunch.

How very different the world would have been if she had married Alfonso Diez after all. To think she only hadn't because he was slightly too short!

'Well, *someone* has hidden it, Daria. It was in absolute plain view on the left-hand side of my desk and now it's gone and it's been *deposited*' – he scrunched up his eyes at the void – 'God only knows where.'

There was little that could be offered to him in response to this. They watched the crisis pass through his body. Then he folded the glasses and dropped them into his pocket. 'Oh yes, Charlie,' he said slowly. 'I . . . saw the thing about you in *The Times* supplement. Of course I meant to show it to you, Daria, but I'm afraid I left it at the office.'

'What *thing*?' said Daria, immediately alarmed. 'What do you leave at the office?'

He winced at the confusion of tenses.

'It's a newspaper article about young London businesspeople,' he explained patiently. 'It partly features Charlie.'

Don't overdo it, Charlie thought, you wanker.

Ordinarily, Daria would have leapt up and kissed her son with pride at news like this.

'Oh,' she said quietly. 'Fantastic.'

Gideon cleared his throat.

'It's been an ideal climate for you lot.'

'Not bad.'

Gideon frowned and rocked a little on his heels. 'Still, everything must come to an end though, Charlie. As I keep telling you.'

'*Do* you? Oh yes, now I think about it I do have a faint recollection of your having said that before.'

'It might be an idea to listen to me, you know? I have a modicum of experience.'

'Well, so do I, actually, Dad.'

'Of a *boom*, Charlie. You have experience of a boom. In my day you actually had to have the money under management before you started making a noise. You lot go and sing a pretty song to the bank and they chuck credit at you as if they've been hypnotised by it. You take a few of the right brokers out to lunch, drop a couple of words in their ear too: bit of scandal about this company, bit of gossip about that one, bit more Cabernet bloody Sauvignon – and lo and behold you've got your market volatility on tap too. Very nice. Quids in. But it's rumour-mongering, Charlie, it's market *manipulation*.' Gideon shook his head. 'Mark my words, it is not possible to sustain a business model that relies on debt and rumour: two *illusions*. At some point one has to face reality.'

Charlie pushed his hands through his hair.

'Oh, for God's sake, not this whole speech again,' he said. 'Not now. Just not now, OK?'

Gideon straightened up. He sniffed. And then all of a sudden he couldn't help being aware that both Charlie and Daria were staring fixedly at the carpet, almost as if they were waiting for him to go. He felt a brief pang of something, a kind of hollowness in his stomach, not unlike hunger. He was uneasy for a moment – but then he remembered his missing yellow file and, feeling angry again, he frowned and took out his glasses.

'Yes, it's late. It's late and I've got a great deal of work to do,' he said, as if this was what Charlie had meant. 'Right. I'll get on, then. Give Leila my best. Is she well?'

'Yes.'

'Good.' He closed the door behind him.

With a fluttering panic which made her scrunch up the cushion beside her it occurred to Daria that Alfonso Diez would be sixty-two in three weeks. *Sixty-two?* He probably got up to pee in the night!

Her eyes filled with tears.

'*Darling*,' she said, 'I am so, so sorry for you. So terrible sorry.'

She began to cry and straining to see him through her tears she realised she had been totally crazy a few minutes before. He was nothing like *Gideon*, for God's sake. Crazy! No, Charlie was and always had been the spitting image of her father. The thick dark hair, the glinting brown eyes. Not Fernando as he had been in the bad days at the end with that dreadful Swedish TV actress, but as he had been in reality, during her childhood.

Daria stood up with her fists clenched, knocking some letters off the coffee table on to the floor. She was afraid she was going to choke.

'What do you *want*, Charlie?' she cried, pressing her throat. 'Hmm? What do you really *want* in your life? Can you tell me? You want this?' She flung her arm out in front of her at the furniture, the hallway. She grabbed a silver peacock from the mantelpiece, '*This?*'

Charlie frowned. 'What are you talking about?' Her face was flushed, she sounded hysterical. This was not what he needed, not what he had come for. He shook his head as if there had been water in his ears. 'No, Mum, I'm sorry, I'm not getting into this. You're living in a fairy tale. Some people have to make money, OK? It's how the world works.'

Daria lowered her hands. A joyless little smile played across her lips, then she nodded slowly, took off her cardigan and draped it on the arm of the chair.

'You know something, Charlie?' she said. 'Your father thinks I am a stupid child – and I think maybe also you do. *Yes*, people have to work, darling – but *how much?*'

He was silent for a moment.

'You're saying it's my fault. Aren't you? First I'm a no-good waster, now I do everything right, only that's wrong too because I work all the time so my wife's unhappy. People work! For Christ's sake she could work too. Anyhow she does work – she's done up all the flats and so on . . .' He shrugged, holding up the palms of his hands. 'She says she *likes* it. She was driving socking great vans of plants around for that guy Jools when I first met her.' He paused, remembering, with a peculiar stab in his heart, a trip to the early-morning market with her, tea and sandwiches in the back of a van crammed with peonies; her excited face. 'Look, she made us a lot of money when we needed it, Mum, and who knew that idiot Jools was going to fuck off to America and ditch their business? Christ, I say business – I mean it was delivering *plants*, it was *gardening*. And what a twat that guy was anyway. I always knew he fancied her. I clocked that one the second I met him.' He furrowed his brow, then he crushed the superfluous anger beneath his eyelids, 'Oh, listen, for fuck's sake – I *had* to get something started, Mum. Didn't I? I had nothing to live off. As you may or may not remember, *he* fucking cut me off with no fucking warning.'

'I remember,' she said. She had told Gideon then: he will hate you. He will also learn this.

Charlie slumped against the cushions.

'So you're saying what, exactly? You're saying she's been miserable all this time? The whole time we've been married? Is that what everyone thinks?' Had they been discussed at parties, at tables in bars? 'Fucking hell,' he said, 'everyone's gone mad.'

Daria stood motionless. She hadn't seen him so dejected since the day he was expelled from Russington. At the time, very secretly overjoyed at the news, she had been intending to zip up and collect him the next day, to take him out for lunch just the two of them – naughty boy! But, quite unexpectedly, he had turned up alone on the doorstep, ashen, dragging his heavy trunk. Aged sixteen, he had cried his heart out like a baby all day, afraid to face *Gideon* of all people. Neither of them had mentioned it since.

Now she felt nauseous with guilt. The truth was, she had done everything wrong. *Everything.* Even her own mother – whose love had been expressed almost exclusively via the purchase of starched little dresses – even *she* had done a better job!

She gritted her teeth. Why had she let Gideon send him away to that place? Why? To that prison with its oh-so-impressive marble hall for the fathers and upstairs, hidden away, the horrible beds, the little signs of violence – scorch marks, splintered door frames, gouge marks in walls . . . What had brought those acts on? She still couldn't bear to think!

'So, this is my dorm, these are some of my dormies,' he told her and she had smiled and waved, deep behind her sunglasses, her headscarf. 'Hello!' They looked up from their comics, they gazed like starved wolves as she went.

'Oh, my darling,' murmured Daria despairingly, 'my *darling*.'

And then, in the seconds it took her to realise she was still holding the hideous silver peacock and to swear and set it down roughly, she had an idea.

Instantly her face broke into a smile. She bit her lower lip and thought hard for a moment, then, smiling again, she rushed over and squeezed in beside him on the window seat. Leaning in very close she gripped his hand and whispered into his ear, 'Charlie, I had the best idea of my life – the *best*.'

'What?' he said despondently. It was a formula of hers. Sometimes the idea was almond ice cream or a glass of cold sherry and olives on the garden steps.

Daria flapped her hand. 'No, Charlie – really. *Really*. *Cariño* listen to me,' she tilted his chin up towards her, '*you take Leila to Spain*,' she said. 'You go to La Campañera! You fix things with Hugo and the fund and all that and – you go! Go for a few months. For the summer. You take Leila to Spain! Time together! Why not?' In her enthusiasm she increased the pressure on his hand and slapped it up and down in time to her words. 'There is peace, there is the village square, there is the sun, there is basil in the garden. And your cousin Jaime is there and his wife *all the same age*! Why not?' Again she bit her lip. She had not felt so excited for years – for decades, perhaps. They would be happy – her son and her daughter-in-law – *she* would help them to be happy!

Charlie's hand sat limp beneath hers. He leant his cheek against the curtain and watched a cat pad across the roof of his car.

'It's impossible,' he said. 'For one thing you don't understand about my work. I can't just leave. It's impossible,' he repeated.

Daria kept quiet. After a second or two he began to speak again, impatiently this time, as if he were interrupting her, 'Oh, for God's sake,' he said, 'I don't know! I mean what would be the point of this anyway?' He pulled back his hand. 'No, no, don't say anything. Don't say anything.' He sighed in frustration – at his mother, at Leila, at the thick haze of feminine emotion that had suddenly made it so difficult to breathe. He pinched the bridge of his nose. 'I could go for a bit. We haven't had a holiday for a few years I suppose and we have just taken on the new guy. Hugo would manage for a while . . . Fuck it, he's capable. He knows the way I think.'

He was silent again – but for longer this time. He stared hard at the cat now lying in the pool of streetlight on his car. It was as still and grey as a lump of stone, almost an optical illusion in its stillness with the branches swaying shadows all around.

She had looked like a stranger when he dropped her off.

'What if she . . . what if she won't come with me?' he said.

Daria stroked his hair.

'*Darling*, you have the character exactly like Papa. You can persuade anyone anything.'

Chapter 4

The drive to La Campañera was a winding uphill road three hours outside Seville into the Andalusian countryside. Charlie and Leila had stepped off the plane early that afternoon into bright sunshine and now, driving the hire car up into the hills, the heat muscled in through the windows whenever they slowed for a bend. Both the boot and the back of the car were crammed with suitcases and books and unopened subscription magazines which there had never been time to read. Charlie's tennis racket jutted through between the front seats making it hard to change gears. On the radio a Spanish voice talked into the air.

For the past few hours, while the narrow road had taken all Charlie's attention, he had seen the valley flash tantalisingly in the rear-view mirror, broadening out, turning from green to pale yellow to burnished gold in the deepening light.

He pulled the car up to take a look at it. It was an astonishing view. The hot wind roared in their ears. 'I remembered this wind,' Charlie said. Whenever it eased off, there was the true force of the heat again with a shove, along with the rasp of cicadas in the hillside behind. 'We'll never get there by seven at this rate,' he said. 'But it really doesn't matter.'

He smiled at her and she felt herself soften a little more. She listened to the cicadas. No, he was right, she told herself. He was. All they needed was to get far away. She smiled back at him and then he looked out at the hills again.

What was it? Had he been too spoilt to appreciate this drive as a child, he wondered? Too bored, too impatient in the back seat with his snorkel and his Walkman and his packet of crisps. Had it always been *this* golden? He couldn't help smiling – at the hills, at the sky, at the idea of childhood. His eyes roamed happily, taking in the hazier, more distant slopes with their ivory inlay of little white villages. Then higher up still, against the horizon, was a ragged lacework of rocks.

Excitement swelled in his chest. Spain, he thought. It was as if a whole area of his brain had gone dark and was now suddenly live with activity again. Here it was right in front of him: site of his childhood adventures with his cousin Jaime, a magic space in which it had been impossible to believe in school and the pouring rain; where his mother wore colourful dresses and sang and his aunt made him chocolate milk.

They got back in the car. After getting lost several times, it was evening when they finally approached the village. Charlie tapped her shoulder.

'This genuinely is it this time.' He pointed at the signpost and in excitement, she sat up.

Ahead of them the road narrowed on the approach to a corner and then there, just ahead of them, was a village built on to one side of a hill. They swept in over the cobbles.

It was more beautiful than Leila had imagined – blinding with whitewash and red bougainvillea, the streets impossibly steep and the houses all toppling into each other like a crowd of drunk friends. She laughed out loud.

'It's *wonderful!*'

'I told you, didn't I? Didn't I say?'

She glanced at his smiling face, then she leant forward, planting her hands on the dashboard and gazing up through the windscreen at a world of dangling things – washing, hanging plants, lanterns. To the left and right were complex glimpses of tiled courtyards and fountains and mosaic walls. Everything seemed to contain a multiplicity of layers, like a Russian doll.

'Oh, I remember all this *perfectly,*' said Charlie. 'That's the main square where most stuff happens. People hang out there in the evening and so on. That's the old clock at the top of the tower which – yep – which *still* says it's two o'clock all the time. There's some crazy story about why they can't change it – all the wine would go wrong or something. Some superstition. It sounds like bullshit but I'm not making it up – it really is like that here. No – I remember it actually. It's something about a *wicked woman.*'

31

'It always is,' said Leila.

'Yes, it was a wicked woman who abandoned her baby. I think maybe she killed herself and no one knew where the baby was. Yes, that's it. This is about three hundred years ago obviously. Anyhow, the harvest was crap that year. Everyone blamed this woman. Why not? Happened at the same time: obviously connected. Eventually they found the child – the little body that is – in the clock tower. Just up there. That was where she'd hidden it. Can you imagine?'

'No. Horrible.'

'Apparently the clock stopped dead as a mark of respect.'

They looked up at the little tower and at the clock face with its rusty hands.

'You mean it's been telling the same time for three hundred years?'

'Funny, isn't it?'

They drove on up the cobbled side street.

'Christ, look at *that*,' said Charlie. He stopped the car abruptly. 'What the fuck's that doing here?'

On the wall opposite was a sun-bleached poster for a strip club in the nearest town. A stocky blonde with black eyebrows coiled a python around her waist and beckoned. The effect was dismal – comical rather than sexy.

'Oh, for goodness sake,' said Leila. 'Aren't they allowed to have sex here?'

Charlie wrinkled up his nose. She was amused by a prudishness she had never seen in him before.

'What?' he said, aware he was being teased.

'Nothing. Just you.'

'Anyway, back to the tour. So, over there on the corner, that's the bar everyone used to go to – La Maja. That's Mourino's restaurant. Over on the other side, just there after the drinking fountain, that's the police station – and when I say "station" I mean it's about three men, two watching game shows and one asleep, so this is the perfect place to murder me if you want to . . . OK, I think it's left here.' He frowned at the piece of paper he was clutching. 'Does that say left?'

'Charlie, you do know I don't want to murder you?' Leila said.

'No? Well, that is a relief. Oh no, sod it – this *is* wrong.' They had arrived in a back alleyway full of wooden crates and an enormous pile of fruit peelings. A cat with four tiny bald kittens regarded them from an upturned bin lid. Charlie reversed back out and down the slope again. 'Fuck it. Never mind – I forgot to show you an important

32

thing anyway. Just through there, if you look back there through the wall, see where I'm pointing?'

'No. Oh yes, got it.'

'That's where the market is on Wednesdays. That's the second square. There are only two.'

Through a carved stone opening backed by an iron grille in a pattern of crosses, Leila could see a fountain. It was surrounded by three lemon trees. Around the square were lampposts with baskets of pink bougainvillea.

'A market?'

'Only tiny.'

'How exciting! I can go and get delicious things there. Bread and olives and honey and stuff. Figs! *Charlie*! I'll have to learn the words.' He was right, she thought – there was no question. Suddenly overwhelmed with optimism, she gripped his arm. 'You know what?'

'What, Leila?'

'This is going to be so much *fun*!'

He laughed at her gently. So, he thought, this is what you look like happy. For a second he allowed himself to be pleased, proud that he himself had brought this about in her. But almost immediately this feeling was replaced by the new gloomy obligation he felt to apologise to her – and by a subsequent longing to escape.

He moved the car off towards the main street.

'I can teach you the words if you want,' he said. 'That's if I can remember them. *Jamon, miel, tomates.*' He lifted the scrap of paper again. 'OK, it's the "second turning on the left after the cash machine",' he read. '*Where*? Aunt Pilar you old bat I can't see a fucking cash machine anywhere!'

'There,' said Leila, pointing.

Charlie accelerated.

In the side street, as promised, was the little hardware shop, which belonged to Signora Montero's son. This was where they were supposed to meet Signora Montero herself to collect the keys. Above it was a faded awning, flapping in the hot breeze. In the window were a variety of hammers and nails. The shop was all closed up now – dim and lifeless inside. Taped to the door was an envelope with the name 'Zavarjelos' on it. Daria's maiden name.

'I don't get it,' said Leila. 'Why didn't she just leave them outside the house?'

'Did you think this was about security?'

33

'What then?'

'Gossip. She hasn't seen me since I was a teenager. Weird as it sounds there will have been talk about us.'

'Oh no, don't,' said Leila, 'I want us to be invisible. Don't you?' Charlie drove back out into the street again. 'Has she really worked for your aunt all this time?'

'Why leave? The place is empty except for a few weekends in the summer. She just dusts and waters the plants and has a bit of a snoop round, I imagine. And Uncle Rodrigo probably gives her enough scandal to live off for the whole year.'

'I bet he's not that bad. No one's *that* bad.'

'Oh Leila, I do love your illusions,' he said, laughing. Then he stopped himself and frowned. 'I'm sorry,' he said.

She looked at him in surprise. On the corner they passed a man holding a bicycle wheel. He stepped out of their way.

'So . . . so am I ever going to meet him, then?' Leila said. 'Rodrigo?'

'Not right now. They're "separating" again at the moment. He's just an old lech, Leila, nothing to get excited about. And not suitable company for *you know who*,' he said, mouthing the words and pointing at her stomach, as if everything they said was being overheard. Somehow his clowning about the baby was always awkward and even a bit sinister.

'Why doesn't Jaime live there – at La Campañera?' she said, changing the subject. 'Seems funny renting nearby when it's sitting there empty.'

'There's a lot I don't know about his life,' said Charlie. 'We may have to bluff when we see him.'

Leila studied his face.

'Why wasn't he at our wedding?' she said.

'Mmm?'

'Jaime. You were inseparable. All your swimming races, your tennis matches. All those photos of you both.'

Charlie puffed out his cheeks. The air came out with a popping sound.

'We grew up? Different countries, different worlds? Also we stopped coming to Spain every summer. I think Mum and Rodrigo had a row, but I always thought it was because of me getting kicked out of school. Jaime came over to London once – but he spent the entire time sucking up to Dad. It was bizarre actually. I left them to it. He'd suddenly got obsessed with becoming this big businessman. Then he got very arsey about going to university in America – "*school*" – wanted

34

me to be wildly impressed all the time. Dad paid some of the fees. I thought it sounded fucking boring. Still do. You don't need to go to university to learn how to start a business.' Charlie squinted through the windscreen. 'Basically I always found him a bit too competitive if you want to know the truth.'

Going much too fast they went round a last corner on the outskirts of the village and then up another street, which eventually became a pair of stone walls. The wall on the left concealed the ragged drop down into the valley. Halfway along it was a little alcove.

Charlie pulled up with a jerk. Inside the alcove, on a plinth, was a statue with a few unlit candles and some flowers.

'And there she is,' he said. 'Say hi to Maria de la Merced. Maria de la Merced says hi back.' Leila shifted uneasily. The glassy eyes seemed to point down directly into the car. 'I got caught trying to nick her once for a bet. Uncle Rodrigo beat me with his fucking belt. Can you believe that? As if he gave a shit about the Virgin Mary. He would have tried to chat her up.'

The tiny mouth was painted rosebud pink. The eyes were bright blue. It was a little girl's dream of a face.

'All that honeysuckle,' said Leila. 'Who puts it in there?'

'Oh, everyone. Even the really normal ones do it.'

She felt the same breathless panic she once had when she watched her mother kneeling in the room at the top of their house. Charlie moved the car off again.

'Right. At long fucking last,' he said, turning on to a dusty uphill track, 'we have arrived.'

The car rocked and bumped upwards and Leila held on to the dashboard. Soon the trees gave way to rough grass and the sky widened out above them and as they left behind the tight knot of the village the white noise of humanity hushed for the sounds of insects and birds.

At the end of the path, over the gateway, was an enormous walnut tree; its shade felt damp and weighty as they drove beneath it. And then came the house. It was lower than Leila had imagined, but far prettier − its walls almost obscured by their load of white wisteria and lavender and dark ivy. Around each window was a calligrapher's flourish of wrought iron. It seemed to creak beneath the weight of its embellishments.

They left the bags in the car.

On the table Signora Montero had left them a note beside some flowers in a vase.

'Dahlias!' said Leila, lifting them up to her nose. 'Grown right here. These are an unusually good colour. It's almost pink, almost purple isn't it? Sort of fizzy on the eye,' she said, aware she was speaking too quickly. He wasn't listening anyway. In the fading light she could make out an open-plan sitting room leading on to a terrace with a glass roof. There were wicker chairs and a breakfast table. Beyond this was the garden.

Charlie studied the note. 'Hello and welcome blah blah blah . . . and then . . . something about the *fridge*.'

He ran down the two steps into the sitting room and turned right along the hallway, at the end of which was the kitchen.

It was as cool and stony and perfect in there as ever. He opened the fridge and on the top shelf was a plate of *pimientos ripieni*, and in the door a bottle of Rioja. Behind him, on the counter, were two glasses and a candle.

'What is it?' said Leila, coming in. 'What's the matter?'

'I think it's supper for two.'

A pan had been left on the cooker to reheat it.

'For us? She made us supper? What is it? Ooh, stuffed peppers – how yummy.' Coming up behind him she slipped an arm round his shoulder and dipped her finger into the rice. 'How incredibly sweet of her. Oh my God, it's *delicious*.'

Charlie put the plate back in the fridge.

'We'll have to have it for breakfast. We can't exactly ditch Jaime now.'

'No. No, of course not.'

'Are you changing? I'm going to.'

'Is there time for a bath?'

He checked his watch.

'A quick one. There might not be hot water, though. I'll check.' He ducked under her arm and opened a cupboard but the boiler had long since been replaced. He found the new one under the stairs in the sitting room.

Leila followed him out, trailing her hand along the wall. It was the kind of floor you wanted to walk on barefoot, she decided – all smooth terracotta tiles.

'OK, there's loads of hot water. I'll get the essential cases out of the car and you go on up. There's a bathroom on the landing just up there. Shout if there aren't any towels but I'm sure there will be.'

Leila nodded. She was suddenly very tired. Holding firmly on to the banister, she made her way up the stairs. Halfway along the landing was a window.

It was a gorgeous tangle of a garden, all rustling with fig trees and wild thyme and pale pink trailing hibiscus. There was a dovecote with wooden shutters. There was an old rope hammock. It would have been nice to go down and lie in it.

But she could hear Charlie dragging the bags up the steps. Taking a last glance at the garden she went off quickly in search of the bath.

Chapter 5

Until the building work on their little hotel was complete, Jaime and Camellia were renting a new house on the main road outside the village. It was set back from the road by a kilometre-long path surrounded by fields. As Charlie drove along the tall stalks crackled in through the windows, brushing their arms.

The gateway was open. In front of the porch lay a dog asleep on its side.

Leila opened her door. It was certainly private out there, she thought. The hills were covered in wind turbines. She moved her shoes around in the dust. Behind her, Charlie unzipped bags, looking for Daria's present. The dog wagged its tail.

'Hello, Spanish dog,' said Leila. It heaved itself up, pushing its old brown neck into her fingers for a scratch. She smiled, liking the live feeling of its fur against her bare legs.

There was a flicker of movement at the front door. Behind the mosquito screening was a shape – a haze of yellow. Her eyes strained. The shape faded. Next moment the screening banged wide open and out down the steps came a skinny, grinning man in battered jeans and a T-shirt, his arms spread wide. Following him was a girl in a yellow dress.

Charlie was still leaning in through the back window.

'*Stranger!*' shouted Jaime in mock accusation, grabbing his collar as if to throw him off the property. Charlie tried to shake him off.

'Hey – let me get out, you idiot.'

'*Already* he's calling me an idiot and he only just got here?' Then Jaime began to laugh. It was a loud, good-natured laugh, which shook the whole of his boyish body, swinging his T-shirt back and forth against his ribs and his flat stomach. It was impossible not to join in. He and Charlie hugged, slapping each other on the back.

While this went on, Leila and Camellia stood by awkwardly, waiting to be introduced.

At last Camellia spoke.

'So, I'm Camellia,' she said. 'You're Leila. Hi.'

'Oh – you speak English!'

'Sure. What did you think?' Camellia was taken aback. 'Yeah, I was a nanny in the US for three years, so – yeah – so I picked it up there. It's rusty – but, you know.' She shrugged, but it was plainly a matter of pride. She had a strong American accent.

'It sounds amazing to me. I've only got this,' Leila said, and without knowing why – perhaps it was in some way to atone for a tactless opening remark – she fished a tatty Spanish phrasebook out of her handbag. It was an old one of her mother's she'd found while they were packing. You never knew where or when you would find things.

Now she wished she hadn't brought it out. It was dog-eared and Camellia would think it was too short to suggest any serious interest in the language. It was possible she would be offended. More offended. To make things worse, before she could stop it, a toffee wrapper unstuck itself from the cover and was caught up by the breeze. For a moment it spun wildly in the air between them and they watched it glittering, both a bit stunned by this apparition. Then Leila caught it and shoved it back in her bag.

'Sorry,' she said. 'Throwing my rubbish all over your tidy place.'

Camellia stared dubiously at the phrasebook. She had been expecting Leila to be older and a lot more pregnant.

'Well, that's OK,' she said with a smile, 'we'll all use English to help you. Not a problem.'

'What a pain. It's so kind of you.'

'Sure,' said Camellia.

Jaime and Charlie arrived beside them.

'Aha,' said Jaime. 'So *this* is Leila.' He raised his eyebrows quizzic- ally and she smiled, liking him immediately. His voice was more Spanish than his wife's. Grinning, he put his arm round Charlie again. '*Enhorabuena*. Carlos. But tell me, how the hell did you persuade *her* to go with *you*?'

Charlie pursed his lips. They were already a double act.

'Mixture of booze and persistence, I think.'

Jaime laughed and thumped his back again.

'Hey, come on, don't do yourself down. I can admit you haven't turned out so disgusting yourself.' He held up one finger. 'Even if I can bet *for sure* you still cheat at cards.'

'I still *what*? This from the boy who glued stones into the hem of my swimming trunks to increase the *drag*!'

Jaime shook his hand as if he had burnt it.

'I never did that. Did I do that? What a *great fucking idea*. But, OK – OK, we can settle this later. Come on now, let's all get a drink before I'm in trouble. Camellia has been stirring things for hours.'

Camellia frowned.

'No I haven't, Jaime, don't say that. He's totally exaggerating. It's nothing special so don't get your hopes up. Just a little meat and some salad, that's all.'

It was a feast. A slow-cooked shoulder of ham lay in the kitchen ready for the barbecue. Beside it were various side dishes – a wild rice salad, some creamy cheeses and a plate of Serrano ham, capers and sardines. They carried it out to the garden where a table was laid.

Feeling useless, having been told to relax, Leila sat with a glass of wine, watching the others fiddle with the barbecue. There was a lot of smoke and Jaime ran about in it fanning clownishly till he suffered a fit of coughing which doubled him up on the grass. Camellia moved him out of the way or shooed him off like a child.

After deciding the barbecue was ready for the meat, Camellia walked back towards the table, smiling and wiping her fingers on a cloth. As she moved her ponytail of dark hair swung out in time at each side. Her yellow dress swished prettily below her knees.

She sat down, flipping the cloth over her shoulder and reached for the wine. It was not difficult to imagine her running a hotel.

'So, you're drinking, are you?' she said, nodding at Leila's glass.

'Oh – just a little bit.'

'Yeah? I didn't. But – wow, I do everything by the book. Forget about me. Jaime thinks I'm crazy. But it's like I'm always telling him – if everyone was so "*chilled out*" . . .' She giggled, but a slight contraction of her eyebrows suggested she would prefer not to have confided this.

Leila reached for an olive. The wine was helping her nerves now and she could feel its warmth in her cheeks. Perhaps it had been for the best they'd come out after all.

She pushed off her shoes and brought her bare feet up beside her on the chair.

'You've got a little boy, haven't you, Camellia?' she said, chewing. Camellia brightened.

'Alberto. My grandpa's name. He's almost three now.'

'Almost three! I don't know why, but I assumed he was tiny still.' Leila tried to imagine that her own child would one day have birthdays, would one day be three – but no pictures came to her mind. 'Almost three,' she repeated.

'Yeah, it's like all of a sudden he isn't a baby any more. You know? He's getting *huge*. I'm totally ready for more – but we can't do anything until this project's finished. I mean we don't want to. Right now we're really too busy, so – you know. So it's fine.' She pulled the cloth off her shoulder and folded it into a square.

'You must be working hard,' said Leila. 'Charlie tells me you're restoring an old tower house in the village. What a gorgeous idea.'

Camellia shrugged.

'It's our dream.' She glanced over at her husband. He was doing an impression of something, waving his hands in the smoke. She sighed. 'Yeah, my dad ran a hotel – over just past Ronda. It's what I grew up with. My dad was basically the perfect teacher.'

Leila took a sip of her wine.

'What fun – doing something together like that. I mean we've made some money selling flats, but we haven't really done it together. It's always been Charlie brilliantly finding them and then me getting on with the practical stuff so it wasn't all wires everywhere and no bath till the second we sold.'

Camellia put down her glass.

'Wait. You don't mean you were actually *living* in these places while you worked on them? Wow, that sounds kind of – exhausting.' There was genuine sympathy on her face. A mosquito circled and she flicked it away. 'But I thought . . . I thought you guys were . . . I thought Daria's always going round telling everyone Charlie's this huge—'

Leila looked down. Her own arms were unpleasantly white against the tablecloth and she folded them into her lap. She felt too tired just then for the intensity of female interaction and wished the men would come over and sit with them.

Camellia leant forward a little. 'Well, obviously you made money out of it – so, you know – so well done! That's the main thing.'

Leila nodded. She felt sure that if she was now asked to describe

41

her existence with Charlie she would simply not be able to. In fact she might burst into tears. This struck her as so pathetic that she made herself sit up straight.

There was another wild shout from the barbecue.

'Oh, God. Leila, could you excuse me for a second? I need to see what's happening over there. What is Jaime *doing*?'

Leila smiled in their direction.

'They're more interested in talking than cooking. It's a proper reunion, isn't it?' But Camellia was already up and off, jogging across the garden.

'*Tienes que girarla*, Jaime! You're going to *dry it out*.'

The stars were out by the time they ate and the sky felt cool and enormous above their plates. They ate hungrily, almost seriously, scraping their plates then soaking up the oil with their bread, taking slices of creamy cheese. But in spite of their pleasure, a silence came down over them like mist. At last even Jaime could not think what to say and the only sound was the wind rustling the foil on the meat.

Camellia relit a candle.

'That's better,' she said – as if that had been the problem. She propped her chin on her hands. 'You know, maybe we can get to know a couple things about each other. Good idea? It's been a long time with you two and I'm guessing you both changed!'

'Not so much,' said Jaime, smiling at his bread. 'He's a little fatter, I'm a little thinner.'

'Because I gotta tell you, Charlie, I did my best to find out but I really don't know what you do. Pilar's descriptions are kinda weird. Is it totally too hard to understand?'

'Not at all. It's just a hedge fund.'

'Una estructura financiera,' said Jaime.

Camellia circled her hand, 'OK – OK, so it's financial. But what exactly?'

'Camellia needs to know exactly,' said Jaime, winking at him.

'*Fatter*,' said Charlie.

'Sorry, man – still cute.'

'What we do exactly, Camellia, is take a risk and then hedge it. So let's say company A is valued at X. We think it's only worth V. So we borrow loads of money from the bank to buy options – like opportunities, basically – to sell it at X. That's a risk, OK? Then we take company B. It's valued at N. But we, in our wisdom, think it's worth Q, so we borrow loads of money from the bank to buy options to *buy* it at N but we don't use them till it hits Q. That's a hedge, right? This is massively oversimplified, but you get the gist. Anyway, then company A plummets to V so now we go back to all the suckers who thought it was worth X and they have to buy the options back at that price. Then company B, bless it, hits Q so we go back to all the suckers who thought it was worth N and they have to buy the options back at N. Legal obligation – very nice. Then we cash in on the difference.'

Camellia glanced from Charlie to Jaime and back again.

'*Perdon?*'

They all laughed. Her timing was good. She was very pretty in the candlelight and Leila could see why Jaime was in love with her.

The old dog came up to the table for leftovers. Camellia made it sit and fed it a scrap from her plate.

'Enough about all that, though,' said Charlie. 'What I want to know is what the fuck happened to your world takeover?'

Jaime leant his head right back so that the Adam's apple stuck out on his throat.

'My world takeover . . . Oh man, *now* we're getting into it.' He shook his soft pack and lit a cigarette. 'To fill this in for you, Leila, I used to have maybe a little different idea what I wanted in my life.' He waved his cigarette hand airily at the house and the garden. 'We grew up in the eighties, right? I was gonna be a *tycoon*.' He gave an idiotic grin and beat his chest like Tarzan.

Wagging its tail, the dog pushed its nose under his hand. Jaime rubbed his head in its fur.

'How about we cut the intro and have a few facts?' said Charlie. 'I thought you were learning all about business at "*school*".'

There was a new tension around the table now.

'Oh, come on now,' Jaime said. 'Do I need to say this stuff? *Everyone* knows this stuff.' He slumped in an attitude of extreme boredom. 'You want facts,' he said. 'Facts, facts, *facts*, the man wants. What should I tell you? What is a fact? So – yeah – so I go to *school*,' he said, winking at Charlie again, 'I walk off this fuckin' hillside out here and it's like: *New York, man!* You got bars, you got clubs, you got . . . *I'm nineteen years of age*. Right? Jaime thinks he got to heaven early.' He let his smile drop and turned his forefinger in a tired little circle. 'So then, you know, you just gotta fast forward a little and – you get what you got. OK?'

Charlie leant forward, furrowing his brow.

'You didn't get kicked out.'

'You *know* this shit. Yeah, just like you with your fuckin' boarding school, Carlos – only I beat you man 'cause I did it bigger. Sure, I got kicked out on my ass and that's when I – how does my mother say it? That's when I "*got sick*".' He waggled his fingers spookily either side of his face.

'What is this crap?' said Charlie. 'I never heard anything. I would have heard something.'

Jaime widened his eyes. He gave a roar of a laugh.

'Are you serious? She didn't even tell *Daria*? You gotta *love* this woman.'

Camellia stood up.

'Can I get anyone some dessert?' she said. 'It's really good. It's this thing I do with peaches.'

'Yes, I'm *serious*, you idiot,' said Charlie. 'Why? What the fuck was wrong with you?'

'Oh, man. Nothing? Everything? Like father, like son, right? I wanted to make lots of money quick. I got involved with this guy – this pyramid scheme.'

'But that's the oldest con in the book!'

'Yeah, yeah. So, anyhow the guy was a crook – *obviously*. So I got in a lot of debt and then everyone had to bail the poor loser out and then I had a kind of a nervous breakdown. OK? Jaime went *nuts* out there for a while . . .' He waggled his fingers again. Then he gave another roar of laughter, slapping Charlie on the shoulder – and Charlie attempted to laugh along with him at this odd punchline. But Leila could see he was shocked.

'Ah, so what? So I was gonna do one thing – and now I'm gonna do another thing. Here I am, back on the fuckin' hillside.' He shrugged, looking up at the stars, 'Do you care? *Does the moon feel sorry for Jaime?*' he shouted. Then he reached across the table and put his hand over Camellia's. 'No. What matters is I got this one now. This one sorted me out.'

'Oh, Jaime *stop*,' Camellia said. 'You're fine now. He's totally fine now.'

She pulled her hand away and then, rethinking this, she moved it back, pushing the hair off his forehead, tidying it.

'I'm sorry *cariño*. You forgive me? She hates when I talk about it.'

'No, I don't. I *don't*, Jaime. I just think it's old history, that's all.' She flinched at her mistake. 'Ancient history, I mean. Sorry.'

Pudding was an effective distraction. Afterwards, Leila went inside to help with coffee. Camellia gave her two cups. She was smiling excitedly.

'I had an idea,' she said. 'I thought maybe you wanna come see Alberto. He's so beautiful when he's asleep. Like an angel.'

Leila was touched. She carried out the coffee. When she came back in, Camellia took her hand and led her upstairs and into the hushed magic of the child's room. They peered round the door. Leila made out lace curtains in the window; a drum; a fluffy owl. A nightlight turned on a stand casting a pattern of butterflies.

'Come on over,' whispered Camellia, gesturing her to the cot. Holding their breath, they leant over Alberto asleep by his bear. He was a beautiful little boy. And how safe and loved he seemed, Leila thought, in the ordered sweetness of the room.

Unable to do anything about it, tears filled her eyes. Camellia turned to her.

'Take no notice,' Leila whispered. 'Please. He's perfect, Camellia. It's all perfect,' she insisted, wiping her eyes.

Camellia touched her arm.

'Hey, come on,' she said. 'Let's go sit down.'

There was a sofa by the kitchen.

'Camellia, I don't know how to apologise,' said Leila. 'Please will you forget all about it? I'm having such a lovely evening. It's just the journey. Maybe it's hormones. You know how it is.'

Camellia nodded.

'Sure. I know how it is. But listen, you don't have to worry so much, Leila,' she said. 'It's gonna be OK. It's natural.'

'I know,' said Leila, trying to smile. 'You're right. You're being so kind. Thank you.'

'Don't be nuts.' Camellia shook her head. The pale face, the hair thick and wild all over the place – in spite of herself she was beginning to like this jumpy English girl. But she was curious about her, too. About both of them.

'So personally, I have no clue why you would want to go to another country right when you're about to have your first child, but I'm *sure* you can make it work. Right?'

'Oh, yes,' Leila said cheerfully. 'No, it'll all be fine. It's the most beautiful house, isn't it?'

Camellia was disappointed.

'La Campañera? Sure it is. Jaime *loves* it up there. Not that we can ever go. But you know what these men and their mothers are like.'

She rolled her eyes. 'Families, right?' She hesitated. 'So . . . so is your mother coming out?' Leila shook her head and, unable to help herself now, Camellia gasped, 'She *isn't*?'

'No. Actually my mother isn't alive any more,' Leila told her, averting her eyes.

'Oh, shit. Oh, God. Now I'm totally embarrassed.'

'Please don't be. How could you know? And it wasn't recent or anything anyway. She died when I was seven.'

'Wow, that's so . . . Who raised you?'

'My dad. Sort of. Really it was Kate – my elder sister.'

As she said the name she felt her whole body clench up with the urge to be off that sofa, to be outside again under the sky, free of this ordinary human curiosity.

'Camellia,' she said, 'you're going to think I'm the greediest person you ever met, but could I have a bit more pudding?'

'Are you *serious*? Sure you can.' Camellia stood up, delighted – Jaime was such a poor eater – always talking, talking, pushing his food around. 'A little more for the baby, right?'

As they came back outside, Jaime stopped what he was saying. He put out his arms.

'Here comes my love! Now,' he said, turning to Charlie, '*what* do we think they were they talking about? How will we place our bets, gentlemen? Hmmm? They were talking about *babies*, I think. Shall we put it all on that one, Carlos? Is *that* the one that'll make us rich? Babies, babies, *baybeeeeez*?'

Camellia put a napkin on top of his head and, in a burst of spontaneous affection, which was plainly his speciality, he pulled her on to his lap, covering her neck and face in kisses.

They had been drinking brandy. Charlie poured himself another full glass. He put the bottle back on the table.

Something on the horizon caught Leila's eye. It began as an indistinct glimmer. Her eyes narrowed. Slowly it became a low haze of light and she found herself staring, unable to speak with a mixture of dread and fascination. It was disembodied – magical. What *was* it? It moved, picking out trees one minute, turning them into fiery silhouettes, then almost going dark the next.

'Leila,' whispered Charlie, 'what the hell's wrong with you? Why are you gazing at the road like that?'

The road, she thought. She had forgotten all about the road. It was nothing more than a truck. A large truck with headlights.

'Sorry,' she said, feeling stupid. 'I . . . thought I saw something. But I didn't.'

She could sense his irritation. She was not surprised. This was exactly the kind of vagueness that drove him mad. What was she doing, she thought, staring into space? It was embarrassing for him. There was nothing to see. Nothing. She settled herself in her chair again and picked up her glass.

But still her eyes wandered back to the road. Parallel to them now, the lorry rushed past, smooth as a jet engine, its headlights sweeping the air.

Chapter 6

Leila was woken by a line of sunlight angling through a gap in the curtains. She turned over, blinking, to find that Charlie was already up. She wondered what time it was. It was very bright. It might have been midday.

She rolled on to her back and instinctively her hand moved down to her stomach, but there was still no outward sign that she was pregnant. Her fingers pressed against her skin. When did it show? It was terrible not to know such basic things. But somehow there had not been time to buy any pregnancy books before they left.

'Oh, I see, you're awake are you?' said Charlie, putting his head round the door. 'I thought you were going to be out cold till the day after tomorrow.'

His hair was wet. There were patches of sunburn above his cheek-bones.

'Have you been swimming?' she said.

'I've been doing all sorts of things. I've brought all the bags in for one thing. Acts of heroism before breakfast. I've even unpacked the books.'

'You haven't. What time is it?'

He went into the bathroom and turned on the taps.

'Bit after twelve,' he called back.

'*Twelve?* My God.'

'Got an urgent appointment?'

She leant back into the pillows again.

'No, I suppose you're right.'

'God, I'm unfit. What happened to me? Jaime's right – I am bloody fatter.' He slapped his bare stomach. 'OK, I'm going to have a shower,' he called. 'There's some coffee downstairs if you want it. Bit cold by now though.'

He began to whistle an echoey tune and then she heard the shower start up. There was a flash of his back in the mirror as he got in.

She stretched and got out of bed. Her head felt heavy after her long sleep but the thought of the garden waiting outside began to fill her with excitement. She grabbed Charlie's shirt off the chair and ran downstairs doing it up as she went.

Ahead of her the glass doors were open, framed with interesting leaves, but with an effort she resisted running over to them and went for the coffee first. There was a carton of UHT milk on the table and she splashed some in. Then she carried her cup out on to the garden steps.

It was eye-wateringly bright. The stone was baking underfoot and she hopped quickly into a patch of shade. She took a sip of the coffee and peered into the sunshine. Her view from the hall window the evening before had not done it any kind of justice. Now, in the daylight, the garden cascaded downhill in front of her and then rose up again in a dizzying network of tiny paths and avenues. Everywhere the eye fell were different plants or bushes or small trees, all of them live and vibrating with bees and butterflies.

It had been a long time since she had lived in a place with a garden. She stood in amazement for a while. Then, remembering herself, she glanced up at the bathroom window and sat on the step to drink her coffee.

The rest of the day passed with odd speed. The shops in the village didn't open until after three so they shared the stuffed peppers for lunch with some figs from the garden afterwards. The figs were sweet and still warm from the sun. The stuffed peppers had probably been better the day before.

Later on they drove down into the village for food, stopping at each of the little shops in the main street for packages of ham and spicy sausage and cheese, for bottled water and tomatoes and aubergines and potatoes and eggs. Most of the women remembered Charlie. They remembered Daria in particular. How was *she*, they wanted to know. Still beautiful? Still the wonderful clothes?

While Charlie spoke Spanish, Leila did her best with the assistants – the self-conscious teenage girls or boys with their acne and their rock T-shirts and their neat aprons – pointing at the food in the glass cases and holding out her hand for them to take the money.

'I really must get on with learning this language,' she said as they got back to the car.

'Why? You're not missing much. Just gossipy village stuff,' said Charlie. 'Don't stress yourself out.'

She put the bags on the back seat. Seeing him climb in and start the engine, she felt a little sting of anger that it never occurred to him that she might like to drive.

It was not long before a routine established itself. On the days they did not go out in the morning, Charlie woke first and went for a swim or a run and Leila slept on, finding his plate and empty cup when she came down. She would discover him under the fig trees reading the paper and would sit cross-legged beside him with her coffee and fruit.

Then the rest of the morning always vanished and after a lunch of bread and salad and cheese, it was three before they knew it. In the afternoon they went off to see something: a bullring, a little museum, a church, a cathedral, a ruin. With a pile of guidebooks and a glass of wine, Charlie had compiled a list and they worked their way through it diligently. Some days they left first thing and didn't get back until long after dark.

With unfortunate timing, Camellia and Jaime had to go away to Madrid, where Camellia's cousin was getting married. Camellia was matron of honour and they were away for two weeks while she helped to arrange the wedding.

'I feel guilty,' Jaime said when he called to say goodbye. 'You only just got here. We should be making sure you guys are settled.'

'We'll do our best,' said Charlie. 'But it's going to be tough.'

'You know what I mean, man. Listen, we'll get together as soon as we're back, OK? I gotta to show you our building site. Our bomb-site. A little holiday from that now, though. Fuck, we need it. You take it easy, too, won't you? Leila should rest. And you, man.'

But there was so much to see – so much to do. Charlie couldn't believe he'd been stuck in his office for so long – that his view of the world had been reduced to a seventeen inch rectangle! They must make a pact, he said, that they would never be too tired to go out, that they wouldn't waste a second of this opportunity. He put out his hand – and Leila shook it, gladdened if a bit dazed by this enthusiasm.

50

It was only at night, lying in bed, their bodies inches apart beneath the sheet, that she thought how much she would like simply to lie in the hammock all morning, reading – or to float up and down the pool, looking at the sky, with the birds singing all around. She would suggest it the next day, she decided. They could spread out their lunch on the table by the swimming pool.

But when she got dressed and went down in the morning there he was, ready with the road map and the next place on the list. Did she want toast? He had already made them some coffee.

Charlie was getting leaner and more tanned by the day. It was all obviously doing him good.

'Sleep tight,' he would say, stretching his foot across the bed at night, pressing his toes on her ankle. Then he would roll over on to his side and very soon his breathing would slow.

Jaime came back from Madrid. Camellia had stayed on, because she wanted Alberto to spend a little more time with the cousins. Enough cousins for him, though – and aunts and uncles and *mothers-in-law*, he said. He'd had enough of family himself for at least a year.

They all went into the village to see the hotel.

'Don't expect too much at this point, OK?' said Jaime. 'Be ready for a work in progress.'

It was one o'clock and everyone had gone home for the siesta. The village was a bright desert. They left the car on the cobbles outside the police station and went up the hill towards the little tower.

Jaime unlocked a wooden door and let them into a passageway. He kicked aside a sheet of polythene. Ahead of them was an inner courtyard with a gallery running round above. Lying about were rolls of insulation, plasterboard, oak beams and bags of cement. There was a lot of work to do.

'Gavin would love this,' said Leila.

'Gavin?'

'Our friend from home. Our friend from another world.'

Jaime swung an imaginary pocket watch in front of her eyes. 'Be careful – it does that to you here. Maybe you'll never go back.'

'We'll go back,' said Charlie. 'I've got a business to run.'

When they got back to La Campañera, Leila went off to the kitchen, leaving the other two on the terrace with cold beers and a bowl of cashew nuts. She had found a recipe in one of Pilar's cookery books, which it was not too hard to understand. All the difficult words had been in the dictionary and she had translated it at night as a surprise.

51

She worked quietly in the kitchen, chopping the garlic, cooking the chicken and rosemary and rice.

They were starving when she carried it out.

'It's an experiment,' she said. 'I hope it's edible. It's "*Paella de Polio*".'

'*Paella de Polio*? So, she's a real Spanish cook now. Wow, this is one of my *all-time favourites*,' said Jaime, tucking the edge of the tablecloth into the collar of his T-shirt.

She served it out for them and Charlie went back for some forks.

'Sorry. I always forget cutlery,' Leila said.

When they sat down, she tasted it nervously. There seemed to be a great deal of rice but the flavour was not bad. A little too much garlic, perhaps.

Jaime leant towards her and put his hand on her wrist. 'OK, so don't *ever* tell her I said this, but it's better than Camellia's. She doesn't put in enough sherry!' He held up his fork. 'And without that, what's the point?'

This formed the basis of an impromptu toast. It was good to have Jaime around. Charlie in particular seemed much happier.

After lunch, Charlie and Jaime talked on well into the evening and Leila went inside with her book.

The next morning, Charlie went off into the village to meet Jaime and the builders.

'The thing is, it's actually a good idea,' he said, knocking back his coffee. 'I genuinely think it could make money. It's just Jaime's figures are a bit of a mess. I'm going to go and meet the head guy this morning. See what's what. The budget needs work and their forecasting's on the fantastical side, but it's nothing that can't be sorted out. I'll spend a bit of time there this week I thought. It's the least I can do really, when I haven't seen him for so long.'

He checked his pockets for something.

'That's great,' said Leila. 'How wonderful you can help.'

'So I'll be back around lunch-ish. Bit later maybe. Don't wait if you get starving.'

'No. OK,' she said.

She listened to the car start up. When he had driven away, she realised she had left her book on the back seat. But it didn't matter. There were plenty of other books. She wandered over to the pile Charlie had made on the shelf by the kitchen door and stood in front of them for a while but none of them caught her eye.

She went over to the sofa and lay down, though she did not think she would fall asleep.

Chapter 7

Carefully shading his eyes, Charlie pushed open the glass door into the garden. Leila was sitting at the table.

'Did I wake you last night?' he said. She shook her head. 'Liar.'

'What happened? Did something break?'

He sat down heavily on a little wrought-iron chair. It wobbled disconcertingly.

'Vase. Great big thing. Don't stress about it, though – she's got a cupboard full.' The chair wobbled again and he jammed one of its legs into a gap in the paving stones. How did his Uncle Rodrigo stand it, he thought. It was all like doll's furniture.

Leila had taken out the middle section of his paper and was doing the crossword. He had never seen her do a crossword before. For some reason this irritated him. Charlie's eyes watered in the sunshine and he wished he had his sunglasses. But he'd gone and left them somewhere the night before. Where? At La Maja probably. When he thought about it he could remember putting them down on the windowsill beside the urinals.

How much had he drunk? More than he'd meant to at any rate. Jaime seemed to get plastered on nothing at all – probably because he was skinny as a girl. Or maybe he was on some kind of medication. He put this thought aside. Anyway, it had been himself and old Mourino who really put it all away – but Jaime was the one who passed out.

For a moment he watched Leila filling in a clue. Her teeth rested on her lower lip. She scribbled out a letter and wrote another one carefully beside it. There were dark circles under her eyes.

He sighed.

'Listen, I know I said I'd make it back for supper. OK? Disgraceful behaviour. I know.' His head throbbed and he pressed his palms hard into the temples. 'If it's any consolation I feel sick as a dog.'

He stared at the main section of the paper. Then with a slight impatience he flipped it open, turning over a few pages. The words flickered without meaning much, though there was something on the sub-prime market in America which looked interesting.

He would have to eat something first, though – and find some painkillers.

Leila took a crust of bread off her plate, broke it into pieces and threw it to the thrushes on the steps. Immediately another five or six descended. He thought of telling her to stop feeding them like that. There were hundreds as it was, squawking all over the place. They had woken him up.

There was a loud noise from the house.

'Christ, now what?' he said.

'What?'

'That ringing. Your phone is it?'

She listened. 'Must be yours.'

He took it out of his pocket and held it up. It was off.

'Well it's not mine either because I can't find it and it must have run out of batteries by now.' She had spoken these last words into her lap. He rolled his eyes at her. Was it six – *seven* phones she'd lost now?

'Well, it must be the land line, then, mustn't it?' he said.

'Is there one?'

'What? Of course there bloody is. It's on the table in the sitting room. Haven't you even noticed it? You are strange, Leila,' he said, feeling angry. The ringing went on. 'Oh, for fuck's sake, who *is* it? Can't they just let us die in peace!'

'You'd better go, Charlie – they'll want to talk Spanish.'

'Me? Forget it. I'm not even up for English this morning. You go. Just say "*Pilar no esta*" or "*murieron en un incendio*," or better still tug it out of the fucking socket.' He dropped his head on to his forearms and groaned. Leila let the pen roll out of her hand. It came to a stop just short of his elbow. 'Or,' he muttered, 'we could just sit here listening to it I suppose.'

'No we can't. It might be important.' Reluctantly, she got up and ran towards the house.

54

Inside the ringing had a deafening, shrill tone. She headed for the table and at last she grabbed it and the noise stopped.

'Hello?' She braced herself for a deluge of Spanish – but there was silence. Then came a hissing interspersed with fragments of a male voice. It was a mobile phone moving in and out of reception. 'Hello?' she said again.

'Leila? Hello? Is that you?'

She had no idea who it was.

'Yes,' she said, 'it's me.' Then she paused. '. . . Hugo?'

There was laughter. 'Fuck's sake. Hugo – from England? Meant to be your husband's *business partner*?'

'Sorry,' she said. 'The line's bad.'

'I thought you'd both vaporised. Where've you been? I've been leaving messages.'

'Have you? I think Charlie's phone's off.'

'Is it. Well, that's brilliant.'

'*Leila?*' said Charlie. His voice made her jump. Having grown curious and hot he had come inside. He squinted at her. 'Leila, who is it?' he whispered.

'It's Hugo,'

He walked over briskly to the phone and she surrendered the receiver to him.

'*Hugo?* How did you get this number? Oh . . . oh right, very resourceful. What? Yes, it is off. Well, because I've got a fucking hang-over, all right?'

She listened to the one-sided conversation for a while. In the garden, the newspaper had blown off the table. Two birds hopped about on her plate.

'What, both of you? Right. I see. Freebie holiday is it? No, OK, OK, just give me a second, all right? Leila?' Charlie lowered the receiver. He raised his eyebrows at her. 'How about Hugo and Gavin come out here for a long weekend. The one after next. We'd love it, wouldn't we?'

The face was taut, luminous. She felt herself nodding at it. He put the phone to his ear.

'Go on then,' he said, 'you cheeky bastard. But you'll have to get a hire car from the airport, I'm not driving down.'

The next two weeks were mainly taken up with work on the hotel. Jaime's project manager, who had secretly taken on two jobs at the same time, had announced there was a major problem with the drainage from the showers in two of the upper rooms and that materials would have to be sent away for from Seville. Charlie went down to find out what was going on and it turned out this was only because he had been attempting to cut costs on the piping.

As a result of these talks, work accelerated and the entrance hall was plastered and even painted by the time Camellia arrived back from Madrid. She was amazed and delighted.

Impatient to start work again she left Alberto with her young cousin some afternoons and she and Charlie and Jaime sat down together going over the figures. It was now accepted that Charlie was helping them 'straighten things out' as Camellia put it: she and Jaime would be lost without him!

Charlie was enjoying himself. Camellia made him some spiced anchovy biscuits to have with his drink in the evening and also a batch of her special white almond ice cream. Giving careful instructions, she told Leila how to make the little pastries that went with it so well. They were only *perfect*, she explained, if you ate them fresh and hot from the oven, so that the ice cream melted against the buttery puff pastry. Otherwise she would have made them herself.

Leila took the recipe into the kitchen and put it on the shelf. There was a bottle opener on the sideboard. She noticed Jaime had started drinking at eleven in the morning. At the front of the house he swung Alberto round in giggling, squealing circles. Charlie and Camellia tapped at their calculators on the garden table.

Chapter 8

It was on the following weekend that Hugo and Gavin pulled into the drive in their red hire car. Charlie was still in the pool and Leila rushed out to the door alone.

Gavin was first on the doorstep. He had his arms full of bags.

'I'm the porter,' he said. 'Hugo's in charge of alcohol. He bought a cellar full in Seville. Kiss me quickly then point me in the right direction so I can dump all this stuff. I have *got* to get a pair of shorts on before we talk about anything. It's baking! Fuck, I thought it would be much like England this early in the summer.'

He looked stifled in his old jeans and checked shirt.

'I think it's quite suddenly got hotter.'

'To scare off the visiting English.'

'I hope not. I'm English too.'

'You're exempt. You've got *Carlos* to dignify you.' He bounced one of the bags off his shoulder and on to his hip. 'So, where to, before I drop it all?'

'Up those stairs. You're on the right just at the top and then Hugo's in the blue room at the end.'

Gavin saluted and set off towards the staircase.

It was true; it had become an incredibly hot day. Wiping her forehead, Leila leant her weight against the wicker chair for a moment. She had slept badly again the night before – maybe just because of the heat, she thought. *Was* it hotter or was it just that the breeze had disappeared, though? It was eerie out there with the trees all completely still like that, she thought.

Charlie came in from the pool.

'Are they here? Have they arrived?'

'Yes. Gavin's upstairs.'

The front door swung open and in came Hugo with clinking plastic bags. On his head was a ragged panama hat and under his arm was a parcel tied with a bow. He looked plump and handsome.

'Greetings,' he said, 'you old waster.' He put the bags down and gripped Charlie's arm. Charlie did the same back. For some reason they never hugged. 'Here – bought you a present,' he said, handing over the parcel. 'Don't say I don't love you.'

Charlie began to tear it open. There was fiddly sellotape.

'Did you enjoy the drive?' said Leila. 'It's stunning, isn't it?'

'Hell of a lot of wind farms, I notice.'

'They're new,' said Charlie. 'All since I was last here. Ugly.'

'Profitable. Can be. Government or private?'

'No idea. Hugo, what is this thing?' At last it came open. Inside the tissue paper was a stack of documents. 'This is . . . is this Swiss stuff?' said Charlie.

'I thought I'd better smuggle it in, in disguise. I did email, but I got no reply.'

'When?'

'Late last night.'

'For Christ's sake, Hugo, I'm on holiday.'

'Yes, but a few of the Swiss have pulled out, OK? I saw it coming. There's some scare-mongering in the markets at the moment. It's just press-driven bollocks. Anyway, I thought you might want to know about it. Or am I wrong? Or is it *banned*?' said Hugo, leaning down toward Leila and narrowing his eyes. At the last second, he turned this gesture into a kiss.

'Nothing's banned,' she said, kissing him back. 'It's lovely to see you, Hugo. How are you?'

He smiled.

'Overworked.'

Charlie began turning pages. 'Fuck, I see what you mean,' he said.

It wasn't long before Gavin came down. He joined Leila on the grass, sitting cross-legged beside her. His legs were long and thin in their shorts. He put an arm round her shoulders and she moved closer to him.

Inside, shouting back and forth to one another, Hugo loaded the fridge with wine and Charlie clattered things in the cupboard by

58

the kitchen door, dragging out the umbrella and the garden cushions, which he and Leila had never bothered with for themselves.

'I still can't believe you don't mind,' said Gavin.

'Mind what?'

'The English invasion. I was a bit amazed when Hugo said you and Charlie had suggested it.'

It didn't surprise her that Hugo had lied.

'Gavin, it's gorgeous to see you,' she said, 'it always is.'

And it was good to see Gavin, she thought.

'Honestly and truly? OK. OK, I'll stop panicking.' He put on his sunglasses. 'My God, just look at this place. There's even a hammock! You must be in your element with all these plants. Have you been digging about? You must've been.'

'No, I haven't actually. There's a gardener anyway and there . . . hasn't been time.'

'Too busy snoozing and reading. Good.' He leant back on his elbows. 'Oh, you two were *so* right to do this, you know? What a relief to get away from the real world.'

Chapter 9

It was too beautiful an evening to cram themselves into cars, so after drinks Gavin suggested they simply walk to the village. They set off down the path, beneath the chestnut tree, towards the church and the clock tower and the cluster of terracotta roofs.

'For heaven's sake, I feel drunk already,' Gavin said. 'Am I the only one? Those gin and tonics were nuclear, Hugo. We will eat *something* tonight, won't we?'

'There'll be food at the party,' said Charlie. 'And we'll eat later. Stop worrying.'

The sky was a purplish blue now, suspended halfway between day and night. Directly ahead of them the sunset had made a bonfire of the horizon and above it, barely clear of the flames, was the palest ghost of a moon.

They reached the cobbled section at the outskirts of the village and Charlie shouted for them to turn right towards the tower house. It had remained both hot and still. Washing hung down with the insistence of plaster, bead curtains seemed to have been caught in a photograph. They walked slowly, past the low open windows with the TVs on and the pans clanking and the children doing their homework at the kitchen tables.

They arrived at the wooden door. It had been decorated with a bunch of red flowers. Sounds of talking and laughter came from inside.

'We're here,' said Leila. She looked back at Charlie.

'Go on then,' he said and she knocked.

A few seconds later there was echoey giggling in the entranceway, then the bolt drew back and Camellia pulled open the door.

'Well, *buenos noches*!' she said. 'A big crowd of English!'

Leila had not seen her tipsy before. She was wearing a blue silk dress with a 1950s full skirt and a string of pearls around her neck. Her hair was up in a bun but a good many strands of it had come down around her shoulders, as if she had been dancing. Her eyes glittered with excitement. 'So, who *is* everyone? Come in!'

Charlie named them in turn as they stepped over the threshold, like members of a jazz band.

'This extremely tall gentleman is Gavin, Leila you know. The man with the million-dollar smile is my business partner Hugo . . . and this is – well, me.'

'Well – you!' Camellia threw her arms round him affectionately.

'Thanks so much for letting us come this evening, Camellia,' said Gavin. 'I do like your party dress.'

'My . . . ? Oh – thank you! Thank you. How charming. You have charming friends, Leila. How are you, *cariño*? Hmm? You look tired.' She was astonished to see that Leila was again wearing one of Charlie's shirts. She also had no make-up on and her hair hung down either side of her face. 'And you're totally welcome here, Gavin. Yeah, it's a big day for us. We're not finished or anything – but we're finally getting *somewhere*. This is our getting-somewhere party. All thanks to Charlie.'

'Is it?' said Hugo. 'Branching out?'

'*Helping* out,' said Charlie. 'Minimally.'

'He's too modest. OK, guys, come get something to drink,' said Camellia. She led them through the second doorway and into the inner courtyard where there were twenty or so other people of various ages with drinks.

Over to one side, on a plank between two piles of bricks, sat Jaime. He was playing guitar, directing the music at two little girls who were tying his shoelaces together. As soon as the others came in, his face broke into its broad grin and he kicked off the shoes and jumped down.

'Who's this racing over?' whispered Gavin.

'That's Charlie's cousin,' said Leila.

'*That's* Jaime? Wow, they're nothing like each other. He's so . . . teenage-boyish. *Lucky* Camellia.'

'What did I do?' said Camellia, hearing her name.

'I was just saying how lucky you are to have found this place.'

'Oh – Jaime's idea. Jaime thought of it,' she said humbly. 'It's basically been a wreck forever. He used to play in here when he was a little boy, getting up to who knows what.'

Jaime came up to them. He had his guitar under one arm and a box of beer under the other.

'Now who's gonna tell me we're not five-star already?' he said.

Hugo took a bottle and Gavin passed another over to Charlie.

'Jaime, you could get *glasses*,' said Camellia. '*Cariño?* Maybe they don't want just a *bottle?* Don't worry, guys, we have glasses. We have plenty glasses if you want them. Also we have wine.'

'Ooh, could I possibly have wine?' said Gavin. 'I'm all fizzy with gin and tonic already.'

'Sure you can.'

'My apologies,' said Jaime putting a hand on his back. 'You want a bottle or a glass?'

They all laughed at his innocent joke.

'I'll get you a *glass* of wine, Gavin,' said Camellia, rolling her eyes. 'Leila, you want one too?'

'Thanks – a small one. Just to toast you. I shouldn't have much.'

'Don't worry, Camellia – I'll help her finish it,' Gavin called after her. Leila nudged him. 'What?' he said. 'I've given up on my attempt to remain civilised and you look like you could do with it to be honest, sweetheart. I've never seen you so thin and dark-circly.' Leila tucked her hair behind her ears self-consciously. Gavin wondered for a second whether to tease her about the enormous shirts of Charlie's which she was swamping herself in, but he thought better of it and put his arm round her instead.

'So. Here we go, guys,' said Camellia, arriving with a tray. 'We have rose, we have red and we have white.'

The place looked pretty, if a little eccentric, with its candles sitting on piles of bricks and its red streamers hanging from the banister round the gallery. Most of the guests stood out in the centre of the courtyard, in the last of the evening light. Over their heads white wisteria framed the edge of the roof and far above was an emerging pattern of stars.

Soon there was salsa music on a stereo. Some of the children began to dance, then the adults. Gavin spun Leila around a bit and then Hugo, who was an unexpectedly good dancer, took over. He and Leila had often danced together at parties in the past, though they hadn't for a long time.

They went round a few times. There was no question he was drunk, but when he smiled and shook his head at her in his usual way, there was a warmth in his eyes. Leila found she was greatly relieved by this and did not want to say she was too tired to dance.

'You know you're still the best dancer of any girl I know?' he said.

'I can't be. Anyhow, it's all about who's leading you. Everyone knows that.'

He spun her round in a tight circle and her skirt flared out. Then he pulled her back in so that she thudded against his shoulder.

'Why d'you do that?' he asked, narrowing his eyes.

'Sorry.'

'No, not that. I did that. Why d'you undersell yourself? "It's all about who's leading you." You have to *sell* yourself in this world, Leila. People fuck you over. People lose respect. It's like dogs. You must know that. What goes on in that head of yours?' He scrutinised her. She smiled at him nervously.

'Christ, don't pass out,' he said, laughing. 'We'll fuck the psycho-babble, shall we? You must be a confirmed lunatic trying to stop Charlie working, anyway.'

Later, Hugo danced with a few of the Spanish girls and then finally with Camellia. They danced well together. Hugo put his hands on her waist and Camellia tipped her head back and laughed and seemed to be enjoying herself. All the children took it in turns to sit on Jaime's shoulders while he did a crazy routine up and down the floor.

Gavin watched, sitting on the wall.

'He's barmy – but he's a bit of a sweetheart, isn't he?'

'Jaime? Yes, he's lovely,' said Leila.

'My God, it's just dawning on me. Is he the boy in all the photos at Charlie's parents' house? He *is*. *That's* the amazing bloody cousin. Charlie used to go on and on about him at school. Drove me wild with jealousy.'

'Did it?'

'Don't laugh. The depths I sank to! I used to mount term-long negative campaigns about all things Spanish. Little subliminal remarks over breakfast: did anyone know that the gunners in the Spanish Armada didn't even know how to reload their guns? Charlie would just carry on buttering his toast.' Leila giggled, able to picture this only too easily.

'Gavin, I can't believe you did any of that.'

'This is because you've always had far too high an opinion of me. Of all men, I slightly suspect. The fact is it's crap, that stuff about hell having no fury like a woman scorned. It's *men* you need to worry about – and the trouble is we're *forever* feeling scorned. By anyone and everyone – not just lovers. Yes, I've always thought we're the ones with the really dangerous vanity. You lot sort of keep an eye on it every day in the mirror. Ours is the hidden kind – goes right down to the core, where the world wars get dreamt up – or the *hedge funds*.' Gavin put his glass to his lips, but it was already empty. He took another from the tray behind him. 'Leila, I'm theorising, aren't I? Why are you letting me? I'm drunk.'

At last the party began to break up. Soon only the English were left, along with Camellia's cousin and her boyfriend in the corner. They were apparently no more than twenty and both a little out of their element in an older crowd, let alone one which was shouting and joking back and forth in English.

Camellia went out into the centre of the courtyard.

'OK,' she said, waving her hands, '*everyone*. Shall we go eat? *Vamos a comer?*' she called out to her cousin. They both stood up dutifully, smoothing down their clothes.

'Camellia, that is a truly *wonderful* idea,' said Gavin. 'You lead the way. Where to?'

'To La Campañera, of course.'

'Oh. Are you cooking, Leila?'

'No,' said Leila. 'Camellia is.'

'Oh. Right. For the whole lot of us, though? Really?'

'Sure. Why not?' said Camellia.

'This is deep self-confidence,' said Gavin. 'You're plainly a very good cook. But hang on a minute – come here, will you? You're also in need of my expert assistance.'

Tilting towards her a little unsteadily, Gavin tried to push some of her dark hair back into the bun at the back of her head. She leant over for him, resting her hand on his knee.

Gavin struggled with the clip.

'Fuck me, this is fiddly. Delicate thingy all tangled up. What *have* you been doing?'

Camellia shrugged. She took another gulp of her wine.

Finding himself unusually impatient, Gavin scooped up as much hair as he could and attempted to cram it in under the tortoiseshell clip, but as he did so it broke into pieces in his fingers and the mass of dark hair fell loose around her shoulders.

He covered his mouth, appalled.

'Camellia, I'm so sorry!' But she was laughing again. She set down her glass. Then she stood, tipped her head upside down and stamping her feet a little, she shook the remaining fragments out of her hair and on to the dirty floor.

Chapter 10

They decided to stop for one drink in the main square before going back to La Campañera.

Even the absence of daylight did not seem to have cooled the village down. It was already past eleven but there were still children's voices in the windless streets; their laughter and their footsteps echoed round corners so that they always seemed to be just a little way off.

They approached the slope down into the main square. Music floated out from the bars and restaurants. The trees were decked out in white lights.

'Is this real? It's a fairground!' said Gavin.

There was a crowd outside La Maja and Charlie and Jaime said hello to a few of the locals before the waitress came over. Hugo insisted on ordering.

'Oh God, just don't get too much,' said Gavin. 'What we need at this stage is food, not booze.'

Hugo waved him off.

There were metal tables to sit at but it was cooler out by the fountain in the square. Leila sat on the edge. A cherub spouted water out of its mouth. In the basin hovered two shadowy old carp. Gavin peered at them squeamishly.

'Eek. D'you think they're alive?'

Above them, the moon wobbled on the surface.

'Where's Charlie?' said Leila.

'Good question. I keep losing sight of him this evening. Still chatting at the bar with Jaime? Oh no, there he is – over there, amusing our serious young friends. Which one's the cousin again?'

66

'The girl, Christina.'

Charlie and Camellia were talking Spanish with them. They were plainly being funny together. Leila had never seen Camellia laugh so much.

In the doorway beside them, some children were playing a game.

'What are they up to? Some kind of a competition is it?' said Hugo, pointing.

'It's courtly love,' said Gavin. 'Two gentle knights vying for the attention of their lady. Don't you think?'

Seconds later there was a fight. The stockier of the boys wrestled the other one to the ground and punched him. One of the waitresses went out to intervene.

'She's a bit young to be causing all that trouble, isn't she?' said Hugo, laughing.

Camellia glanced over. She clicked her tongue.

'You gotta remember this is *Spain*, Hugo. We know we're women pretty young out here. *Very* young.'

'Is that so?' he said.

'Uh-huh.'

Leila noticed how beautiful Camellia was this evening; how her eyes flashed and her pearl necklace shone against her dark skin. A lot of men were looking at her.

'Don't get me wrong, Camellia,' said Hugo, 'but I'd say that gives you an unfair advantage.'

She winked at him and he ground his cigarette out under his heel.

The girl arrived with the wine. Then straight afterwards another girl arrived with a tray of shots. There was general groaning at Hugo, but except for Leila, they all clinked glasses and drank.

It was past midnight by the time they set off for the house. Camellia and Jaime stopped for their car and the food. Then Jaime sped up the road behind the others, hooting and swerving and flashing the lights to get through.

While the rest of them sprawled out in the garden, Camellia put on her apron and made her fish stew. When it was ready, she laid it out on the table in the kitchen. There was a green salad and warm bread to go with it. Beside the bowls sat the stew in an earthenware pot. It was rich with chorizo and potatoes and monkfish and the colour of the tomatoes was set off by green herbs.

But no one was hungry any more.

'I think the trouble is, it's too beautiful to eat,' said Gavin.

Camellia seemed not to care. She threw off her apron.

'Ah, we'll have some later. What's the difference, right?' she said.

They wandered back out with their glasses. On the kitchen table, the stew congealed in the moonlight. When it was certain everyone was safely outside, a cat climbed in through the window, jumped on to the table and dragged off a large piece of cod.

It was not long before Jaime took out his guitar. Leila could hear him singing as she made her way up to the bedroom. He had a beautiful voice; quite high, almost feminine at times, she thought. She would have liked to listen to him, but her eyes were closing with exhaustion.

Clutching his plate and a wine bottle, Hugo sat down beside Camellia at the garden table.

'Now don't you dare throw any of that marvellous stew out,' he said, steadying his chair. 'I'm planning to have it all for breakfast.'

She let him refill her glass.

'I'll join you,' she said. Then she widened her eyes and giggled through her fingers.

'I can't think of anything nicer, Camellia. Better leave some for that skinny husband of yours, though, hadn't we? Don't you feed him, then?'

She blew the hair out of her eyes.

'Jaime is just like that. It's how he is. We tried the protein drinks – we tried the weights. It's how he is.'

They both glanced over. He was cross-legged, playing alone now, his face tilted up at the stars.

'Not a lot to hold on to,' said Hugo. 'If you know what I mean.'

Camellia's elbow slipped a little off the edge of the table.

'He loves me,' she said. 'You know?'

'Yeah, I know,' said Hugo.

A barely perceptible breeze wobbled the pearls on her earrings. From the end of the garden came a series of screams followed by a loud splash. She wrinkled her nose.

'Are they *swimming?*'

'Are they? What *is* the world coming to?'

'It's gonna be nice and cool in the water I guess . . .'

'Too much like exercise for me. Life's too fucking short. It's too fucking short to spend half of it forcing yourself to do things you

68

hate, Camellia, when you spend the other half forcing yourself *not* to do things you know you'd love. Cigarette?'

'I quit. Two years ago,' she said. Then she propped herself up on an elbow. Hugo smiled. He handed her one and struck a match.

On the table were two glass lanterns with candles rippling light up into the white umbrella. In the surrounding darkness were velvety petals and leaves thick and glossy with juice. The garden at La Campañera was so beautiful it was possible to forget the existence of the house altogether.

Some figures made their way across the grass.

'Hey, who's coming? Who's this?' said Camellia, shading her eyes. 'Is it Charlie?'

'Didn't you *hear* me?' came the voice.

'It's Gavin. *Hear you what?*'

With him were Pablo and Christina. Christina was unable to walk straight. Their hair was wet. They each carried their shoes.

'*Hear me what?* Honestly, you callous pair. Sitting here calmly when there's been an attempt on my life. For your information I have been *hurled ruthlessly* into the water *five* times. Horrible. Just like being at school again. Pablo and Christina rescued me. Charlie's still out there doing perfect dives, insulting the gods. It's all a bit demoralising. Any more of that wine? It's meant to last the weekend, Hugo. Are you *smoking*, Camellia?'

'Optical illusion. You're imagining it,' said Hugo.

'Of course I am. That time of night. Anyway, we've come inside to escape. There's a pool table somewhere, isn't there?'

'Uh-huh,' said Camellia. 'Just across from the kitchen. The light switch is out in the hall in this kinda little box. I can come show you if you like.'

'You know, I think I can find a light switch. Actually it's very import-ant I believe in my practical abilities to this extent. Pablo? Christina? *Vamos a casa?*'

Camellia laughed.

'Oh I see, you're all talking just fine now, are you?'

'As long as we stick to being grateful for things or suggesting we go inside. Actually we've discovered Pablo speaks a bit of Italian.'

'So you know Italian, Gavin? That's great.'

'Well, not exactly, no. I know Latin.'

'*Latin?*'

'Laugh if you want, but this is the essential purpose of an English

69

public school education: no stone unturned, a *comprehensive* inability to communicate.'

'Oh, stop whining,' said Hugo. 'I hate all that crap. It gives you a lot of good stuff too and you know it: contacts, team stuff. You get what you fucking pay for in life.'

'Ah, well, some of us went for free, actually,' said Gavin.

Hugo knocked back his wine.

'Just like my little fucker of a brother, Sam. Didn't anyone tell you, top of the class doesn't count out in the real world?'

'No! No, they didn't. My God, that explains so much. Thank you, Hugo.'

Gavin took two of Hugo's cigarettes and Christina and Pablo followed him into the house.

The room with the pool table was musty. They settled themselves on some beanbags and in the attitude of extreme seriousness initiated by Pablo, they smoked two of his joints together. Then Christina fell asleep on the floor.

Following this, there was a moment of self-consciousness, then Gavin and Pablo played a few games of pool. They won three each and shook hands. Then Gavin got some beers from the kitchen. When he came back, Pablo was rolling another joint.

'I feel like a bit of a wanker not having something to offer you in return,' Gavin said. Pablo attempted to follow what he was saying and Gavin frowned into his lap. 'Why didn't I finish those tapes? I had French ones, too, somewhere.' He pictured the atrocious cupboard in his hallway – the old newspapers, the unopened bank statements. 'Why don't I ever finish *anything* these days, Pablo? I'm sure I *used* to finish things. Did I?'

'*Mi dispiace*, Gavin,' said Pablo, '*ma non capisco.*'

It was such an innocent face, Gavin thought. Young and pink-lipped, but strong-jawed at the same time. Beautiful, really.

'No, no. *Mea culpa*,' he sighed.

They both drank some beer. Christina lay sprawled on the floor nearby. Her head was now tilted back at an angle over the beanbag and her arm was wedged under her chest.

'Oh, now hang on, poor girl,' said Gavin. 'Life should definitely be better than that.' He lunged to get out of the beanbag, which was surprisingly difficult. Pablo put a hand on his arm.

'Gavin – OK. *OK*,' he insisted, smiling. Gavin flopped back down again and it was only after a few seconds had passed that he became conscious Pablo's hand had remained on his arm. For a moment, feeling the butterfly pressure of the fingertips, his mind raced.

The world was a symphony of subtle cultural differences, he told himself. In Russia men kissed each other hello three times, in India they walked hand in hand down the road. He'd read an article somewhere about it. The *London Review of Books*, was it? The *Times Literary Supplement*? Which? Why couldn't he remember?

And then, in surprising detail, he found he could remember Josh, the man he'd been seeing in London, and wondered if he was the monogamous type.

Then he scrubbed his face in his hands. He was drunk. Plastered. He was also very dizzy. As if to anchor himself, he brought his hands down on to the beanbag with a thump.

'You know what? I'm actually too young for this crap,' he said. 'I know, I know – you haven't got a clue what I'm saying, but through no fault of your own, Pablo, you're making me feel like some grotty old perve.'

The boy smiled questioningly. It was such a generous mouth – deep pink, the lower lip a little plumper, the top one protruding slightly in a wicked little curve.

Gavin lurched to stand up, but as his legs straightened out he found he was unsteadier than he'd realised and without making much effort he collapsed into the beanbag again. Then Pablo leant over, pushed Gavin's shoulders back against the wall and kissed him full on the mouth.

After no more than a few seconds Gavin shoved him away.

'What are you *doing*?' he said, idiotically, but before Pablo could respond Christina began to cough in the background.

'*Pablo? Me das agua*,' she muttered.

Pablo went over to her and, finding it strangely much easier to do so now, Gavin stood up and stumbled out into the hall.

It was blinding out there. The smell of fish stew from the kitchen was faintly nauseating. He leant back and tried to stop his head spinning and then, feeling his heart sink at the sound, he heard footsteps and in the corner of his eye he saw Leila's pink skirt come round the corner.

Wishing for some reason that it had been anyone else on earth, he turned to face her.

'Leila. You disappeared,' he said brightly, realising this for the first time.

71

She looked dishevelled – as if she had been asleep.

'I was only upstairs,' she said.

'Oh.' He made a concerted effort to focus on her face. The wall light kept merging with her cheek.

'I suddenly flaked out. It's cooler upstairs,' she explained.

'Is it? That's odd. Isn't it meant to be the other way around?'

There was something strange about him, she thought – some quality she had not seen before. It was an unnatural exchange. Gavin tried to smile at her. His mouth felt crooked.

'I fell asleep,' she said, 'and now I feel like I've missed everything.'

'You've missed nothing. Nothing at all. You had precisely the right idea. We should all go to bed. *That's exactly what we should all do.*'

Leila fiddled with the end of her belt.

'Gavin, are you all right?'

'Me? Yes! Why? We've been – we've all been playing pool.'

He stood aside and Leila saw the cues in corroboration of this. Camellia's cousin and her boyfriend were on the beanbags. There were a lot of beer bottles around them. Christina looked unwell and Pablo was stroking her hair.

'Where's Charlie?' she asked.

'Charlie? Oh . . . um, outside I think. Probably still swimming, knowing him. Yes – don't ask, it seemed a good idea at the time.' Gavin paused. He drew his eyebrows together. 'Leila, I know I'm pissed but you seem . . . you seem so *pale*,' he said, holding back what he had meant, which was 'unhappy'.

She sighed impatiently at this.

'Everyone keeps *saying* that. I'm not pale. I'm fine. I just need some fresh air,' she said, hurrying back towards the sitting room.

The idea of fresh air was absurd in that heat. When she had reached the end of the corridor, she slipped round the corner and leant against the wall, out of Gavin's view.

It was oddly dark in the sitting room. It struck her that she had never seen Gavin do anything wrong or unkind before and for the first time she wondered if there were sides to him she didn't know. Then she shook her head forcefully. What was the matter with her? He was drunk and a bit stoned – that was all! Couldn't he enjoy himself on his holiday?

Then she noticed that one of the lamps had been knocked over by the far wall. That was why it was dark. She had thought the room seemed distorted in some way when she came down the stairs and, as if she had imagined something more complex and sinister had accounted for this, she now put her hand on her chest in relief. It was only the light. She went over and straightened the shade and switched it back on and the room took on its ordinary shape. Almost immediately the bulb went with a faint popping sound.

Exasperated, she turned towards the garden.

There was no one in sight. It was like standing in front of a blank cinema screen, she thought – only there were no characters in the film. Or was that someone lying on the rug? She couldn't tell.

But it didn't matter anyway. She wanted to find Charlie. She had woken up knowing she must find him and talk to him straight away. Tugging the door open as softly as she could and avoiding the usual route over the lawn, she set off towards the pool by the footpath.

She had bare feet and the stone was warm and rough. At the top of the slope the bushes rustled as she pushed her way into them and then she could smell jasmine and there was moonlight through the branches and she stopped to look up at the sky.

Why had they never been out here at night, she wondered? She and Charlie could have sat out there under the stars. It would have been fun. She began to walk again, picking her way through carefully. There were so many things they hadn't done. Why had they never even brought out the white umbrella for the garden table? It was so much nicer with it. They hadn't even bothered with the cushions for themselves.

For a moment, she pictured all their boxes in London, still taped up. Her stomach clenched.

In the distance she could hear laughter and she came to a stop. Ahead of her was the pool house spot-lit against the sky. In front of it the water was a glowing rectangle of blue, rocking, slopping against the sides as if it had just been disturbed. The red lilo bobbed at one end. Then there was another shout and a smile came to her lips as she watched Camellia in a yellow swimsuit run headlong across the foreground and dive backwards into the pool. Now Charlie came out of the pool house, half dressed, a towel round his neck. He stood on the side.

From all his running he was as strong and lean as he had been when they got married, Leila thought. She felt a wrench of physical desire for him. An old longing. He was saying something and Camellia was laughing again. She splashed water at him and he leapt to one side. Then she put up her arm and he hauled her out and they talked for a minute, facing each other, Camellia's back towards Leila, the dark hair streaming down her back. And then in a curious movement, in which at first Charlie appeared to be seeing if there was something stuck in her eye, he put his hand on the back of her head and tilted it towards him until it eclipsed his own face from view.

Something cold moved across Leila's feet. She jumped back violently, knocking her elbow on a tree trunk, assuming immediately that it had been a snake. She stared down at the ground in terror, trying to make out where it was. It might still be waiting, coiled up, ready to bite, she thought.

But there was no sign of anything – not in any direction. There was not even a track – just the parched, cracked soil, which the gardener never remembered to water.

Why hadn't she been up there to water it herself, she thought? Poor plants!

And then she knew was going to be sick.

Dropping the long stick she had picked up on the way up the path, she turned around and ran back towards the house, her eyes filling with tears so quickly that her legs and her long skirt were a thudding blur beneath her. The sky was a faded blue-black and the trees in the garden were dense and there was still no one around – except over to the right, on the old rope hammock, where she spotted Jaime, playing guitar to the moon.

She was sick into the hedge. For a few moments afterwards she sat on the path, trying to stop crying, trying to hear splashing – trying to remember splashing, to imagine splashing, as if by projecting this sound in all possible directions, she might impose a simpler story on the last ten minutes and choke that lurid flower of a moment out of existence. They might all have been swimming races, she thought. Hugo might have been out there with them – and Jaime. But she could see now that it was Hugo's shape she had noticed, slumped on the rug on the grass.

She ran silently back to the house, in through the doorway, past the corridor, in which she caught a glimpse of Gavin giving water to Christina, across the sitting room, and over to her shoes by the door. She pulled them on, catching the hem of her skirt under her heel and tugging it free again. She wiped her eyes with the back of her arm. Outside, the cars were lined up on the drive. But it was no use: the keys were all in the bowl by the kitchen.

She opened the front door and walked outside.

It was much brighter on that side of the house. The moon was very close – and the stars. As she ran through the gate, the leaves of the walnut tree shook cool and silvery above her.

Chapter 11

Leila kept running until she reached the road. To the left, it wound off towards the village. On the right-hand side where the wall began was the little altar still flickering in the darkness. She had noticed it earlier when they walked up. Someone had tidied it and put in new flowers and little oil-burning candles. Camellia's cousin had made the sign of the cross as they went past. Then the boyfriend had done the same.

She shivered, and then she clenched her fists in frustration with herself. Why did it bother her so much? A few candles and a stupid doll gazing out at a brick wall! But it was no good – it was like the horrible story about the clock tower, which had meant she could never bear to look at it, let alone go inside and take *photos* as Charlie had.

Turning her head frantically, she spotted the road off to the right behind her, which led up into the hills and towards the villages she could see from their bathroom window. Starting to cry again, she ran towards it, scrabbling up the sharp incline, bunching her skirt in one hand and grabbing fistfuls of long grass to pull herself along.

Soon the road levelled a bit and she was able to walk in the centre of it, stumbling a little after the exertion. The sickness had gone now, and with it the desire to cry. The wind was going again, she noticed – though perhaps it had always been strong all the way up there. La Campañera was not the only place on earth, she thought.

The higher she got, the stronger the wind became. Soon it swelled down over the hills in waves, pulling her brown hair back in a line behind her, plastering her skirt to her legs. And then every so often it would stop and all was quiet again for a bit.

It was in one of these pauses that she became aware of the sound of a car. She didn't turn round but began to walk faster, her heart going hard, her teeth clenched. Perhaps Gavin had seen her run past the corridor, she thought. Perhaps he'd met Charlie on the way back from the pool and told him: *Leila ran off like a madwoman*, and now he and Charlie and even Camellia were all driving around together searching for her.

But the picture was too disturbing to think about.

The noise of the engine continued intermittently. It was impossible to tell if it was ahead or behind. Becoming curious, she stood still and listened and then in the instant she saw her own shadow illuminated from behind, growing long and thin ahead of her, a car careered round the bend, swerved at the sight of her and spun into the ditch, knocking her off the road.

For a few seconds there was silence; then there was the wind. Then the car reversed up the bank again, spraying earth over the tarmac and without stopping, it turned in the road and sped back the way it had come, bouncing down into the valley, the radio chorusing through the open window.

It was a couple of minutes before Leila moved. There was a pain in her ribs but it was not a bad one. The car had in fact barely touched her, but she seemed to have fallen some way. On to what? She tried to make out where she was. It appeared to be a sort of grassy ledge or promontory. The wind was almost deafening now. She tried to sit up but couldn't.

She felt a strong desire to know where she was. She was definitely above something, she decided. Just beyond her, behind the long grass, was where she sensed the edge was or the drop. She rested for a moment and then crawled towards it and then there beneath her was a vast plain floodlit by the moon as if it were a football pitch.

She held her breath. It seemed to go on forever, she thought. For ever and ever. And at regular intervals, as far as the eye could see, it was covered in hundreds and hundreds of mechanical crucifixes, their arms all moving in unison.

Chapter 12

There was a bowl of nectarines by the window. In front of this was an oven tray with some biscuit dough moulded into five splodgy dog shapes. Beside this was a dummy and some bottles, their teats sitting before them, all recently washed. Outside the window, Jaime, wearing Camellia's sunglasses and hat, rode up and down the grass on the lawnmower.

In a cloud of scent, Camellia came back into the room. She was blossomy and sweet – she mingled with the cut grass.

'Oh,' she said. 'Actually, Charlie, we don't let our friends smoke inside the house any more? We made a kinda rule about it when Alberto came.'

Charlie eyed the end of his cigarette. He stubbed it out in the sink.

'Finished it anyway,' he said.

'God, I don't know how you can even *want* to smoke,' said Gavin. 'This is without doubt the worst hangover I've ever had in my life.'

'You always say that,' said Charlie.

Camellia squeezed a few of the nectarines. She chose one and began to peel and cut it up for Alberto's lunch. The yellow and coral-coloured skin unwound in a curl from her knife. No one spoke. It was very quiet. Then without any warning a bird flapped in wildly through the open doorway and shot back out again.

'*Jesus Christ*,' said Gavin. 'Gave me a fucking heart attack.'

Camellia closed her eyes for a second, then continued to cut up the fruit.

Now Gavin looked at Charlie and then at Camellia and then back at Charlie again.

'OK, so this is a pretty odd situation,' he said. 'I mean, wouldn't you say?' Camellia put her knife down. She turned on the tap and washed the juice off her hands. Gavin sighed. 'Well, is she awake then or what?'

'She never slept,' Camellia said. 'She's still crying.'

They had been able to hear the crying earlier – but not now.

'Oh, God. Oh, *God*,' said Gavin. 'How can such terrible things happen?' He rested his elbows on his knees and scrabbled his hands through his hair, which was already wild and messy from this treatment. 'You should be up there *with* her, Charlie,' he said. 'You should both be at *home*, surely – at La Campañera . . .' He had made this remark several times now in the hope of triggering anything approaching an explanation – but it hung limp in the air once again. On the lawnmower, Jaime droned towards the open doorway, curved and droned away again. 'Why didn't she want to talk to *anyone*, though – at the hospital? That's what I don't understand. Even you, Camellia, if not to a man. And it just does seem *strange* not wanting to go back to . . . Oh, I've got no idea. I mean it's all covered in bottles and fag ends at La Campañera, isn't it?'

Camellia sat down with the tray of biscuit shapes on her lap. She neatened the doggy outlines a bit, careful not to obscure their naïveté, then she began to push in tiny raisins for eyes, a row of almond halves for collars.

'What can anyone say to her, Gavin? Seriously. You know? I actually lost one a few years ago. It takes a woman time to . . . I don't think a man can understand it anyway.'

Gavin put up his hand. 'I'm quite prepared to believe it,' he said.

It was the first time Camellia had told anyone about her baby. Even her mother didn't know. She and Jaime never mentioned it. She peered out at him – in her floppy sunhat, her Jackie-O glasses, clowning as usual. Her lips tightened.

Charlie scraped back his chair.

'I'm going up now,' he said.

Camellia opened her mouth to speak but closed it again and turned away.

They listened to him leave the room. When they could hear him on the stairs, Gavin said, 'And they genuinely think this wasn't *anything* to do with that car?'

'No. The baby was already dead.'

Charlie knocked softly on the door and opened it. He had expected her to be in bed but she was on a chair by the window, her legs up and folded to one side. She was wearing a white cotton nightdress of Camellia's and she looked oddly Victorian, her hair scraped back off her face. She was visibly startled by him.

'You're up,' he said. It smelt of Camellia's scent in there too − she must have tipped on half a litre of it, he thought. He walked inside a few steps and stood by the bed. On the bedside table was a photograph of Camellia in her wedding dress. In front of this was one of her breastfeeding Alberto.

Charlie thrust his hands into his pockets.

'So are you in pain?' he said. Leila shook her head. 'Good. Painkillers are working then.'

'No, there just isn't much pain.'

He smoothed an imaginary crease on the bedcover and sat down. On a tray beside him were a brioche and a cup of coffee, both stone cold and untouched.

'Oh, yes,' he said, after a few moments had passed, 'they let the boys go, by the way. Only temporarily of course. The one driving didn't even have a licence. He was *fourteen years old*. Joyriding in his dad's car. The other one was Mourino's nephew, would you believe it? Little shits. At least they had enough of a conscience to report it even if they didn't fucking check if they'd *killed* you. Mind-blowing really,' said Charlie, 'leaving you stranded. *Animals.*'

He was working himself up, she noticed.

The daylight outside the window was still a shock to her.

'They didn't mean to knock me over,' she said.

'Well − no. The point is they did.'

'I was walking in the middle of the road.'

'I can't believe you're making excuses for them!'

'I'm not,' she said.

Beneath the window, Gavin walked across the garden, shading his eyes. Camellia came after him with a plate of tortilla slices and a jug of something pale green and full of ice. They sat down cross-legged on the grass. Jaime stopped the lawnmower and joined them. Camellia pulled the hat off him and tidied his hair. Jaime put the hat on Gavin. Gavin took it off and laid it on the grass. They began to eat. Then Camellia got up and ran back to the house for something.

'Is everyone here?' said Leila. 'Downstairs?'

'Hmm? Oh − no. No, Christina and Pablo went home straight from the hospital a few hours ago when we knew you were OK. Hugo drove them. He's back at the house now. Out cold I should think.'

Leila nodded.

'Well. So, you're not in any pain, anyway,' Charlie said again.

'No.'

Her face was pale, vacant. Her eyes were red with crying. She looked pitiful, he thought – and yet he wanted to shake her, even to see her cry out. He pressed his thumbs into his temples. What was happening to him?

'Why are we *here*, Leila?' he said. 'We shouldn't be here; we should be at La Campañera.'

'Why? Why *should* we?'

'Because at the moment it's our home. This is not. This is someone else's house.'

'Everywhere's someone else's house,' she said.

Charlie stood up.

'Listen, it's *awful*, Leila, it's fucking sad, but it *happens*, OK? Lots of women have—'

'Yes,' she said, 'I know all that.'

Camellia came back with napkins and a plate of fruit. Jaime was wearing the hat again.

'*Leila?*' Charlie insisted.

'What?' And for the first time she turned to face him. He looked terrible – greyish beneath his tan. His face was drawn and exhausted, his hair was greasy.

'It just seems a bit strange, that's all.'

'What does?'

'You insisting on coming back here.'

Her hands felt cold, her body felt cold.

'Why?'

His eyes tightened as if he were bringing something very far off into focus. Then they loosened again. 'It just does,' he said, and seeing him straighten up a little as he spoke, Leila was bizarrely reminded of a village policeman she had once seen topple off his bike. Amazed by her own reaction, she found herself beginning to laugh. She leant back in her chair and laughed soundlessly – almost painfully, until she was breathless and the laughter became crying and she put her head in her hands.

It had probably been dead inside her for a week, they told her.

Through the net of her fingers she saw Charlie's legs cross the room

– bare, tanned and muscular in their shorts. He stopped beside her. She could smell the leather of his belt. She could hear him breathing.

'*Leila?*' he said and willing herself, as if her own face were the heaviest thing she had ever lifted, she raised it to him. She was crying convulsively now, her shoulders shaking with each breath; she struggled to see through her tears. He was holding something out to her but she couldn't make out what it was. He was pressing it at her, pushing it into her hand, and as she unfolded her fingers and looked down, she saw it was his handkerchief, crisp and white – a neat square in her palm. There were his initials looped formally in the corner: *C.G.B.* for Charles Gideon Bell. Every few years a new set from Daria. It had always amused Gavin: only Charlie carried handkerchiefs in this day and age.

She tightened her hand around it, crumpling it up in her fist and then, quite suddenly overwhelmed by anger, she leapt up, tugged the window open and threw the handkerchief out into the air. For a second it flashed against the sky, then it sailed down slowly, past the kitchen window, coming to rest on a tomato plant.

'Leila, what the . . . why the . . .' Charlie began angrily, but even though she had still not turned around, something in her posture served to silence him.

Suddenly his legs felt terribly heavy and he sat down and rested his hands on his knees. It was a posture he'd once sat in on a roadside somewhere, after his motorbike crash.

Out in the centre of the lawn, the others continued to eat and talk, unaware of the scene behind them or the little patch of white in the flowerbed.

'I'm going back to England,' she said.

'What? *When?*'

'First thing tomorrow. It's already booked.' She gestured at the laptop on the table. 'I'll come back and get a bag while you're all out at supper.'

Charlie absorbed this – the fait accompli, the order to get out of the house. He licked his dry lips.

'How will I . . . explain it?' he said.

'You'll think of something, Charlie. You can always make people believe anything.'

Chapter 13

London was close and dirty and warm – but it was not hot like Spain. It was eight in the evening and Leila sat on a plastic bench at a bus stop. Not knowing where to go, she had taken the airport train to Victoria, because the buses there went everywhere. Everywhere had turned out to be overwhelming and now she sat on the bench and watched them come and go. The traffic was incredibly loud. In her bag were keys to the flat in Marylebone, but even if she had not been sure there would still be a constant stream of viewings, of strangers with tape measures and grinning estate agents, she would not have wanted to go back there.

She had told Jaime and Camellia she was going to stay with a friend. They would have passed this information on to Charlie. Who was this friend, she thought? There was no one. Everyone would have wanted explanations. Everyone belonged to her life with Charlie.

After some minutes had passed she opened her handbag and took out her wallet, finding something tucked inside it. It was a piece of paper torn out of a menu and on it was scribbled an address. She had carried this scrap around with her for nearly two years now, ever since a girl called Shona had handed it to her across a bar. Shona had been at Cambridge with Gavin. For no apparent reason Shona had mentioned a friend of hers called Catriona who lived with a girl called Kate who was always going on demonstrations. And Leila had known immediately that this was her sister.

How had she known? It was ludicrous. But she had been certain.

And now here she was, contemplating doing in reality what she had so often imagined. Was it even possible? she thought. Could there really be anything so ordinary as a doorstep at the end of the series of pictures in her mind?

It was a long bus ride there through the evening traffic. Leila rested her forehead against the glass. Drains passed, cars passed, bikes passed. London was on its way home from work. After the emptiness of rural Spain she felt she had never seen so many people, all engaged in a cycle from which she felt strangely detached – getting on, getting off. They crowded up to the door at the bus stops, with their brief cases, with their shopping bags of spaghetti and yoghurts and mince, their tired children, their newspapers, their mobile phones. 'I'm on the bus. I'll be back soon.'

The sky turned a pale brownish colour and a light rain fell for a while, dotting the pavement. Then it brightened again.

Leila got off the bus. It was still daylight but the air was cooler now after the rain and she took a cardigan out of her bag and wrapped it around herself. It was a cream mohair one – only grabbed from the drawer as an afterthought. She was glad she had brought it. The small leather bag was almost empty in her left hand. She had packed very little; but it had been too hard to imagine what she might want or need. She had also been afraid that Charlie might come back un-expectedly and she had rushed round La Campañera like a thief. Had she even brought a second pair of shoes?

She stopped to check the address on the scrap of paper again, though she knew it by heart, then she began to walk down the road. The flat was in an ex-council block in the middle of a tree-lined street near Bayswater. It was a tall, grey brick building, U-shaped, with two entrances, one marked 'Flats 1–40', the other 'Flats 41–80'. Number 37 was third bell from the top. 'Catriona Dean' read the label. No sign of Kate. Leila pressed it anyway and waited and as she did so it occurred to her in a cold flash that Kate would plainly have moved in two whole years and that she was now standing on a stranger's doorstep. Any second now there would be an agonising conversation with someone who would want to know why she was there, who she was, how she knew Kate. She imagined running back up the path and down the road to the bus stop again.

And then there, quite unmistakeably after so many years of silence, was her sister's voice on the entryphone.

'Yes?' She was crunching something – an apple, crisps. 'Yes? Hello?'

Leaning right into the box, cupping her hand around it as if she were whispering not into wires and plastic but right into her sister's ear, Leila said, 'Kate, it's me, Leila.'

She waited. Then very slowly she sank back on to her heels. Behind her a man walked up the path, thudded a sports bag on to the ground and let himself into the other entrance. Then there was a buzz and the door opened.

Leila went in. There was a concrete floor, a smell of Thai cooking, a lot of stairs. Kate looked down from one of the landings above.

'It is you,' she said. Her voice spiralled quietly down the staircase.

Leila began to climb. It was three flights all covered in frayed green carpet. Her feet plodded on to each stair, her mouth increasingly dry with fear, and she began to wonder if she would even be able to speak when she reached the top. Then there was Kate standing a few feet off, face straining as if she was being asked a difficult question.

'You're all . . . different,' Kate said. 'You look taller – but you can't be, obviously. Your hair's so long.'

Kate was older, thinner herself. Her hair was cut short, side parted, tucked behind her ears. She was wearing jeans and red trainers, a pale green T-shirt. In her hand was an apple the same colour as her shoes. Leila smiled nervously and pointed at it.

'You still like those, then,' she said.

Kate frowned at the apple and deposited it on the table just inside the door.

'Leila, what the fuck are you doing here?' she said. There had always been something about Kate's eyes which was difficult to meet. She laughed. 'Oh no,' she said, 'I hate to disappoint you, but you can't just go silent and gaze at the carpet. I'm afraid that's really not an option right now.'

The voice was angry – defensive; its territory had been invaded.

'Kate, I'm *sorry*,' said Leila desperately, and then in spite of all her intentions, she was unable to stop herself for one second longer from thinking how sad everything was and she began to cry, covering her face with her hands.

Kate observed this for a moment. Then, drawing her eyebrows together into their two habitual furrows, she walked inside the flat leaving the door open behind her.

Leila followed. Inside was a small sitting room with windows at one end. There was a sofa and two chairs, a coffee table. Uncertainly, she sat on the arm of the sofa. It was a few minutes before she could stop crying. Kate sat opposite her in silence. At last Leila wiped her eyes, felt for a tissue in her pocket and blew her nose.

'Thank you,' she said.

'What the hell for?'

'I don't know. Letting me sit here and cry, I suppose.'

Kate grunted.

'You look awful, you know? White as a sheet. Have you eaten?'

'No.'

'What, not all day?'

'Actually, no. I couldn't on the plane.' Leila looked off distract-edly around the flat. There was a tiny balcony, a tiny kitchen, one bedroom off to the side. That appeared to be it. In the room they were in there were the two unmatching armchairs, the old sofa she was sitting on and a dining table with a couple of wooden stools. To her right was a TV resting on a hatbox and a bookshelf behind it crammed with books. In the centre of the far wall was an electric fire surrounded by tiles and above this a mirror with some postcards propped against it.

'The plane,' said Kate. 'I see.' She took a very deep breath. 'Right, well, you obviously need some food. I'll give you some food.' Leila glanced at her in surprise and Kate leant down and retied her trainer. 'You won't get any meat here, though, I'm vegetarian,' she said.

'Oh no, that's fine – that's fine. I . . . *thank you*, Kate.'

Kate went off to the kitchen and began to crash things around.

'Don't expect much, OK?' she called out, 'It's just some veggie shepherd's pie.'

'It sounds amazing.'

'It's just leftovers, Leila. You want some lemon squash?'

There was silence for a moment. Kate leant out of the kitchen doorway.

'You're crying about the lemon squash, aren't you?' she said. 'Oh, for fuck's sake. Just about *everyone* had it when they were children. Still sentimental as ever, then – God help you.'

It was not long before Leila sat at the table in front of a huge plate of shepherd's pie and a glass of squash. She lifted her fork. She almost wanted to laugh. The unearthly moment, which she had imagined so many times in so many different ways, was now overshadowed by the simplest physical need. Perhaps it was for the best, she thought – they were both glad to have the distraction.

She ate quickly, gulping the squash, and the colour returned to her face.

'*Chew*,' said Kate. 'My God.'

'Sorry. It's so good, though. I can't *tell* you how good it is.'

Kate rolled her eyes.

'Anyone would think you hadn't eaten for days. Here, have some more bread. You probably want *ketchup*, don't you?'

Leila grinned at this little remembrance. Kate avoided her eyes.

'Yes, please.'

'I'll get it then.'

When Leila had finished eating, Kate brought out some tea and they stood on the balcony with their mugs.

It had become a nice evening. There was a smell of greenery in the air from the trees at the front of the building. Leila glanced down at the hand on the railing beside her – it was pale, long-fingered; it could almost have been her own hand. This was really Kate, she told herself, Kate standing, Kate breathing beside her. Just ten hours ago she had been in Jaime's car, on the way to an airport in Spain. Just twelve hours before that she had been sitting on a hospital bed while Charlie translated for the doctor.

She took a gulp of hot tea. Beneath them in the courtyard between the two halves of the building stood a boy in baggy tracksuit bottoms and a baseball cap. He was drinking Coke, talking on a mobile phone. A dog scratched around in the bushes beside him, cocked its leg and let out a stream of urine across the paving stones. The boy stepped over it.

'*Oi!* Hey, you in the hat,' shouted Kate. 'It's not a dog's toilet down there, you know? Yes, go on, pretend you haven't heard. We all have to *live* here, though, don't we?' She tutted and rolled her eyes. 'No respect,' she said. 'No respect whatsoever.'

A stereo came on in one of the flats below and some dub music went out into the courtyard. It was less a balcony than a ledge they were standing on – just a foot deep, most of which was taken up with empty plant pots and a few dead ferns whose leaves scraped across the ground.

Kate lit a cigarette and puffed three expert smoke rings. She put her trainer up on the railing.

'So I notice,' she said, 'that you've got a ring. On your fourth finger.'

Leila curled up her hand self-consciously.

'Yes.'

It had not occurred to her that Kate might be with someone herself. She did not want to talk about Charlie.

On a balcony opposite a woman was hanging out her washing. Kate pulled her trainer back from the railing with a jerk.

'Am I making *conversation* with you? This is insane. I mean, OK, you needed something to eat – I gave you that, I could hardly *not* give you that when you look like you're going to pass out – but what the hell are you doing turning up here like this? Why *now*, when my life's finally . . . *Why have you fucking done this?*'

'I . . . I didn't mean to *do* anything. I just didn't have anywhere else to go.'

Kate looked at her clothes, her shoes.

'I don't believe you,' she said.

'I mean this was the only place I felt I *could* go.'

Kate laughed.

'Oh, come *on*. We haven't seen each other for . . .' she waved her cigarette, 'since another life, since the entire planet was different and there was a different sun and moon and different animals wandering the earth . . . and this is the *only place you felt you could go*? I find that somewhat hard to believe.'

'Kate, *please*. None of that was my choice. It wasn't my choice not seeing you. I *never* said I didn't want to see you.'

Kate crouched down, putting out her cigarette in a pot full of many other stubs.

'The fact remains,' she said. She blew out her smoke. Then she stood up again, her thin body all stiff and taut, and went back inside. Opposite the doorway was an armchair with stuffing coming out at each side and she threw herself into it and crossed her legs, her trainer jogging frantically.

Leila waited in the doorway. In a matter of seconds, everything seemed to have changed.

'Do you want me to leave?' she said.

Kate threw up her hands.

'Do I . . . Do I want you to . . . you come here with *no* warning, you come here and you stand on my doorstep and you burst into fucking tears and—'

'Because if you want me to leave then I can just—'

'What I *want*,' Kate interrupted, 'what I want is for you to have some sense of how *strange*, how *violent* it is just to fucking beam in here from Mars or wherever it is you live. I want you to at least see that.'

'Marylebone,' said Leila. 'I've been living in Marylebone.'

A TV came on in the next-door flat. It was impossible not to be aware of the closeness, the warmth of other lives. There was a round of studio applause, some tinkly music.

Leila pulled her cardigan around her and moved just inside the

88

doorway. Gavin would be on the way back to London by now, she thought, and Hugo. Charlie would be alone. She leant back, pressing the palms of her hands against the wall behind her. There was rough wallpaper on it, lumpy beneath her fingers. It was the kind of wallpaper used to cover uneven plaster.

'You know you walked right in front of my car, once?' she said. 'A few years ago.'

Kate glanced up.

'*When?* I didn't.'

'About four years ago – on a zebra crossing near the Earl's Court Road. You crossed the road in front of me. I just sat there and watched.'

'It wasn't me. It was somebody else.'

'You were wearing this blue coat with a furry collar. You looked . . . tired.'

Kate shivered and folded her arms across her chest.

'I was tired,' she said. 'I was very, very tired. I . . . don't have that coat any more.' Then in another jerky movement, she pulled her legs off the table and leant her elbows on her knees. 'Oh, for God's sake *forget* this, just *stop*, OK? Can't you understand I don't want to *know*? This little anecdote – it's something out of a whole box of things I don't want to trawl through. And do you have any idea what it's like, thinking you've been spied on?'

'I wasn't spying! Why would you see it that way? Always the most horrible interpretation.'

'Always the most . . . what were you *expecting*? You thought you'd track me down and turn up here and I'd throw my arms around you and we'd be magically transported into some misty reconstruction of the past?' Kate's voice became louder – it rose to a shout, 'because if you want the past, Leila, you're welcome to it. I want nothing to do with it. I endow you with my share of it in fact,' she said, offloading an imaginary armful in Leila's direction. Then, as if she had a bad headache, Kate pressed her hands against her forehead.

Just like their mother, both of them became pink very easily if ever they were angry or upset, but in Kate's case the flush spread over her neck and even on to her arms and chest. At times it could even become a rash – sore and itchy, lasting for days.

She took a deep breath.

'A plane. You said you'd been on a plane.'

'Yes.'

'Where from?'

'Seville. I've been away with Charlie.'

'*Charlie?* Is *that* who you married? Not that one with the leather jacket, thought he owned the world? Did you fall for all that, then?'

They had only met once. Charlie claimed not to remember what the row had been about.

'Yes, him. We've been living in Spain for a bit to see if we could find a way to make things . . . and we couldn't. So I'm here.' Leila closed her eyes. 'The important part of the story is I was pregnant – but I lost my baby.'

Kate buckled slightly at this, as if she had been thrown an object far heavier than it had looked.

'When did that happen?'

'Two days ago.'

'I . . . I'm sorry.'

'Thanks.'

'But – oh, look, as horrible as that is I'm afraid I still don't see why you're here. Where the fuck do I come in?'

Leila looked up at her imploringly.

'You come in because you're my sister, Kate.'

'"Your *sister*" – like it's a magic spell!'

'It is in a way, isn't it?'

'No, it *isn't*. For God's sake. Listen, I *explained*, Leila – I told you this was how I wanted it. Did I or did I not? An end, I said, a line: big and fat and final. I told you that. I know it sounded harsh – I know it *hurt* you . . .' Kate stood up quickly and went over to the mantelpiece, 'but when it comes down to it we can't get crippled with fucking guilt over these things. We just *can't*. We have to fight for ourselves in this life. There's no choice. It's self-preservation – it's a natural instinct, like . . . like horses protecting their hooves so they can run. Haven't I got the right to choose who I see? *Haven't I even got that right?*' she shouted.

Leila stared at the dirty plate on the table, the empty glass.

'People can't just disappear.'

'Oh? Why not? Because Leila says so?'

'Because you're my sister.'

Kate stamped her foot.

'Stop saying that! You never were logical, were you? That's what's called a circular fucking argument.'

'But we're family.'

Kate snorted.

'What are you on about? She broke all that and you know it. It was broken anyway – even before she went. *Please*, Leila. You're living in a fantasy world. You always have. When did you last speak to Dad? Or Aunt Jane? They're both still pissed out of their brains, I imagine.'

'They're *different*, Kate. Dad and Jane are different. You and I are . . . we were in it together. We did everything *together*. Don't you care about memories at all? Don't you even remember? You loved me, you looked after me when Mum was . . .'

'When she was what, Leila? What? Off her face?'

Leila flinched.

'New Delhi', 'Peru', 'Paris', she read. The postcards were evenly spaced along the mantelpiece.

'Remember how we used to dress up in her things?' she said. 'Those amazing dresses and all her high heels? Remember that floppy red hat?'

Kate shook her head and puffed out her cheeks. She threw herself down again heavily, recrossing her ankles on the coffee table.

'I remember you were completely mad. You used to make me turn that awful old fur coat of hers inside out so you could lie down in it and go to sleep.'

'It was to get closer. You did it too.'

'Only sometimes. Not like you.'

'We wanted to *be* her. We could never get close enough to Mum, could we?'

'No.'

'She was always sort of there but not there . . .'

'Yes, well that's alcoholism for you.'

'What happened to her pictures?' Leila said. 'All the paintings? What happened to them? I never knew.'

Kate shrugged.

'He burnt them.'

'*Burnt* them?'

'Yes. For fuck's sake – how have you managed to avoid knowing this stuff, Leila?'

'I . . . I don't know. I just have.'

'One of your tricks.'

'It's not a trick.'

'Isn't it? What are your dreams like? All sunshine and picnics?'

'Not at the moment, no.'

91

Kate uncrossed her legs. She laid her hands on the arms of the chair.

'No. Look, I'm sorry; you've . . . been through a lot. Here, have a biscuit,' she said, pushing a tin towards her – and quite unexpectedly, they both laughed. Kate's eyes crinkled up at the corners in the old way. Leila sat down. She took a ginger snap.

'This isn't what I thought it would be like,' she said.

'No? Well, I'm sorry to disappoint you.'

'You *haven't*. You haven't disappointed me, Kate. Why would you think that?'

The biscuit tin was rectangular, rusty at the corners with little horses round the edge. She picked it up.

'Isn't this the one we . . . ?'

'Mmm? Oh, I've kept a lot of old crap. Fuck knows how, through the dark ages, but I have. Maybe it's kept me,' said Kate.

Leila studied her sister's face – a finer-boned, fiercer version of her own, the eyes a lighter grey and sharp with intelligence, the trainer still jogging almost as if she was running even as she sat there.

'Why didn't you want to see me?' she said. 'Kate?'

'You know, you haven't exactly been beating my door down either. Ever considered that? You even knew where I lived.'

Leila thought for a moment.

'You're right. Why didn't I come before? I don't know. I was scared I suppose.'

'Of *what*? Not of me.'

Leila laughed.

'No idea. Anyway I did go looking for you once – about five years ago. I went to your school and they said you didn't work there any more. There was this woman with bright red hair. She said you'd "done a vanishing act".'

'Angela. Silly old cow. Well, she was right. That's exactly what had happened. You should have accepted the explanation. Why didn't you accept the explanation, Leila?'

'Because it wasn't an explanation.'

'This is *life* we're talking about, what are you after – algebra?'

'People always have to go *somewhere*—'

'I can assure you they don't,' said Kate.

Leila put out her legs rather stiffly in front of her.

'You think I'm naïve, don't you?'

92

'Do I think you're naïve?' Kate scrunched up her mouth. But then her eyes closed softly as if whatever had come to mind had sent a wave of pain through her body to which she could only submit. 'No. That would be impossible. But . . . somehow you've – you've patched things together. Well, good for you. Your world's solid. You think people are all sort of mysteriously connected,' she said, and then something occurred to her and she leant forwards, nudging Leila's bag with her shoe. She smiled. 'But having said that – where's hubby anyway? Aren't we being a teeny bit of a hypocrite?'

Leila felt her face become hot. She pulled the bag towards her. 'All these years, Kate,' she said quietly. 'Haven't you wondered about me *ever?*'

'Oh, Leila, you don't have a clue what you're asking. You've no fucking idea, have you? Where I went, what I've been through.' Kate clenched her fists in her lap. 'Yes, of course I've *wondered* – of course I have, but the brutal truth is it didn't seem worth it. And I was busy, very, very busy. It's a full-time job, heroin – then there was booze. Oh, my gorgeous light switches: *click* and the world goes off! For God's sake, stop looking so frightened, you knew that's where I was heading.'

'I knew you'd smoked it. With that guy – that guy with the yellow car . . .'

'A guy with a yellow car? You knew it was more than that.'

'You injected yourself, then?'

Kate laughed.

'Once or twice, yes. Then I stopped that and started drinking.'

'Like Mum.'

'Yes, funny that, isn't it?'

'No, not so funny,' Leila said. 'And – and now? Are you . . .' she trailed off.

'You mean *am I still a junkie? Am I still a drunk?*' Kate took out her cigarettes again. 'No, I don't drink or use any more. Now I'm a sedate lady with an adopted cat and a job and *colleagues who know nothing about all that crap* and a desire to keep it all *very fucking simple.*'

'And do you still paint?' Leila asked. The question had come out of nowhere. It seemed to startle Kate more than any of the others.

'What? No. God, no. Not for years.'

'That's a shame. You were good.'

Kate narrowed her eyes.

'No, I wasn't. What are you talking about? You don't know about painting, Leila. You think everything's so easy. You live in a dream world.'

Chapter 14

There was still anger in Kate's voice but it was of a different quality now – it was showier and therefore safer, part of the familiar drama of her personality. Leila peered around the flat again. There was definitely only one bedroom.

'So you . . . you live here on your own then, do you?' she said.

'It's a friend's place. Catriona. But you know that – I'm assuming you met her somehow. She seems to know everyone in fucking London, that girl. Anyway, she's got a French boyfriend, lives with him mostly – in Paris. They keep this place as a "*pied à terre*", as they call it. Very grand. I pay them a bit of rent and look after the cat. If they ever do come back, which happens about three times a year, I clear out for a bit and kip on someone's sofa. So it all works very nicely.'

As if it had been waiting until its presence was formally announced, a strange cat now came round the corner and rubbed itself against Kate's chair. It was silverish grey, short-haired – a Siamese, perhaps. As it moved round the edge of the chair, Leila saw it only had three legs – the fourth was just an inch-long stub. It hopped gracelessly, mewing and rubbing its neck. '*Doesn't* it, Jude?' said Kate. 'We're a match made in heaven, aren't we, you grumpy old sod? Catriona calls him Crosspatch, but I've renamed him Jude, patron saint of lost causes.'

Kate scooped the cat up under her arm and went out to the balcony, lighting a cigarette as she went. The cat's soft weight rested on her hip and she leant her forearm on the balustrade, raising it every so often and blowing the smoke out across the courtyard. The pose had the natural look of habit.

The opposite building was in shadow now and there was an unquestionable chill in the air. The breeze rustled the dead ferns. Kate rubbed her arm, scattering ash off the balcony. The cat hopped down.

'Heartbreaker,' she said, and when she had put out her cigarette and turned around she saw that Leila had fallen asleep. A look of great weariness passed across her face and then, very quietly, Kate went to her bedroom, pulled the duvet off her bed and laid it over Leila. Grabbing a coat from the cupboard, she went and lay down herself.

It seemed very early when Leila woke up. There was a smell of toast and coffee and Kate came in with a tray and set it down on the table. Her hair was wet and combed down. She was dressed in a cream shirt, jeans and the same red trainers.

'It's five in the morning,' she said. 'I'm doing the early drop-in this week. Want some breakfast?'

'No, thanks. Um – not right now.'

Leila rubbed her eyes. Kate scooped out some marmalade with her knife.

'Mind a bit of radio? It's the news.'

'No, no. Not at all.'

They listened for a bit to the radio headlines. None of it meant much to Leila.

'Further trouble in the UK housing sector is expected as house prices continue to slide. The sub-prime market in America continues to be cause for—'

'Kate?'

'Mmm?'

'Where do you work?'

Kate took a mouthful of toast, a sip of coffee.

'I thought I said last night.'

'No.'

'Oh.' She took another mouthful. 'I work in a . . . it's a charity. It's a drop-in centre for "teenagers and young people". There's a bit of a drugs and alcohol emphasis – so there are counsellors. It's very new so you won't have heard of it or anything. It was set up a year ago by the wife of the guy who started Summerdale's.'

'The supermarket?'

'Exactly. "*Keeping you healthy a-a and wealthy*",' she mimicked. 'Their son ran off when he was fourteen. Junkie. They spent a few years searching for him – TV appeals, ads in papers, you name it. Gold bullion makes no difference though, obviously. Found him dead near the canal off the Harrow Road in the end. He'd been living in a cardboard box.'

'That's terrible.'

'Mmm. Anyhow, Mrs Summerdale started the foundation in his name. Something concrete to do with the guilt, I imagine.'

'And what do you do there?'

'Me? Oh, anything and everything. Fundraising officially. Bit of admin, bit of computery stuff.'

'Wow.'

'Hardly that.' Kate gulped her coffee and brushed off her hands. She checked her watch. 'I'm going to be late.' Carrying the second half of her toast in her mouth she went around the room, picking up the things she needed: a notebook, two pens, a small shoulder bag, a jacket. 'Use the bath and stuff obviously,' she said.

Experiencing a dismal, plummeting sensation, Leila saw that any minute now she would be alone. 'I must buy you some more food, Kate,' she said.

'Don't be stupid.'

'No, I must.'

'It would only have gone in the bin if it hadn't gone into you, Leila.' Remembering something, Kate opened her bag and searched through it hurriedly for a moment. Then she rushed back into her bedroom and came out with something in her hand. It appeared to be a necklace. She put this carefully into the bag, did it up and went out into the hall. 'Right, I'm off,' she said. She jangled her keys off the hook and then, as if she had been debating whether to say it or not and for her own obscure reasons had only just decided that she would, Kate paused in the open doorway. Her fingers pressed the lock in and out.

'I was thinking,' she called back, 'if you want to stay one more night, Leila – if you need to I mean, then that would be OK. You've . . . well, you've had a shit time. Anyway, I've put the address of the place where I work by the toaster in the kitchen. I keep a spare key for this place there in case I get locked out or something. If you want to drop by at lunch, then you can and I'll lend it to you for today. My break's at one. Do it or don't, though. Your call.'

The door shut firmly and the flat was quiet.

Leila stretched out her legs. This was Kate's sofa, she told herself. Kate's book was just there on the table. This was Kate's duvet lying on top of her. Kate's cardigan was lying on the chair. She smiled. The cat came back in through the open window and she put out her hand to it but it hopped past her obliviously towards the kitchen for its food.

Chapter 15

There were two entrances to the Thomas Summerdale Centre, one on the high street between a cash machine and a Chinese takeaway, the other, which was through the basement garden and needed a code, was down a path straight off the Hillford estate.

Leila stood by the railings on the high road. On the pavement in front of her, a pile of slumped bin bags gave off an overpowering smell of ginger and vinegar. A truck pulled up and a man jumped out of it, hauled the back open and reached in for a crate of bottles.

Leila shivered. Her cotton skirt and T-shirt were not nearly warm enough for the English weather. She had thought of buying some-thing, but had not wanted to use the card with both of their names on it – or even to take it out of her wallet. If she didn't buy anything more expensive than food and tube tickets, she had enough cash to last her for a little while, and even though this too had originally come from their joint account, it had been taken out over a month ago, when they were packing for Spain and things had been very different.

She went down the steps. At the bottom was a plaque, which read 'Thomas Summerdale Centre For Young People, in memory of Thomas Summerdale, 1989–2006'. The door was open. Inside there was a waiting area with plastic chairs and a few magazines. There was a smell of new carpet. On the right was a reception office behind a window. There was no one in there and the door was locked. To the left of the office was a pair of swing doors leading on to a hallway. Leila peered through the glass: it appeared to be deserted out there too. Everything seemed very new. Along the length of each wall were pin boards covered in leaflets and flyers and as she pushed her way in a breeze carried through from the street behind her and set them all off. For a moment, the walls seemed to be alive.

Some way along the hallway was a corridor with rooms off at either side, their doors propped open with plastic chairs. Leila peered in cautiously in case she was interrupting whatever it was that went on there. But each of these rooms turned out to be empty too. In the one at the end there was a whiteboard. Here and there fragments of words had survived the swipe of the cloth:

'Respe . . . em . . . ntrol . . .' she read. It smelt of school.

There were hurried footsteps behind her.

'Excuse me? Hello? Excuse me?' came a voice. Jogging down the stairs was a plump, compact woman with white hair, eyebrows raised in an expression of polite concern. 'Sorry, who are you?' she said, 'I saw you wandering around.'

'I . . . Oh, I'm Leila, Kate's sister.'

The woman caught her breath. Her face was round and friendly. 'Kate's sister?' she said smiling.

'Um – yes, she told me to meet her here but I'm a bit late—' Leila checked the clock on the wall. 'Oh God, half an hour late actually, and . . . I didn't know where to go. There wasn't anyone out on reception.'

'Ah, no, well there wouldn't be. It's lunchtime. You won't catch anyone working through lunch break. They're all down in the canteen, sweetheart. I'll take you if you like – I need to go down there anyway and check the rotas. I'll just lock up the front entrance. I'm Janice, by the way.' Her round face broke into another smile and, feeling lost behind a time lag, Leila shook herself a little and smiled back.

As if she was determined it was going to be summer, Janice was wearing a turquoise T-shirt, cotton trousers and espadrilles. Her hair was a cropped glossy white and in her ears were wooden earrings in the shape of parrots on swings. Leila watched her bolt and padlock the doors.

They went out to the staircase. The banister was newly varnished and smooth to the touch. On the wall at the top was a framed photograph of the opening of the centre. A lady in a green hat cut a ribbon across the front steps. Beside her were a very thin, elegant woman and a man, slightly distant somehow, holding an umbrella over them. In the background was a small crowd.

'Janice?' said Leila.

'Yes?'

'When you came down, you said you saw me wandering around.'

'I did, yes.'

'But you were upstairs . . .'

Janice smiled. She put a soft hand on Leila's arm and pointed up at the ceiling. There was a CCTV camera with a red light, winking. 'Highly controversial, but we've got them now so there we are. I was on gold-fish duty upstairs,' she said. 'You've arrived on their first day up.'

They had reached a hallway, which was also a sort of crossroads. To the right was another office and ahead was an archway into a wood-floored canteen, divided by folding doors. The doors were not quite closed in the middle, but it was impossible to tell how much of the room lay beyond them. In the first part the overhead bulbs were off and the only source of light was the windows on to the basement garden. Leila made out paving stones and a few benches out there, but no plants. It was drizzling again.

'Oh dear, now what's this? Sorry, I won't be a second,' said Janice, stopping to examine a chair. The legs were loose and she tightened them with a screwdriver. On the underside was a scrawled drawing of two breasts. 'Funny. I wonder who's done this again,' she said curiously. She rubbed it with her handkerchief. 'So strange. What's the point? That's what beats me. It's not like writing your name. I understand when they do the tags – I see why you might do it if you feel like no one notices you. But why would you want to do that?'

'I'm . . . not sure,' said Leila.

They both stared at the drawing for a moment. Then Janice turned the chair over and checked the one beside it.

Leila cast her eyes around the canteen. There was a rail for trays and a serving hatch. There was a padlock on the hatch.

A burst of laughter came from the other part of the room. Janice pushed the chairs back into place. 'Serious lot round here,' she said, smiling. 'It's the end of the week.' And then walking off ahead and turning herself to one side she slipped in neatly through the folding doors. Leila did the same.

Facing them was another wall of pin boards and leaflets, which formed a narrow corridor. Then the room branched off abruptly towards the windows and broadened out to the right.

From the amount of noise they made, Leila had expected to see more people, but in fact she could only make out five over Janice's shoulder. There were sandwich wrappers and crisp packets on the table in front of them. There was a conversation going on and none of them had noticed anyone come in.

'Just one more jiffy,' Janice whispered, stopping to read a list on the pin board, and as Leila waited behind her, she thought how contained and private this group ahead of them were. There was something sanctified and unapproachable about them, like the staff in the staff room at school.

This was Kate's work; these were her colleagues, she thought; and as the seconds passed it seemed increasingly likely that Kate would see her coming all the way down there as an intrusion.

She ought to have waited upstairs! That was obvious now. But how could she get out? Janice's plump arm hung just inches away but there was no simple way of touching it and saying she would wait upstairs. The others would hear.

She could see Kate. She was sitting with her back to the window. Beside her there was an empty seat and then one occupied by a sunburnt-looking man who was raising his eyebrows at her, waiting for a reply.

'Because it's *espionage*, that's why,' Kate said.

'Such a dramatic way of putting it, Kate,' he said. 'Always a drama, isn't it?'

'And when even a place like this does it . . . well, it's *the end of privacy*. Let's face facts, it ended ages ago really. You only need to go to the cash point to see that. It's the Orwellian nightmare come true out there. There'll be identity chips next; fingerprint readers; cameras that scan your iris; radio-frequency tagging—'

'*Kate*,' said a grey-haired woman with her back to the corridor, 'you're being "like that" again. You said to tell you, love.' Kate threw herself back in her chair with her arms behind her head. 'Now look, Mike,' the woman went on, 'as usual I've no idea what she's on about but I'll tell you what – she's bang on about one thing: it is spying and for the life of me, I can't see what's wrong with that. It's common sense. You've *got* to spy on them otherwise they'll nick everything, won't they?'

'Oh, Kerry,' sighed Mike. 'You're not doing wonders for the moderate case there.'

Kerry shrugged.

'No? Well, I'm sorry about that, love, but I grew up on this estate and for all your counselling degree and wotnot – well, *I know what I know.*'

'All right, all right, I'm not arguing with you. Wouldn't dare.'

'There's a good boy, then,' she said. She held out her packet of biscuits to him. He took one. 'Oh, go on with you, you know you want two.' He winked and took another.

'Kate, love?'

'No thanks.'

'Oh, treat yourself, Kate,' Mike said. '*Try*. Have a biscuit.'

'I don't *want* a fucking biscuit,' said Kate.

'Dear me,' said the man at the head of the table, 'things are deteriorating.' He flattened both hands out broadly, as if to contain the situation. He was quite young, but there was something paternal about him, Leila thought.

Then, with a rustle of paper, Janice let go of the list and, suddenly becoming aware there was someone behind her, Kerry spun round in her chair.

'Who's that? Who's there?' she said. '*Janice?*' she put her hand to her chest in a curiously old-fashioned way. 'Give me a heart attack looming up out of the shadows like that. As if I didn't have enough to contend with round here.'

Leila could see her face now – even from the end of the corridor, where she was still standing, trying to hide from Kate for as long as possible. Kerry was younger than Janice, about sixty perhaps, she thought. She had small, sharp features and hair pinned up in a bun.

'Law and order up there, is it?' she asked.

'All is peaceful,' said Janice. 'And our bike gang seem to have moved on to other pastures, Dan.'

'Oh, that is good news,' said the man at the head.

Kerry noted the smile that passed between them.

'See? Pay for themselves in *days*, those cameras,' she said.

'Well, it . . . it might have been because of the visit Dan paid to the mothers, Kerry,' said Janice. 'Anyhow,' she went on, before the other woman could speak again, 'I just popped down to check the rota was up for next week and I've brought along a visitor for Kate. Now where's she . . . oh, there you are, love. Lost you back there. Everyone, this is Kate's sister, Leila.'

With an unfortunate crackle of drama, Janice beckoned her out of the passage and into the open room.

'I thought you were going to meet me outside,' Kate said. 'At one.' She tried to stand up but somehow her jacket got hooked over the back of the chair.

'The tube stopped in the tunnel,' Leila answered, nonsensically.

'*Did* it?' Kerry gasped. She put a hand to her throat. '*Claustrophobic*,' she said. 'Why ever did that happen?'

'Oh, now watch it, Kerry, or you'll get her going again. She'll tell you it was a government plot.'

Kate stopped struggling with her jacket.

'Take the piss all you want, Mike, but I'm telling you there's technology—'

'*Technology*, is there?'

'Yes. For watching people. It's being developed as we speak.'

'*As we speak?*'

'Yes.' The jacket came free.

At the corner of the table was another man who had not yet said anything. He was dark-haired and pale, bent low over his food. Mike leant in towards him.

'You going to put us out of our misery?'

'No, he isn't. Leave him alone. James isn't speaking this week,' said Kate.

Mike gave him a nudge.

'Go on, James, be a sport. Give us a bit of scientific fact?'

At this the dark-haired man balled up the foil from his sandwiches and scraped back his chair. 'No,' he said. 'And you know, sometimes I wish everyone would stop asking me this kind of stuff – even if it is meant to be funny.'

There was silence. He frowned into it. He was tall and very slim. Forgetting to throw away the foil, he pushed past Leila and Janice and through the folding doors. His trainers squeaked out through the canteen.

'Oo-ooh,' whispered Kerry, 'now you've upset him. You've done it now, Mike.'

The man at the head of the table pushed his own chair out too. He was not tall himself, though his very broad shoulders gave him presence. His hair was reddish. He laughed and shook his head.

'You've said nothing, Mike, don't fret. Honestly, James is all right, Kerry. You don't need to make everyone walk on eggshells like this. It's the fuss that bothers him.'

'I agree,' said Kate. 'There's nothing worse than everyone pussy-footing around you.'

Kerry swiped a spoon round the remains of her cherry yoghurt. Then she stood up too. She was angular, Leila noticed, fine-boned. Her face was unlined but weary, the little brown eyes darting, like an animal in search of predators.

'Don't mind the rabble,' she told Leila pointedly. 'I'm Kerry, by the way. So you're Kate's *sister* are you? Haven't you got gorgeous skin?'

Kate took Leila's arm.

'I'll be out in the garden if anyone wants me,' she said. 'Not that anyone's allowed to want me for another ten whole minutes.'

Mike tipped the last of his crisps into his mouth and crunched. 'In the garden,' he said. 'In the rain. When are you going to give up, Kate?'

'Give up? Actually, I'm thinking of trying to smoke more, Mike. Treat myself a little.'

Now the reddish-haired man made his way firmly round the table and Leila noticed that under his sweatshirt he was wearing the stiff white collar of a priest. Assuming she had imagined it, she checked again and he saw this and smiled at her directly. She was embarrassed.

'Leila,' he said, putting out his hand, 'I'm Dan. Pleased to meet you.'

'Right,' said Kate, 'I need my cigarette.'

At the back of the kitchen there was a side exit on to the garden. It had stopped raining now and there was a smell of wet concrete. Fat drips fell from the guttering on to the paving stones. The sun was bright and very pale. Kate lit her cigarette.

'Kate, I should apologise,' said Leila.

'Should you? Why, what have you done?'

'Barging in like that. I should have waited upstairs.'

Kate waved a hand.

'Forget it,' she said. She took a drag, sucking her cheeks in, then she blew a few smoke rings, all very thick and neat. 'Thanks.' Leila watched her sister's fingers pick at their own nails, the short hair blowing about in the breeze, falling into her eyes and then lifting out again. Kate appeared not to notice this. She bit her lip distractedly. 'You know what I really want,' she said, 'is for someone to please, *please* tell me why I keep letting that *something* guy get to me? I mean you saw him. *Mike.* You saw him, didn't you? I mean, he's a bloody *counsellor*, too. You'd think he might know better even if I don't. But he always just somehow – he pisses me off and I end up saying shit I don't really mean.'

Leila nodded.

'I've got people like that,' she said.

'You! Spare me. You've never lost your temper in your life, Leila.'

'What? I *have*. Of course I have.'

Kate blew a few more smoke rings. Her eyes narrowed. 'What happened to your gardening business anyway?' she said.

'My . . . Why would you suddenly ask that?'

'Dunno. Just popped into my head. Why, what happened?'

'Oh, nothing.' Leila put her hand on the bench, but it was too wet to sit on. 'No, I . . . I never did it in the end,' she said, wiping her fingers on her skirt.

'What d'you mean? It was all set up and running, I thought.'

'Well, yes, it was – it was. But then Jools's mother got ill. You remember him? You did meet him once. He bought us those ice creams he was crazy about. Jools was the one who really started it – I just sort of tagged along. Anyway, he went off to live in America. In California. That was where his mother lived.'

'Jools . . . Jools . . . Oh yeah, I liked him. That stupid tattoo on his arm. "*These*, ladies, are the best ice creams in the *Western world*."'

'That's him. Everything was always the best this or the best that. Literally everything.'

'Why did you stop doing it, though? You could've carried on, couldn't you – even if he did bugger off to America. You had the van – you must have had clients, surely.'

Leila put her hand out to touch the bench and then remembered she had already done this.

'Oh yes, well we did, but basically Charlie had this amazing business idea and we needed to raise money so we were very, very busy with that. We were buying and selling flats. We've only just stopped really. I did them up – that's been my job, I suppose. Sort of. There wasn't time to do the deliveries as well, going off to the markets and stuff, doing the bouquets. It got too much. So in the end I . . . let it go.'

Kate snorted.

'I get it,' she said. She finished her cigarette and stubbed it out on the ground. An aeroplane went past overhead. They both looked up.

'So, this is where you work,' Leila said.

'Yes. This is where I work. Where I *live*, more like it. You're not seeing it on a typical day though.' Kate stood up and went back inside and Leila followed her out to the office by the stairs. There were two small desks in there and some filing cabinets. There was a calendar with cats on it: two kittens in a teacup. On every available flat surface was a pile of folders. Moving one of these aside, Kate sat down and began to open the drawers. 'No, normally there are lots of kids here, obviously, but we're having to close up two afternoons a week at the moment – not to mention working all bloody weekend. As you can see we're reaching bureaucratic meltdown. It's mainly these dim-witted government forms. You have to be checked constantly if you're a private charity or they take away your registration. It's the forms, and the fact we lost a member of staff in *circumstances I won't mention.* Anyhow, fanatical as she is, Kerry can't do it all on her own. No, she does a nightmare job actually – none of us give her enough credit.' Kate rummaged in the bottom drawer and then closed it. She tried the other desk.

'Ah. Here we are.' She held up a couple of keys on a plain key ring. 'My kingdom,' she said, chucking them across the room.

Leila caught them and Kate sat back in the other desk chair, drawing her eyebrows together and clicking the mouse. Her computer sprang back to life.

Leila stood by the filing cabinet, holding the keys.

'Kate, I . . . don't know how to thank you,' she said.

'Mmm? Oh, then for goodness sake don't. Now hang on, I'm sorry: *forty* emails? *How?* Do these people not eat lunch?' Then, as if she had just remembered Leila was still standing there, she glanced up briefly, 'I get back around eight thirty,' she said – and then she began to type.

Leila stepped backwards, knocking her heel into the bin. She whispered a hurried goodbye and then she went out and up the stairs again and back on to the street.

Chapter 16

It was nine before Kate came in. The front door opened and Leila sprinkled Parmesan into the risotto and stirred it hurriedly. Turning back a few times, uncertain whether the rice would stick if she left it on the heat, she then rushed over to the draining board for the plates.

Kate came into the sitting room and put her bag and jacket on the chair.

'Well, well,' she said, peering through, 'you're cooking something.' She came in and leant over the saucepan. 'What's this, then? God – it's my mushroom risotto.'

'"Tuesday night risotto". Exactly. I haven't made it for years.'

She turned the heat on and began to stir again. Kate frowned and glanced round the kitchen. On the sideboard was a shopping bag with aubergines and tomatoes and so on – all the ingredients for the shepherd's pie she had told Leila not to bother replacing. Beside this was a cheese grater and a pile of cheese on a plate.

'Is that Parmesan?' she said. 'Parmesan's not vegetarian, you know?'

'*Isn't* it? I thought all cheese was . . . Oh, God, I've put it in the risotto already. What an *idiot*.' She put down the spoon. 'I've ruined it.'

Kate observed this display for a moment: the slumped shoulders, the hands covering the face, and, feeling another wave of exhaustion heavier than she had felt for a long time, so heavy in fact that she had to rub her eyes to open them up, she said, 'No, you haven't, don't go mental.'

'I *have*.'

'You haven't, Leila. Listen, I let myself off a bit every so often, OK?'

'You don't. You're just saying that.'

Kate came across the kitchen, picked up the spoon and put it back into Leila's hand.

'Yes, all right, I am just saying that. But finish it off and serve it and I'll go and put on something clean.'

They ate at the small table together, Kate facing the window.

'That was good,' said Kate, putting down her fork. 'I never used parsley like that. You're a cook, Leila.'

'Don't be silly, I'm not. It's people who don't even need recipes – that's how you can tell. You always did it all so beautifully. All my birthday cakes. That heart-shaped one with the strawberries on it when I was ten.'

They sat silently for a few seconds.

'Are you going to keep doing that?' said Kate.

Leila stared into her lap.

'No. Sorry. It's just that things keep coming into my head.'

'Like the risotto.'

'Yes.'

'You know if you'd come a year ago I wouldn't have let you in?'

'I thought you might not this time.'

'I don't even know why I did. To tell you the truth, I almost didn't. But it was like something in me sort of thought *fuck it*, just *press the button*. You know what I mean? As if that was all there was to it. It was that voice; that little devil in your left ear. But on second thoughts, you probably have an angel though, don't you, Leila? Anyway, next thing I knew there you were in the hallway, like a ghost.'

Leila pushed her plate away.

'You keep saying that. Like a ghost. I wasn't *dead*, Kate. I haven't been dead.'

Kate stood up and then sat down again on the arm of the sofa nearby.

'No, I . . . I know. I know that. You're right,' she said. Her eyebrows drew together and her brow crumpled into its two furrows again. Her thin face was drawn and exhausted. 'Oh God, Leila, I'm knackered,' she said. 'OK? I'm knackered and I've got to be up at five again tomorrow.'

'For the early drop-in.'

'Yes, exactly. For the early drop-in.'

Leila stood up and began clearing the plates and seeing this, Kate clenched her fists.

'Why are you doing that? For fuck's sake you don't have to *do* all this. Buying stuff, cooking – tidying the place up. You've even hoovered. It's not necessary.'

'But I like it. I want to.'

'You don't *like* it. Christ. Listen, you don't *owe* me anything, Leila. No one owes *anyone anything* in this life, OK? Parents, children, brothers, sisters: it's a clean slate. We do what we need to, to survive. We try not to harm anyone, they try not to harm us – fine, all well and good – but we don't *owe* one another. That's the deal, that's the way it works all right? So you can forget it if this risotto . . . this . . . this *hoovering* is all about some kind of guilt.'

Leila put down the plates.

'Why are things always "all about" something completely different with you? I won't do it if it annoys you, though,' she said.

Exasperated, Kate took out her cigarettes. She put one in her mouth and patted all her pockets for matches, but there were none in there. Where the hell were they? she thought. She glanced angrily at the mantelpiece and then at the shelf in the kitchen, then the hall table. But as if in doing this she had forgotten what she was searching for, she took the cigarette out of her mouth again and held it unlit in her lap.

'So, what's your plan then, anyway? Tomorrow, I mean. Won't that husband of yours be *frantic*? Won't he be calling all your friends?'

'No. He won't.' Leila stood up again, lifted the plates, flinched, put them down and then, flattening her lips and frowning, she snatched up the salad bowl and carried it determinedly through to the kitchen.

Kate closed her eyes. She folded her arms across her chest and listened to the sound of the taps going on, the leftover salad scraped into the bin. Well, she thought, it was good to have a full stomach. This at any rate was true. She was often too tired to eat when she came in, too tired to cook anything just for herself and simply went to bed hungry. She opened her eyes and her trainer dug an indent into the thick carpet: a curved line, half of a circle, her own body behind it.

Her expression had softened a bit.

'Leila?'

She came back in, a drying-up cloth in her hand, soap foam clinging to her wrist. 'Yes?'

Some of the foam fell on the carpet in a blob. Somehow, Kate thought, it was typical of Leila not to notice this. Jude the cat hopped up on to the sofa behind her and Kate ran her hand over his bristly fur. She sighed deeply.

'OK, so listen,' she said, 'I don't need to know *any* of the details, right, but are you telling the truth when you say you've got *nowhere* to go?'

Leila tossed her hair behind her shoulders.

'I'm not sure,' she said.

'Right. Which means what exactly?'

'What is "nowhere to go"?'

Kate laughed bitterly.

'There are kids I know who would spit at you for saying that.'

Leila dried the bubbles off her wrist. 'Would they?' she said. She put the cloth down. 'Would they have thought we had somewhere to go when we were little?'

Kate felt her whole body tensing again. 'Oh no. I've made myself very clear – I'm not getting into that. Nice try.'

'"Nice try"? What do you think this is? I'm not trying to *trick* you, Kate!'

But it was no good. As if an alarm had gone off and she had been told to gather valuables and evacuate the building, Kate grabbed her things: bag, jacket, book and went over to the bedroom, her bag thwacking against the doorframe. But instead of going in and slamming the door, she threw it all in a heap just inside. A red apple rolled out of her bag and came to a stop by the wardrobe.

'OK,' she said. 'OK, all right, you're not trying to *trick* me. Whatever it might seem like I'm not actually trying to chuck you out on the street either. I'm not a total bitch, OK? I'm just . . . incredibly fucking tired.'

'You work hard, Kate.'

'Yes I do. I do work hard.' She rubbed her eyes again. 'Still, God knows I can't complain about that, can I? How *else* would I maintain this lifestyle of frivolous excess?' Kate turned round, throwing her arm out, and Leila smiled: my sister.

It was now that Kate spotted the matches. There they were in plain view on the coffee table. How was it possible to have missed them? She took out her cigarettes again. They were French matches, from the last time Catriona had been back. *Café des Artistes* she read. Pretentious fucking place. And he was a confident bastard, that boyfriend. *Philippe*, she thought, with his golden-coloured eyes and his hands groping over Catriona all the time. Was that what she really wanted? But she loved him, she said. '*Adored*' him.

Orgasms, Kate thought. There were just three matches left.

She turned round again.

'OK, listen,' she said. 'There's something I thought of. Christ, I can't quite believe I'm saying it but I've apparently gone mental so what the fuck? Now, maybe I've got it all wrong, maybe I haven't. Jesus, you look like you're about to be sick, Leila. Don't freak out, it's nothing terrible. It's just – well, unless that little bag of yours is lined with diamonds or something, I'm assuming you could do with earning a bit of cash. Now don't get excited – it's nothing much, but there is a bit of work you could do at the centre if you're interested. It wasn't my idea – it was Janice's, oddly. She's right, though – we've been needing someone to do it for months. Someone literate and – cheap. Look, it's five days' work, seven at the most, so it's not a big deal. It's just those files. It won't exactly sparkle on your CV, but it'll earn you a few quid. I mean – whatever. That's if you want it,' said Kate, 'because I could be way off. For all I know you could be a millionaire.'

'I'm not,' Leila said. She didn't dare look up at Kate directly. 'It sounds – it sounds good,' she said softly.

'Fine then. Turn up after lunch tomorrow. I won't be there – I'm out all afternoon, but Kerry'll show you the ropes. Just don't expect to be riveted, that's all.'

She went out quickly on to the balcony. There was a warm breeze out there and, as if from nowhere, a smell of blossom. Stretching a little, she put one foot on the bottom rail, then the other and then for some unknown reason she found she had an urge to lean right out into the evening air. All of a sudden she felt strangely light; her arms tingled. Above her, the sky was clear and there were even a few stars.

It's going to be warmer soon, she thought.

Beneath her in the courtyard, the boy with the baseball cap brought out his dog to urinate again. Kate laughed to herself and then, leaning a little further over the rail so that her hair swung forward over one eye, she called out, 'Good evening,' and gave him a kind of salute.

The boy glanced up at her momentarily and then continued talking into his phone.

Chapter 17

'Aren't they a pair of little cuties?' said Kerry, unhooking the calendar and tilting the photograph towards Leila. 'So tiny – in a teacup! Breaks your heart. I love cats, me,' she said. She drew a big red tick across the previous day and rehung the calendar. 'Always have. It's a passion. Our feline friends. You're either dogs or cats, aren't you? My brother's wife's got a dog. Awful great thing with all dribble – *drool* – hanging out of its mouth all the time. Jumps up on you, rips your tights up. Awful. Neil only keeps it to please her. He'd have a nice cat if he could. D'you like dogs, Leila? You look like someone who prefers cats to me. Yeah, I see you with a little ginger. Or a little tabby, maybe.'

Carrying armfuls of files they went out of the basement office and back up to the one out at reception. Kerry nudged the light switch with her elbow.

'We had a cat when we when we were little. Kate and I did,' said Leila. 'I mean, it wasn't really ours but we used to feed it. It was a stray.'

'Was it? Oh, that's so *sad* when you see that. Breaks your heart . . .' Kerry trailed off. She pushed the door open and put her stack of files down on a shelf, her face becoming curious. 'So, where did you two grow up then? Round here was it?' she said.

'No. No, we grew up in the countryside. Well, not really the countryside if that makes you think of somewhere all wild and open. In Kent, we grew up in Kent.'

'Did you?' Kerry sat down and nibbled her biro. 'What did your dad do, then?'

'Solicitor. He still is.'

'Is he? Hasn't he retired yet? Some people just go on and on, don't they? Makes you feel guilty. Mind you, I thought "part time" was going to be a nice balance. Less of a shock than stopping work altogether, was the theory. *Little did I know.*'

They both cast their eyes round the office at the files. There were even more up there. Kerry stood up and heaved a pile of them on to her desk.

'So what is it all?' said Leila.

'You name it. Some of it's notes for the kids – you know, records for whatever they're doing: mental health stuff, sexual health, drugs counselling. Some of it's crime bits and bobs – if they're on community penalties, if they've been cautioned or ASBO'd. Some of it's about this place, though: where we are on fire inspections, hygiene inspections, environmental health. Oh, the lot, Leila. They make your life difficult, this government, I can tell you. Kate's right on that. Anyone would think we were trying to do harm, not give these kids something decent in their lives. Something with a bit of structure.' She opened a ring binder on her desk, flipped a few pages over and then flattened her lips. 'Oh, *Janice*,' she said, 'I ask you. You can hardly read what that woman writes sometimes. For the life of me I don't see why Dan keeps giving her so much responsibility. It's not like she's been here any longer than anyone else. I'll have to redo this quickly, Leila, it's the food orders and it wants posting this morning or we won't have lunches next week. *I shall just have to redo it,*' she said.

Snapping out a crisp new form from the drawer at her knee, Kerry began to write.

There were voices outside. Leila made out two figures coming down the front steps. They tried the door, shaking it a few times. There was a loud knock.

'*Read the sign please,*' murmured Kerry, without looking up. She reached for a calculator and began to tap.

There was some muffled talking, another shove of the door and then they went back up the steps and disappeared.

It was silent out in the corridor. Kate was at a meeting and everyone else was apparently working on the top floor. There were no counsellors in, except Mike, who was doing his records. It was another 'admin afternoon'.

Leila noticed the sole of her boot was coming loose. She pressed it and decided it would last for a bit. It was two o'clock. The clock on the wall had a loud tick.

'Kerry?' said Leila. 'Could I ask you something?'

'Shoot.'

'Is Dan – is he really a priest?'

Kerry looked up and smiled.

'Yes he is. Catholic. Kate's not filled you in much, then? Well, there's a surprise.' She folded the form and put it in an envelope.

'So this is a sort of . . . religious centre, then.'

Kerry put her forefinger against her lips.

'*No.* Gawd, no. Get caught saying that and you're shut down in a flash. It's *interfaith*. We've got a room with prayer mats for the Muslims. There's signs go up when it's Jewish holidays – or Hindu. You have to or there's an unbelievable stink. Dan's here because Ann Summerdale wanted him but we have to make sure it's all represented. Dan's very discreet. He has to be. It's his way, though.'

'Ann Summerdale,' said Leila.

'The woman who started it. Out there, in the big picture.'

'Oh, yes – yes, of course.'

'Pots of money. Most miserable woman I ever met in my life. She's never in these days. Lives abroad mostly – in Germany where *he* comes from. I never warmed to him. We get a call every now and then but it's not what she hoped it was going to be, I don't think. I do get that impression. Not that the centre isn't as good as what she wanted, but it didn't bring her son back, I guess. I think she liked it when the papers were asking about him for a while and there were all pictures of him and that. Just after the place opened this is. Brought him alive again for her, I should think. But it's all quiet now – obviously. Had to be. Anyway, it's all in his memory, so that's something, isn't it?'

The phone rang and Kerry put up a finger again and answered it.

'Thomas Summerdale?' she said. 'Oh no, you're *joking*. When for? Well, has it been paid for then, or what? Well, of course. Well, yes. Thank you. Yes, thanks.' She put the phone down and rolled her eyes. '*Knives and forks,*' she said. 'Do we want them delivered? No, we want you to keep them and give them all to your grandma for Christmas. Crazy,' she said. 'What the hell anyone nicked all the cutlery for in the first place is anyone's guess. Anyway, enough of that. Let's get you stuck in, shall we? Bit of filing to start with. Alphabetical order.'

It was four thirty before they took a break. Kerry had been out of the room most of the time and Leila had worked her way through a large stack of records, each of which needed to be filed under the correct name. Many of the names were new to her, beautiful names whose origins she couldn't guess: 'Tunde', 'Ilias', 'Jiwad'.

Kerry set down two mugs and a plate of mini-muffins.

'Ooh, you've done quite a lot. You're a hard little worker, aren't you? Like Kate,' she said. 'It's impressive. It's a nice quality in a person, that.'

Leila smiled nervously and pulled her cardigan round her.

'Well, sit down then, love. You are allowed to take a break.'

Leila dragged the other chair over to Kerry's desk and took a mug. The tea was strong and milky. Kerry chose a mini-muffin and took a bite. She sighed contentedly while she chewed, then she swivelled her chair round a little to face Leila.

'Aren't you having one, then? Go on,' she said, '*choc chip*.' Leila took one and Kerry seemed pleased. 'Well,' she said. 'You and Kate close then, are you? See a lot of each other?'

'No. We used to. But we lost touch for a while. That's probably why you didn't know about me. It's OK, I know no one knew Kate had a sister. I've been . . . away.'

Leila took a small bite of her muffin.

Kerry nodded gravely, savouring this piece of information. 'Oh well, it's nice for you to get together then, isn't it?' she said. 'Family reunion.'

There was a knock at the door. Relieved not to have to continue the conversation, Leila swivelled round in the hope it was Kate or even Janice, but it was only the strange, quiet man, James. He seemed younger than he had the day before – in his mid-thirties, perhaps – but there was a heaviness about him, as if he was dragging a great weight behind him as he walked and you felt tethered to it yourself when he was around. His shirt was very creased, as if he had slept in it, she thought.

'Kerry,' he said. 'I've been on the phone to the council like you told me to and they did eventually give me the right person.'

'Oh, yes. Right. Good. So, what's the latest?'

'They're coming on Monday. It was only a confusion because they thought it said Thursday on the form, not Tuesday. They faxed me a copy. It was quite hard to tell.'

'Oh, you are *kidding* me. All that fuss! Who wrote that letter, then?'

'Who? Oh, I'm afraid I don't know that.'

'Well, they should be *ashamed* of themselves. If you can't *write* properly you shouldn't be doing the letters.'

Not responding to this, James seated himself at the other desk. His face was slightly sweaty. Feeling Leila's eyes on him, he looked up briefly and his lips flattened out in what was either a half-hearted smile or an expression of resignation. Leila wondered if he was ill.

'Right-o. Back to it, then,' sighed Kerry. 'Photocopying for me. I shall take this up with me. Maybe just one more of these. Just a little one,' she said, taking another mini-muffin and dropping it into the pocket of her cardigan. 'You all right with those files, Leila? Know what you're doing?'

'Yes, I'm fine. Thanks.'

'Leave you to it, then. Take five, though – you've earned it.'

Not wanting to disobey Kerry, Leila sipped her tea for a while, unsure whether to say anything to James or not. It seemed weird to sit in a room near someone without speaking at all, but then perhaps this was just because she had been used to chatting with John and Myron all the time while they painted the walls. They even sang along to the radio. Myron did improvised descants. This was obviously very different. This was the real world, she told herself.

No, silence was good. It was serious. She was not used to an office environment and didn't know how to behave, that was all. It was probably normal not to speak for hours at a time.

There was something comforting about the simple, repetitive filing. She got back into the rhythm of it quickly. Also, she thought, strange as it sounded it was good to work near someone who didn't want or expect anything from you, not even good manners. He was just a human presence, she thought, a faint animal warmth.

Here I am, alive, Leila told herself. She remembered the face of the Spanish doctor. He had held her hand.

But I am alive, she thought.

She read the name on the next sheet of paper: 'Ling Kiang, aged 15', and suddenly she felt so grateful that she was still there: breathing, seeing, standing, holding a piece of typed paper, that she was almost moved to tears. To be near Kate, to have simple work to do, which was even of some use – she could not have expected anything so good after all that had happened in Spain.

She lifted another stack of files and opened the one on the top.

It was not until well after five that there was any sign of life in the rest of the building. Then there were voices out in the hall. James was uninterested and continued to type. Leila tried to make out how many there were out there. It was either two or three, she decided. The male ones were hard to distinguish, but after a minute or two the female one was unmistakeably Kerry's. She coughed a few times.

'Sorry. Summer cold. The injustice of it,' Leila heard her say. 'Anyway, back to what we were talking about. Look, I had a word, all right? Like we said. But you've got to let people . . . What I'm saying is, I did mention it, though. In a roundabout way.'

'Well, yes, you *did*,' said a male voice. It was Dan, Leila thought. The priest. 'And I'm sure that'll be an end to it now. I'm sure everything will be fine now.'

'It will. It'll blow over. You'll see.'

'No, I won't *see*. I'm sorry, but I'm afraid I've got to disagree with both of you,' said the other voice.

'Oh dear,' said Dan. 'Have you?'

'Yes, I'm sorry, Dan, but I have. There are reasons why you do things a certain way, OK? Not to use too much shrinky jargon, but it's about *boundaries*. You break that and the trust goes, the value goes. For some of these kids this is the only place they come to where there are any boundaries at all. Abuse, violence – you know how it is. This is a *refuge*, even if they're just in here for a game of pool. The adults have to be *safe* here. And no, I'm not saying anything *like that*, I'm saying it's about the way things are *perceived* by very vulnerable teenagers.'

'It's just concern,' Dan said.

'It's still doing the wrong thing.'

'OK, Mike, OK – I can see you're angry about this.'

'I'm not angry. Don't make this personal, Dan. This is about a colleague; I'm flagging something up about a colleague's professional conduct, that's all.'

'It's more than a flag,' said Kerry.

'It's a flag.'

'A red one, then,' said Dan.

'OK, a red one. Yes, OK, I feel this very strongly. You can't just decide to do it your own way here – it won't work. And all right, yes, you do start to wonder about the . . . motivations.'

Dan's voice was clearer, firmer now.

'Mike, OK. Let's drop this now, all right? I'll have a word if it seems necessary. But in all likelihood what Kerry said will have done the trick.'

'You think so? That'll be a first then, because I've never seen Kate back down on anything yet,' said Mike.

There was a pause.

'Oh, for goodness sake,' said Kerry. '*Tea break*. I don't know about you two, but I'm parched.'

'Tea. Yes, good idea. Excellent idea, Kerry. A cup of tea.'

They moved on, their footsteps going down the stairs towards the canteen, their voices becoming fainter.

In a kind of daze of confusion and embarrassment, Leila glanced over at James to see if he had also heard this, only to find he was staring directly at her. She felt her face becoming hot and red and he looked down again, picking up his pen and beginning to fill out the form in front of him.

'Date and place of birth', he read. He copied the details neatly from the screen. 'St Mary's Paddington, London', he wrote, then '08/09/1993'. And then he stopped. With a jerk of frustration he saw that after filling in more than thirty of them perfectly, he had now written his own name, of all things, at the top of the form.

He drew a sharp line diagonally across the page. Then he screwed it up into a ball and threw the whole thing into the bin.

Chapter 18

Staying with Kate was not what Leila had imagined. They barely saw one another. Kate was mostly back after eleven at night and after eating a plate of whatever Leila had cooked, generally while standing up in the kitchen, she went straight to bed. She went out very early too. It seemed that even when she wasn't on the first shift at the centre, she left before seven. Sometimes she appeared to go running, sometimes not – but Leila knew better than to ask about this.

Five days passed. Then six. Leila had finished the filing and the ground and basement offices were transformed. She had unquestionably done a good job. Having spoken to Dan about it, Kerry asked if she would like to take over on reception for a bit, just answering the phone and the door and checking the appointment books, while they found a replacement for the woman who had left them in the lurch. This would then free Kerry up for the more urgent administrative stuff which was what her job was actually meant to be about. Not that you'd guess it, she said. It wouldn't take longer than two weeks to advertise and do the interviewing – three at the very most. Until then, there was a bit of basic work on offer.

Leila told Kerry she would need to ask Kate, but in theory she would love to do it.

'Three weeks?' Kate said, fiddling with the tuner on the radio. 'I see.' The station fuzzed into place. It was an opera. She shrugged. 'Well, it astonishes me to say it, but it doesn't bother me too much. It's not like I thought it would be. *Nothing* like it, thank God. Shit, this is beautiful – listen to that tenor, would you? Oh, wow, I mean just *listen*.' Kate's eyes opened slowly again. She poured herself some water.

'No, it's all right you helping out at the centre. Fuck, it's even OK you sleeping here,' she said. 'You've stopped hoovering all the time for one thing and – well, we aren't getting under each other's feet. That's what matters.' Leila thought of saying that, other than when she arrived, this was the first evening they had actually seen each other, but immediately she thought better of it. 'Even so, when it comes to you crashing here, we'll have to take it day by day, OK?' said Kate. 'No binding contract. Not that there is such a thing.'

The soprano's voice trailed silkily across the room. The cat loped in clumsily, lapped at his water bowl and went out again. Kate turned up the volume. She stretched. Her arms were very long and thin, like stalks in the wind. Leila remembered her learning ballet steps from a book when they were young, practising them in the kitchen. She had been too little to join in, but Kate had let her hold the book.

'So, what's for dinner, then?' Kate said. 'I assume you've bought something special. Oh God, look at you – I'm joking, Leila. Remember joking? No, you're all right – I'm out again anyway.'

'Are you?' Leila said, unable to conceal her disappointment. She had in fact bought something special.

Kate put a cigarette in her mouth and headed out towards the balcony.

'I'm sure you'll survive,' she said. 'You're a big girl now.'

In the bathroom later that night, while the taps ran, Leila took the keys to the flat in Marylebone out of her wash bag. She felt ashamed of her dishonesty – but then was it really dishonesty? she thought. She couldn't go back to that place – with its unopened boxes and that poor bonsai she had got for Hugo, which was probably dead on the sideboard by now. No, she couldn't go back – there was no question in her mind. She wrapped the keys in the handkerchief again. Then she took off her wedding ring and put it in there too and hid it all away.

Chapter 19

At long last, the weather began to improve. Leila found a way to walk through the park a bit on the way to the centre. Kerry had paid her for her first five days' work up front and she had bought herself a pair of jeans and a pretty skirt and two blouses from a charity shop. She also found two new ferns for Kate's balcony on a market stall. Then she sat in the park with the shopping bags and a slice of watermelon. Pale hazy sunshine came through the lime trees. The watermelon was sweet and cold. Her hair hung loose down her back and over her shoulders, the light picking out the gold in the thick brown waves. It seemed amazing that London was so large that she could sit there without anyone knowing where she was: not Charlie, not Gavin. Not a single person who was a part of her normal life knew where she was. The night before she had sat in a café with her book and a glass of wine, like a tourist.

On the grass nearby two children were playing a game with an old-fashioned hoop. They were immaculate, combed down, like something from a fifties film.

The children at the centre were very different. On her first full day, she had watched them come in. They were boys mostly – boys with their jeans tugged down, their caps on sideways, their jackets slouched off one shoulder. Everything they were outwardly seemed to express a desire not to be contained; to be just a little lower or slightly more to one side than expected. They were poised, contorted even, not unselfconscious for even a moment; the way they walked or stood never failing to convey the values of the world they had just walked in from. Be aware, be manly, make it all look like you don't give a shit, their bodies said. They were adult long before their time, but then they were children, too – and so they came in, to play pool; to see the various counsellors; for their life skills courses in cooking and cleaning and paying the bills.

Leila began to know some of their names. There was Zane, with the little straggly beard, Clint, with the red bandanna hanging out of his back pocket and Nathan, whose lips and tongue were bright blue from the sweets he was always chewing. They eyed her suspiciously at first, but after a couple of days they simply walked past.

Then, out by the drinks machine in the hall, one of the older boys spoke to her. He asked what her name was.

'Leila?' he said. 'Leila. Where your mum get that name from innit? That's like a name off of a song. Yeah, I know that song . . . I know that song . . . "*Don't break my heart, Ley-la*,"' he sang. '"*Don't you say goodbye, don't you tell me a lie . . .*"' It was a good voice. He nudged his friend and winked. 'Check it, yeah blud, this the chick from out the song we got here. She be the original.' He was good-looking, sexually sophisticated in the agonised, fraudulent way of a boy who has modelled himself on older brothers. His friend was taller, emaciated, with a nervous laugh. They were both black – about fifteen. Leila took the apple juice carton out of the dispenser.

'*Oh* yeah,' he said. 'My girl's sweet like apples. You *know* it.'

She smiled back at him. 'So what's your name?'

'Romaine. Ain't no song. And this here hoodrat's K.J.'

'Pleased to meet you.'

The doors of the centre opened for appointments at 10 a.m., except for three Thursdays and two Wednesdays a month, when there was someone there for the early hours. Ann Summerdale had wanted it to open early every day, but there simply wasn't enough money, particularly since the burglaries. No one appeared to mention the burglaries. There had been various measures taken to increase security since then, but it was a policy Ann Summerdale had insisted on, that during opening hours, the front door was always unlocked – even if there was now a CCTV camera over it.

By Leila's third day she had understood all that she needed to do and was quite comfortable at her desk by the window at reception. She could see whoever came and went. Mostly Kerry had been sitting at the other desk, but that morning she was out and Leila was printing envelopes alone.

'Hello, excuse me?' said a girl's voice. 'You in charge here?' Leila put the envelopes down and turned round. In the entrance was a small, very slim white girl of about fourteen or fifteen. She could have been no more than five foot two. 'You're new,' she said. 'They fire that other one then or what?' Her hair was scraped back into a high ponytail and her eyes were heavily outlined with kohl. She wore hoop earrings, a halter-neck top and on her bottom half were pink leggings and little high-heeled sandals. Her feet were tiny, Leila thought – as small as a child's. The arm of her jacket trailed on the floor.

'Yeah, so I come for my appointment but the guy's not there, yeah?' she said. 'Is he not coming then or what? Thinks I got fuck all to do he can just *blank* me if he wants. It's rude, you know?' She had the indefinable accent they all had – a mixture of cockney and various African and Asian elements.

'Sorry, I don't know what you're talking about. Who was your appointment with?'

'Shrink. Drugs guy. *Stacey Clark?* Dragged my ass out of bed for it too. That's fucking *long*, man – not showing up.' She wobbled a bit on her left heel. 'So is he not coming then, yeah? I can go back to bed now? Or they gonna give me some shit off the school for this 'cos I ain't having that, right? He don't show up then it's his problem. You get me? They ain't putting that shit on me.' Her little handbag tapped against the door. She chewed her gum. She was a pretty girl, her features even and childlike in spite of the black kohl and the mask of foundation. '*Stacey Clark?*' she said, drawing up her eyebrows impatiently.

'I'll find out what's going on,' said Leila. 'Was your appointment with Mike?'

Stacey nodded – but it was as if, as soon as something was being done about her protest, she had lost all interest in it. She began to pick off her nail varnish.

After searching a bit for it, Leila brought out Mike's appointment book and ran her finger down the list. Stacey's name was not there. Having seen this happen a few times now, she turned the page.

'Oh yes, here you are. It was yesterday,' she said. 'Yesterday at two.'

Stacey stared and chewed, apparently unaffected by this news.

'You look like someone,' she said.

There was a buzz at the back door. It was the electricians who had come to fit the new alarm on the back gate.

'Won't be a second,' she told Stacey.

The two men made their way through the canteen and up the stairs to the reception.

'Afternoon. Anderson Security?' said one of them. 'We've come to do you a Zentro 2000? Booked by a . . . Kerry Rogers,' he read. 'That you?'

'No, I'm not Kerry, but she told me about it. Thanks. D'you need a signature?'

'Here and here.'

They stood with their toolboxes, feet apart. Leila took the clipboard to sign and as she did so, out of the corner of her eye, she saw Stacey leave, the arm of her jacket dragging behind her. For a flash she wished she could run after her, but there was no point; Mike was fully booked.

There was something so sad about her having come on the wrong day, Leila thought.

The two men gazed out after Stacey too and then the taller one turned to his friend and winced playfully.

'Here,' said Leila, sharply pushing the clipboard back into his hands.

When they had gone, she sat down on a plastic chair, her heart still beating hard with anger. She was almost breathless. She put her hand against her chest as if to slow it down. *Calm down*, she told herself. They had only looked at a girl. A girl she didn't even know. But she was such a young girl, such a small girl even in her high heels – like a child dressed up in its mother's clothes.

She took a deep breath and checked the clock: it was one forty-five already. She had lost track of time again and nearly missed lunch. She locked up the office and made her way downstairs and through the canteen, which was peppered with teenagers now, all lingering over their trays. The serving hatch was still open and the hot lights glared down on Sean and Pat, the cooks.

Without much interest, Leila chose some salad and cheese and a few bits of bread. She carried it through to the staff section.

'Oops-a-daisy,' said Kerry bumping into her in the corridor. 'You're not only getting your dinner now are you? You must be *starving*. Enjoying those envelopes too much? You're a funny one. You tuck in, girl, you've only got ten minutes' break left, bless you.' Kerry peered at her plate. 'Ooh, didn't you want the chicken, then? It's not bad today. Get yourself a bit of chicken, go on. But no – there I go interfering again. You enjoy what you've chosen. Nice bit of salad and what is it, cheese? Is that cheddar?'

'I think so.'

'Oh, I didn't spot that. Probably only just put it out. Typical. Anyhoo, there's only James and Mike in there, so it's quiet. Kate's still out.'

Leila took this in with a mild disappointment. Mike and James, she thought. Mike was so earnest and for some reason when he did tell a joke it always missed her slightly, so that she laughed too late, not having understood the punchline. Rather than putting him off, this only seemed to have made him more determined and now she felt nervous as soon as she saw him in case she would be required to laugh. James was basically irrelevant, he spoke so little – and Kate was always out. The person she would quite like to have seen was Janice, with her round smiling face and her straw bag as if she was always going on a picnic. But she had obviously missed her chance.

She went out into the room. James was at the far end of the table. Mike was sitting in the window, reading a magazine, finishing a Mars Bar. He raised his hand.

'Salutations, Miss Leila. How are we today?'

'Fine, thanks,' she said.

'Electricians are here, I see.'

'Yes.'

They were out in the garden, a stepladder propping open the gate.

'That only took two months, then.'

She sat down and began to butter her bread intently, hoping he would get bored and turn away. A few curiously weighty seconds passed, and then he went back to his magazine. She ate silently for a while, eyes fixed on her plate. Then Mike stood up and yawned and stretched. He chucked his magazine on to the table with a slap.

'Right, I'm done. That's up for grabs if anyone's interested. There's a good thing on Israel,' he said.

Unsurprisingly, James said nothing to this. Mike picked up the magazine and tapped him on the head with it. Then he went out, whistling something.

Leila went back to her plate. She didn't mind being around James when there were other people there, but there was something tiring about being alone with him, she thought. She cut a piece of cheese and put it on to her bread. She ate a forkful of lettuce. Her own chewing seemed very loud.

With relief she heard someone coming into the corridor and then to her surprise, James grinned.

'I thought you must have gone back to bed,' he called out.

'What are you on about? I can hack it with the best of them.'

It was Dan.

'Hi, Leila. Taking a well-earned rest? All right, mate,' he said, sitting down beside James, rocking his shoulder. 'If we are still mates, that is.'

'We're still mates. Sort of.'

'We on for tonight again, then?'

'Amazing you ask. You don't think you're getting away with it, do you? I'm going to win it all back.'

'Is Nick coming again?'

'Should be. Susie isn't very impressed apparently. I had a funny text.'

'No, well I'm not surprised. You can't blame her. Two nights in a row. I think that constitutes putting asunder.'

'Well, it's your fault for clearing us all out like that. You and your direct line to God.'

'Wow. Have I got a direct line?'

'Your own personal one, plainly. You do not get a full house, a straight and then a Royal bloody flush any other way. Soak it up, Dan, some of us poor sods didn't even get given the number.'

'You've got his number.'

'Oh no, *don't* do that. Don't get all *priesty* on me, I've just eaten.'

'All right, all right. Calm down. Anyway. So, eight o'clock tonight then is it? Should I bring anything?'

James got up with his tray.

'Bottle of communion wine?'

Dan rolled his eyes.

After James had left, the atmosphere felt calmer. Dan shook up a carton of strawberry milk.

'So, Leila – we haven't spoken much. How are you finding the place?' he said.

She put down her fork.

'It's great.'

Dan smiled.

'Great? Is it? Nice to hear some enthusiasm. We're all a bit jaded – except the unstoppable Janice, obviously. But no, it is great, you're right. I'm glad you're enjoying it.'

'I like feeling useful,' she said.

'Oh yes, I agree wholeheartedly. It's essential. Who was it that said, it's one of life's big secrets that all we do of any value is the stuff we do for others?'

'I'm not sure,' she said. She still found Dan a bit frightening. What did it mean to be so young and a priest? She couldn't help

127

imagining there must be something strange that had driven him to do it.

Even so, he had a friendly, broad face with freckles and blue eyes. His hands were broad, too. He looked like someone who spent a lot of time outside, which was not what you imagined of a priest.

He took a bite of his pear.

'Kate's out fundraising again, is she?'

'I haven't seen her but I think so, yes.'

He chewed.

'She's so *good* at it,' he said. 'We had someone before who never really had it in him, I think. That sort of . . . *fire*, you know?'

'Yes.'

'Kate's got a lot of that.'

'Yes, she has.'

He smiled at her again and then, leaning over the table, he pulled Mike's magazine towards him. He began to read the Israel piece.

Leila found herself disappointed.

She tried to imagine Dan as a teenager at school. Had he always wanted to be a priest? Had his family made him do it? It seemed somehow incredible that people were still becoming priests – young people, particularly.

In the other part of the room, people were throwing away the trays and going back upstairs. A group of girls stood out in the garden talking. One of them began to dance – it was a caricature of someone. The others laughed.

'Dan?' she said. 'Are you and James old friends?'

He looked up.

'That's perceptive of you. Yes, we were at school together.'

'I can't work out what he does. He isn't a counsellor, is he?'

Dan found this so funny he had to cover his mouth and swallow.

'No, James isn't a counsellor. He's a surgeon.' He took the last bite of pear then threw it into the bin. 'I'm guessing you're now wondering why we've got a surgeon working here, aren't you? He's a volunteer – so we won't have him for long, sadly. He's taking some time away from work – a sort of . . . sabbatical,' Dan said, wiping his mouth and standing up quickly 'Anyway, he very kindly let me persuade him to sort out our computer system here and our website. He's one of those people that can do all that and make it look easy. Aren't they annoying?' He checked his watch. 'Oh, how did that happen?' he said. 'I've got a

128

meeting with the imam of the local mosque in fifteen minutes. I must get back up there.'

'Me too. Not that I'm doing anything so important.'

'Hey, Leila, you're doing a lot for us. Don't underestimate it. We were beginning to think we'd lose Kerry in a sea of filing.'

They went back out into the canteen together to throw away their trays.

Chapter 20

At 5 a.m. the roads around Bayswater were empty, except for the occasional lorry or coach. Queensway, so busy in the day, with its Lebanese takeaways, its Chinese herbalists, its clothes emporiums promising everything you wanted for under £10, was dirty and silent.

Kate had been awake since three. For a while she had tried doing the silly visualisations, which had never once worked, then she had thrown off the covers and stared out of the window. But there was nothing to see. She went out to the kitchen and made herself a cup of tea – but it was far too early to want it. She tried to read a bit but found she couldn't concentrate. Now she stood beside the sofa, watching Leila sleep. She fastened her watch. She was dressed in trainers and shorts and her hair was scraped back behind a headband. It was the third time she hadn't slept that week – but for some reason her body didn't want to. For some reason it seemed that when everyone else's body closed down for the night, hers went on humming and buzzing and beeping like a frantic computer.

Well, that's just me, she thought. So what? Fuck off.

She laid her fingertips on the back of the sofa. Leila breathed softly in her sleep. Her hair trailed off the edge of the pillow, a few strands of it reaching the carpet. How had it happened? Kate thought. How on earth had it happened that this person she had dreaded seeing so much for literally years was now here, in her home, was now even working where she did – even if it was only for a few weeks? It was insane. But then life was just like that, she thought – it regularly was the thing you could never have imagined that ended up happening. And how often this impossible thing, which if you'd been told to

130

expect it you'd have said no way, not without reversing the laws of physics or something, how often it turned out to have been less than a millimetre away from you all along, behind a veil of – nothing.

It had been that way with addiction, she thought. It had been impossible – *unthinkable* – to imagine a life without vodka, without syringes or pipes, without the filth and grime in that unforgettable kitchen, the 3 a.m. scenes, the repulsive compromises of every level of your human dignity . . . and then there she was, living it. There she had spotted herself one day, pouring milk on an ordinary bowl of cornflakes, a radio on in the corner. Whoosh: *life*.

Imagination was not really what was required. What was then? There was blood and sweat obviously – oh yes, there was always blood and sweat, she thought – but maybe there was also some element of fate. She looked down again at Leila's sleeping face, beautiful in the dawn light, the right arm cushioning her cheek. Maybe there genuinely was. Outside on the balcony, the two new ferns blew about in their pots. There seemed to be a new watering can out there too. What else had she gone and bought?

Kate bent over and tugged her laces tight, tying the bows in a double knot. She put the backpack on, snapping the straps in close around her waist. Then she went noiselessly out and down the stairs and it was only once she was outside and had shut the main door behind her and leant back against it, hearing the latch click shut, that she realised she'd been holding her breath. She let go of it all and immediately her lungs snatched for more air. Her temples pulsed and her vision was blurry for a moment.

It was good to be outside, she thought. The air was fresh and even though there was sunlight already, the world still had that silverish blue quality which her years of insomnia had taught her to appreciate.

She rubbed her hands to wake them up and set off at a jog. In every house there were drawn curtains, darkened rooms. The weight of sleep lay across the road; it was sleep that made the leaves rustle so quietly, sleep that made the parked cars so still.

I am the only person on earth, Kate thought.

And then she began to run, her long, thin legs carrying her on, out through Leinster Terrace, past Porchester Gardens, on towards Queensway and Hyde Park and the Bayswater Road. Here and there a light was on, but there were no cars on the road, no one to be seen at all, not even a dog. And then suddenly there was someone. An old Indian man hauled up the cover on his shop. The cover rattled noisily into place. Beside him were stacks of newspapers, all tied up with string.

Like a falling object or a spark or flame, Kate caught his eye as she passed and he watched her lean shape bobbing in and out of visibility above the car roofs, on past the ice rink and the steak house, past the tube station, towards the main road.

Ahead of her, across the Bayswater Road, the park was beautifully empty too and over the ground was a thick mist three feet deep between the trees. She ran up to the railings. It was an image from a fairy tale. In an hour it would have burnt off, but for now a little unreality was still permissible, she thought, before the logic of daylight applied.

She kept running for over an hour. She ran faster and further than she normally did, making a great loop all the way round the outside of the park. She did not even stop when the sweat poured down her face and her chest began to hurt. There is a pain, she thought, noticing it. She pressed it with her fingertips. But why stop? What is pain? she thought. It was just her body arguing – her body fighting, as it always fought, like a wild cat in a bag.

And then, having reached the railings outside the centre long before she realised it, she put her arm out towards them, hunched over double and began to cry.

The crying was uncontrollable. It was convulsive, violent as vomiting or choking; it held her and shook her and had her gasping for breath. Tears streamed down her face and she glanced left and right, horrified in case someone should see. But there was no one around. Of course not, she told herself; it was not yet 6 a.m. There were just Mr Wing's stinking bin bags on the pavement beside her.

She bent over again, or rather the crying bent her and her shoulders shook and her mouth moved wordlessly as if in expression of some deep grief.

In the window above, Mike appeared with a cup of tea in his hand and then moved back quickly, away from the glass.

At last the crying passed. Kate wiped her arm across her face. She wiped her arm on her shorts. She straightened the backpack and went down the steps. She let herself in and flicked on the lights and made her way upstairs. There was a shower on the top floor. She took out her bottle of soap and her shampoo and her towel. She put the clean clothes on the chair. Then she washed quickly, scrubbing her face and her neck and her scalp – and dried herself off. She combed her hair down flat and clipped one side of it back, out of the way.

Then she leant into the mirror. Her own face looked back at her, pink and clean, but with awful dark circles under the eyes. Even if her body didn't seem to want rest, she certainly *looked* tired. She stared for a moment and then put her fingers against her temple and pulled up the skin. Her cheek lifted, along with the corner of her mouth. She did the same on the left – and then, abruptly losing patience with this, making a flapping gesture at the mirror as if it was asking her something she didn't have the time to answer, she turned away to search for her socks.

Once dressed, she went down to the basement. The neon lights buzzed and flickered on in the kitchen and she put some bread in the toaster. She tugged open the fridge. There was no margarine, only a vast brick of butter. She would go without. She didn't much care: what she wanted was coffee anyway. Her sanctioned stimulant. There was a small amount of jam left in the jar and she scraped this on to the toast and put the jar into the recycling bag. Then she carried her plate out into the staff area of the canteen where the mugs and the small kettle were kept.

'Morning,' said Mike. 'Crikey. I didn't mean to scare the shit out of you.'

'You didn't.'

'Because it looked like I made you shoot out of your skin.'

'You didn't. It's fine. I'm fine. You're here for the early drop-in,' she said, remembering as she spoke that it was a Thursday, not a Friday as she'd thought.

'I am. Only no one turned up as usual. We really should stop bothering with it in my opinion. Or scale it back.'

Kate checked there was water in the kettle and tipped some instant coffee into a mug. The teaspoon clattered on to the sideboard.

'Even if only one person comes every few months, Mike, it's still worth doing. Ann Summerdale might be full of crap, but she was right about the early hours of the morning – it's a special time. It can be the most dangerous time on earth. If something's going to go badly wrong, it's then.'

Mike exhaled. He drummed his fingers on the tabletop.

'You speak from experience?' he said.

'What?'

'Mmm? Oh, nothing. Didn't mean to pry. No, anyway, maybe you've got a point.'

Kate glanced at him sceptically. She bit into her toast.

'Aren't you even going to sit down?' he said. 'It's murder on the digestion, that.'

She rolled her eyes but sat down anyway, putting her plate down heavily on the table, her foot on the next-door chair. The kettle began to boil.

'Milk?' Mike said, pushing the carton towards her.

'Don't take it. They do horrific things to cows.'

'Do they? Who does? Vitamin D though isn't it? Calcium. You need it for your bones, girl.'

'My bones'll survive.'

'Cows more important?'

'Yes,' Kate said.

Once replaced, the kettle rumbled on for a while and was quiet. Mike got up for a refill himself.

'So,' he said, 'your *sister*, hey? That must be nice for you.' Kate's eyebrows twitched. She continued to eat. Mike threw away the tea bag and sat down again. The silence continued for a moment. Then he said, 'How's work, then?'

'Work?'

'Fundraising. Application time is upon us. You've been out and about a lot from what I hear. How's that all going?'

She raised her eyes.

'It's fine, thank you, Mike. We seem to be on course for another Bentingdon grant at any rate.'

'Oh, that's good. Well done you.' He dropped two sugars into his tea and stirred. 'My third cup.'

'*Shocking*,' said Kate.

He smiled at her.

'Slippery slope?'

'Inevitable.'

He sipped.

'What about the rest of it? How are the life skills classes going?'

'How are the . . . Mike, you're very interested in my career all of a sudden.'

'Hey, I'm being friendly, that's all. I thought the classes were a good concept. An interesting idea. I saw all your drawings and stuff. You're a bit of an artist, aren't you?'

Just then, Kate noticed a tiny screw lying on the floor by her foot. It was the kind of thing that ought never to be found but the light had caught it by chance. She picked it up and examined it closely.

'No, I was just interested how it was all going down with them, that's all.' Mike went on. 'Because you've got a few tricky customers, haven't you? Kate?'

'It's all going very well, thank you, Mike. All of it.'

'They're coming in for them, then, are they? Attending.'

'Most. One or two aren't brilliant.'

'Oh?'

Kate ducked under the table. She checked the hinge to see if the screw had come from there, but it hadn't. She was not surprised – it was far too small to have come from anything but a gadget of some kind. There were Mike's legs, stocky in their jeans, planted solidly a few feet off. 'One or two?' he repeated. She watched the toes scrunch up and relax again in his right shoe.

'Yes,' she said, emerging, 'one or two. Right, I'm going to get some emailing done in peace now before the Kerry whirlwind sweeps in.'

She threw the rest of her toast in the bin, picked up her coffee and plate and went out with them towards the office by the stairs.

Mike shook his head at her back. He sighed. Then, opening his bag and rummaging about for a moment, he brought out an egg and sausage sandwich with extra brown sauce.

Chapter 21

Only six of the ten had turned up. They sat behind the tables in their jumble of slouched clothes, their hair scraped back or gelled into tufts or hidden beneath caps. The phones were mostly off.

Kate cracked another egg into the bowl and whisked.

'Then what you do,' she said, 'is take the chicken breast and dip it in the egg like this.' She lifted it and put it into the bowl. It disgusted her to handle the meat – but it was a requirement. It was for them, so it was justifiable. 'Then you just wiggle it around a bit to make sure it's coated—'

'Oh, no way, that is proper grimy, man! Raw egg. That is *nasty*. I'm telling you – that is *nasty*.'

There was muffled laughter – but it was without any of its usual life. It was a strange atmosphere today, Kate thought. Two of the tallest boys, Romaine and K.J., were missing, and the room felt emptier as a result. A couple of them stared out of the window or fiddled with mobiles under the table.

The phones were her great enemy. Each time she saw the little lights go on or heard a beep, her throat tightened. 'Where are you? Come back!' she wanted to shout. The games, the text messages – all their invisible exits.

But there was no point in asking them to pay attention again and again; it only undermined your authority in the end. It came across as begging. She would just have to find a way to be more interesting, she told herself.

'Then,' she continued wearily, 'then you put it in the plate of bread-crumbs so they all stick, see? You turn it over like this – and then

136

they're ready to go. That's it.' She laid the three chicken breasts on the foil and sprinkled them with salt and pepper. Then she put the baking tray into the oven. 'Right, now we've got to set the timer. *Or*,' she said, 'or what can you do if there isn't a timer?'

'*Use the one on your phone*,' said Clint. She wasn't surprised he sounded so bored. She couldn't think how many times she had repeated this pearl. But you foresaw fires for them – you saw black smoke chugging out of tiny high windows.

'Exactly. Use the one on your phone so you don't forget how long it's been in there for. You got it, Clint.'

In spite of himself there was a flicker of pride. He adjusted his cap to offset it.

Kate handed out the recipe sheets.

'Oh, check it – we got little pictures again. Not bad. You should try a spray can, Miss.'

'I'd like to,' she said, truthfully. She had always understood this desire. She looked at him, at his strong face with its scarred lip, its pale blue eyes. 'Why d'you always call me Miss, Clint? I'm not a teacher and it makes me feel about a hundred and eleven. Kate's fine.' A clean wall, neighbours appalled, she thought: very appealing. She straightened up. 'Yes, there's a special place you can go to do it over in Kilburn. Have you been there?'

But the bond had broken instantly. She might have guessed it would. He sucked his teeth at her.

'Some shithole, they give you a space this big, wash it off next day. Stay in bed, innit.'

She turned back to the others.

'OK,' she said, 'so what's the most important thing about chicken?'

'Gotta be jerk chicken,' said Nate. 'If you want me round your house. None a this breadcrumbs.'

'Rice and peas!'

'No way, man, you want that shit *fried* with some hot sauce. Not too much so your nose running and shit – just right. You don't want no *jerk's chicken*, man – forget about that. That's fools' food,' said Clint.

Always the rivalry, always the fantasised home-cooked meals, Kate thought.

'The most important thing about chicken,' she began firmly – but as her mouth opened to form the next words, she felt all of the melancholy of the early morning pelt down over her like hailstones. 'The most important thing about chicken, is you've got to wash your hands carefully after you touch it.'

They finished at one. It had not been a successful lesson. By the end they were all talking, distracted – disappointed in her: another person in their lives who had failed to represent order, to maintain coherence. They packed up their things, took their little bit of cooked chicken and began to file out. There was no lunch on offer in the canteen today; it was an admin afternoon.

'Stacey?' Kate said, catching her in the doorway. 'Don't you want any chicken? There's a piece here for you.' She held the plate out.

'What? Oh, no, I'm good thanks.' She turned to go. She was wearing baggy tracksuit bottoms today – so large they seemed to belong to someone else. There were burn marks down the legs, a stain across one knee. She had seemed listless throughout the lesson, her eyelids drooping at times.

'Are you?'

'What?'

'Are you OK?'

Stacey turned round properly.

'I'm feeling *sick*, yeah? I don't want no chicken because I'll *throw it up*.'

Kate set the plate on the sideboard again. Her heart sank. She sat down on the edge of the desk.

'So you're drinking again,' she said.

Stacey laughed.

'Yeah I'm drinkin'. I *like* drinkin'. Drinkin's *nice*. Vodka's *nice*. Maybe you should try it some time: might make you fuckin' *loosen up* a bit,' she said. Then she frowned and flipped her shoe back and forth against her heel a few times. She crossed her arms.

The frown made no difference to her face – she still was doll-like in her prettiness. Her little halter-neck top emphasised the fragility of her upper body so much that the baggy bottom half made her seem like two different people stuck together.

'Stacey, you know it's one of the conditions. If you start drinking again you'll have to go back in front of the magistrate.'

She looked Kate straight in the eye.

'Yeah. But someone's got to tell them though, haven't they?'

Kate rubbed her hands across her face. It was thundery outside. It was humid and there was a heavy grey sky. Good weather for running in.

'Did you at least see the drugs counsellor this week?'

'Missed my appointment, innit.'

'Oh, Stacey, you didn't.'

She widened her eyes. '*Yes, Stacey, I did*. Big fucking deal. What's he gonna tell me, fuck's sake, Kate? He's gonna come round my place, tell me how I can sleep with that shit going on next door, that fucking techno bullshit tunes all hours, people coming and going for business twenty-four-seven? And I gotta do what I gotta do.'

Kate's fists clenched.

'No. You don't have to do it. There's another life for you. He should be in jail. They both should be.'

Stacey uncrossed her arms. She leant forward very slightly.

'If you report it I'm not talking to you no more. Never. I should never of told you.'

'OK,' said Kate. 'OK. Sit down.'

'No. I can't. Look, I gotta go, yeah? I'm late.' Stacey hopped off the table. Then, softening a little, she walked up to Kate, stopping just a few inches away from her. She reached past Kate's shoulder, towards the table and took a piece of chicken from the plate.

Her skin was still as perfect as a child's. Kate's eyes closed. She smelt of strawberries. *What are you late for? Where are you going?* Kate thought.

'Stacey, can I . . . give you something?' Kate scrabbled in her handbag. 'Hang on, it's a . . . it's a new phone, sorry.'

Stacey leant back against the wall. 'You're giving me your phone number?' she said.

'Yes. I haven't actually *got* the phone yet, but here's the . . .' she trailed off, seeing Stacey's grin. Then she tore out a page from her address book anyway, leant over it and copied the number out, folding the page cleanly. 'It's a work phone. I don't have a personal phone; I hate them actually. Nice being uncontactable. Anyway, here you are,' she said, dropping it into Stacey's top pocket.

'Thanks,' said Stacey. Immediately Kate began rummaging in her bag again and Stacey walked out of the room.

Kate sat down and rested her head in her hands. Right away there came into her mind a series of images: Stacey walking into a road drunk, Stacey listless in a chair, Stacey being hit by a man Kate could hardly bear to give life to even in thought.

But she was letting her mind run away with her. Why was she doing that? She put down the paper cup whose rim she had been tearing to pieces.

Teach them how to clean the fridge, teach them how to make

themselves an omelette, teach them how to pay their bills, she told herself. Life skills. The fucking irony of it, she thought – but this really was what she was there for. Another in a long line of little cosmic jokes.

She shook her head. Still, it was no good sitting there being sarcastic at God; she had work to do. The lessons were a very small part of her job after all. It was the fundraising she needed to turn her mind to now, she told herself. She must get the Bentingdon proposal finished by the end of the week. There was a lot of work to be done.

But as firm as this inner voice was, it faded to nothing and Kate's fingers moved unconsciously towards the paper cup again. As she picked it up, she imagined Stacey walking up the ramp through the car park into the huge expanse of Hillford's forecourt, with its high-rise blocks on all sides, its windows like a million insomniac eyes, all staring at once.

She had once watched this scene in reality. It had been after the first time they spoke, when Stacey had cried desperately and, in a moment that had arisen so naturally, so beautifully that it was not to be argued with, they had put their arms round each other, breaking all the rules. And afterwards Kate had found herself racing upstairs to the shower room window at the top of the building.

There she was. There Stacey went: a little dab of pink on an enormous grey canvas.

But *what* did she walk back into, Kate thought? Into the void, into the black hole of addiction, that was for sure, into that place of incalculable density where even light got sucked down and crushed.

But the truth was there was this and there were things even Kate couldn't imagine.

'I don't understand. Who lets these men in, Stacey? *Who?*'

'My mum.'

Chapter 22

The next day Kerry, James, Mike and Janice had gathered round the table in the office on the second floor. Kate came in late, carrying a file under her arm. She was wearing a suit jacket and skirt.

'Sorry, Guv,' she said, nodding to Dan. He gave her a warm smile in response.

'Only just got back?'

'Uh-huh.'

'This was the Bentingdon lot again?'

Kate grimaced.

'That bad?'

'Oh, they're all right. I'm whingeing. They're just a lot of old pompous businessmen who fancy themselves as *philanthropists*. It was bearable – just long. How they *love* hearing themselves sound noble – and boy can they get stuck in when it's all offsetting that guilt about their naughty little offshore trusts. Still, it's your actual cash money, isn't it,' she said, 'and this is what matters in life.'

'Have we got it, then?'

'No. No, I wish I could say that. Believe me, you'd know it if we had. There's a lot of competition, I'm afraid. But then, I'm a fierce opponent.'

Dan smiled at her.

'I've no doubt you are.'

She pulled up a chair opposite him.

'You look whacked, honey,' said Kerry.

'Do I? I'm not.' Kate rubbed her eyes as if tiredness was something she might be able to wipe off.

'You're overworked. Like we all are, poppet.'

Dan brought out a box.

'*Not* speaking of being overworked, but your phone's arrived,' he said.

'Has it. Oh, how fabulous,' said Kate.

'Now listen, in all seriousness, *don't* be worried – you won't start getting called on a Sunday afternoon or anything.'

'This is only because I'm usually here on a Sunday afternoon,' she said, taking the box.

'Ooh, let's see. Is yours silver?' said Kerry. 'Mine's only the black one.'

'They're all the same model, I think,' said Dan. 'They were meant to be.'

Janice leant her elbows on the table. She had the parrot earrings on again; they bobbed on their swings.

'Excuse me? Sorry. Does anyone mind if I start? I'm so sorry to be impatient.'

'Janice, you are the least impatient person I've ever met,' said Dan. 'I only wish I could be more like you.'

Kerry gave an audible sigh.

'I hate to interrupt, but Janice, if you've got something to say, then say it, would you? I've got work to do.'

'Well it's . . . I've had an email from Ann Summerdale.'

'Right. *And . . .*'

'I'm afraid there's a bit of bad news.'

'Oh, God. Now what? My hot water this morning – *now* what?'

'There's no nice way of saying this. There really isn't.' Janice pushed a hand through her hair. It bristled between her fingers like cut straw. 'We all know what's going on in the world financially. Meltdown, they call it, some of the papers, don't they? These words. Who knows? Anyway, the fact is, Ann and Peter are not going to be putting the usual amount in this September. It's the share price or something – of the supermarkets. They've lost a lot of money what with the stock market. They're only doing half this year.'

There was silence.

'Come again?' said Mike, blinking. '*Half*? Is this a joke?'

'No.'

'I thought this was "*the most important thing in my life*",' he said, doing an impression of Ann Summerdale which sounded more like the Queen. 'It's in their *son's* name for Christ's sake. In his *sacred* memory.' He turned to Dan, 'What the hell's going on?'

'Mike, sweetheart, it's not Dan's fault. Why are you getting angry with him?' said Janice.

'Because he knows them. He knows Ann and bloody Peter. Ann loves him. And I'm not getting *angry*, I'm just asking.'

'Ask away but it's a complete and utter shock to me too, Mike,' said Dan. His blank face confirmed this.

Everyone took it in for a moment.

'Why *this*, though?' Mike went on. 'OK, they've been hit; OK, they've lost money like everyone – the papers are full of it. But for Christ's sake, couldn't they cut back on gold-plating a yacht or something? Why *this*?'

'What does this actually *mean*?' said Kerry. 'Can everyone stop shouting for a second and could someone please just tell me what this *means*?'

In fact no one had been shouting, but the accusation had a sobering effect. Kate took a deep breath.

'It means we need the Bentingdon money just to stay open,' she said. 'And there are over twenty other charities in the running.'

'Well, no, hang on,' said Janice, 'because that was the other thing she said actually – on a more positive note.'

'Oh, *now* she tells us,' said Kerry. 'When we've all had a stroke.'

'Apparently there's this other grant you can get from the Bentingdon people. This is as an addition to the one we're going for.'

Kate frowned. 'It's for equipment for people with special needs,' she said. 'And that's exactly what you have to use it for – every penny. Even if we did need it and even if we were lucky enough to win it, we'd have to use it all to put in another stairlift or whatever. What's Ann Summerdale on about?'

'Not that. Not the disabilities one. No, there's this other award for creativity or something.'

Everyone looked at Kate.

'Yes – it's for charities with a focus on the arts. Drama and so on. Singing.'

'*We've* got a drama club,' said Kerry.

Kate's face coloured. 'No, I'm sorry – this is actually pretty offensive, OK? I do know how to do my job. I get us money any way it's possible, right? I know every grant and subsidy there is in England, Scotland and Wales. Anything we're eligible for: I'm in there like a wolf. I've read all the small print, I've looked into every possible loophole. We're *not eligible* for this grant, OK? No one even turns up for the drama club! Even if we were all about singing and acting, we've missed the application date by two months. More in fact.'

'Well, this is what Ann was saying, Kate. You see, she knows this chap what's-his-name – I forget his name – who runs the trust. What is his name?'

'Andrew Lucas,' sighed Kate.

'Yes, she knows him – he's a friend's husband or something – and what she's saying is when she's over in a few weeks' time she could arrange for him to visit.'

Mike laughed incredulously and shook his head.

'Hush-hush sort of thing? Nudge nudge, wink wink?'

'Oh *no*, nothing like that, I'm sure. Ann won't have meant that.'

'Bless you, Janice. Shit,' Mike said, 'the other bloody half.'

Kate put a hand on the table. 'What would be the point of this visit anyway?' she said. 'To what – view our extensive singing and drama workshops in action?'

Janice seemed dazed. 'He's a . . . patron of the arts, Ann said.'

'So we could rustle something up for him? Sing for our supper?'

'Well, not singing necessarily. It could be anything. He likes all art, apparently.'

'That's not what Kate meant, Janice,' said Kerry.

'Yes, I know that. I'm sorry. I . . . I see now I hadn't understood what Ann was saying.'

There was another taut silence.

'It's degrading,' said James. Everyone stared at him. As usual he spoke into his lap. 'I'm only temporary here so I shouldn't get a view, but I think you've got no reason to resort to dishonesty and that's what this sounds like.'

'I agree,' said Kate. 'I agree with him. You may not say a lot but at least you talk sense when you do, James.'

'It's all very well being all fancy and idealistic when you're not going up the spout, but maybe beggars can't be choosers at this moment in time. With all due respect, you're a *surgeon*, James,' said Kerry. No one was sure what she meant by this. James pushed his chair back.

'Look, we've made a good case for the money already,' said Kate. 'I actually can't believe Ann's suggesting this. She's so above board, I thought. God, you never know people, do you? The fact is, even if we did sink to it, I don't think that old bastard would be in the least bit impressed by some kind of faked-up spectacle, anyway. All that would happen is he'd think it was incredibly *vulgar*.'

Mike snorted. 'I suppose you should know.' He clicked the lid of his pen on and dropped it into his bag.

144

'Sorry? *I* should know? Why's that, Mike?' He shrugged this off. 'Well, you obviously meant something.'

There was no response.

'Goodness me. Goodness me,' said Dan, rubbing his hands. 'I think we're all slightly in shock. I know I am, anyway. We should probably reconvene. Why don't we? Shall we meet again tomorrow afternoon? It's not as if anything will have changed by then unfortunately, but we may all think a bit more clearly about it. Let the shock wear off a bit. Shall we do that?'

There was subdued agreement followed by the packing away of notepads and a fumbling for jackets and bags.

'What did you mean, Mike?' Kate said. Her voice was very clear above the noise.

'Mmm? Oh, for goodness sake,' he said. '*Nothing*. Just that they're, well they're your sort, aren't they?'

'My sort?'

'You know what I mean, Kate – don't make a big thing out of it.'

'Kate,' said Kerry.

'No, Kerry,' said Kate. 'What's your actual point, Mike?'

'I don't have one. It was a casual remark. Ever heard of a casual remark? Ever relax for a second? It was just that you might have a better understanding of how these types work than say Kerry or Janice or I would for example, that's all.'

'I see. And why's that, Mike? How have you decided that? What are you basing that on?'

'Kate, sweetheart,' said Janice.

'No, I'm fascinated. What exactly is it that makes Mike think I'll have some particular connection with the people on the board of the Bentingdon Trust?'

With a sort of half smile hitching up one side of his mouth, Mike began to put his notepad back into his bag.

'My God. This is all about my accent, isn't it?' said Kate. 'The immense significance of my fucking accent.' She stood up. 'Why me? Why not Dan? We don't sound so different, do we? Or does he get away with it because he's a man of God? Or a man? For fuck's sake, you know nothing about my life, Mike. *Nothing*.'

'Yes, that's true, Kate. You're right. None of us knows a single thing about you, do we?'

'OK. We're all upset. Let's meet tomorrow,' said Dan.

Chapter 23

It was stuffy and humid. As he went down the stairs, James pulled the collar of his shirt away from his neck. Janice smiled and went on ahead of him, the perennial smell of lavender trailing after her, a sort of beach bag over her shoulder. Kerry, Dan, Mike and Kate were still talking in the corridor above. He had felt no desire to stay with them. It was a relief to be out of that room. He never felt comfortable at the meetings. He knew Dan only insisted on his attending them to make him feel welcome, to make him feel he was 'one of them'. It was misjudged. He would have preferred to get on with the web stuff quietly. He ought to say something to Dan about the meetings. It was stupid doing something to please Dan, which Dan thought was being done to please him.

For a nasty second he thought he heard one of the group on the landing above calling his name, but he had imagined it.

He fiddled with his collar again and went round the corner to reception. Immediately his heart sank. He had forgotten that Kate's sister would be working in there. She gave him one of her smiles and he did one back and then that was done and he sat down at the desk.

For ten minutes or so, there was quiet. Then the phone rang.

'Thomas Summerdale? I'll just see if I can find out where she is. Could you hold please?' said Leila. 'Um . . . James? Sorry to bother you, but do you know where Janice is? It's someone about the camera on the back gate.'

James put his pen down. He struggled to remember where Janice had said she was going. She had definitely told him. He frowned. Why couldn't he remember anything? Twice he'd asked Kerry what date it

146

was earlier. And he'd left his lunch behind yet again today. He could never remember *anything* these days. It was inescapable.

Is that true? he thought. Or am I imagining it?

He became conscious that Leila was waiting.

'Out,' he said abruptly, feeling impatient with himself.

He saw the chin jerk inwards slightly, towards the neck: hurt, offence.

'Oh. Right. Thanks,' she said. 'Hello? Yes, I'm sorry, but she's . . . she's out at the moment. Yes, I'll tell her of course. Singer,' she said. 'Patrick Singer.'

She put the phone down. Neither of them said anything more and they continued to work in silence. Every so often one of the teenagers came down the steps and either went off to the basement to play pool or came in saying they had an appointment. Leila brought out the relevant book and then they waited in the hall to be called in.

Later on she began doing some of the photocopying. It was a clunky old machine and, hearing it grind into action, James wished she would do something else. It was such an irritating noise and he couldn't go off and work elsewhere because he needed the computer and the others were all taken. He was trapped. He observed Leila standing by the copier. She had her back to him. She was slightly taller than Kate – healthier, less bony, he thought. Her clothes were more female somehow. She pressed a button. There were a few beeps and then, when nothing seemed to happen, there were a lot more beeps, and then rather than letting the machine warm up, he heard her begin to press the buttons impatiently.

'Damn it,' she said, after a bit. The inevitable had happened and James looked quickly back at his screen. There was a crunching sound and another series of beeps. 'Oh no, *please* don't do that. Be nice to me. Go on – *please*,' Leila said. From what James could hear, she was now tugging the trapped paper out at the other side. He kept his eyes on the flashing cursor. There was a frenzied whirring, and then a final-sounding clunk.

'Oh no,' she said, 'I've jammed it.'

Right away she regretted saying this out loud. Now James would feel obliged to come over and offer his help in some way, she thought. Her face began to burn. She tried to tug the paper free.

'If you keep doing that you'll make it worse,' he said.

She felt her neck becoming hot. Even her hands were hot.

'I'm such an idiot. Who can't work a *photocopier* for God's sake?'

James stood up. 'We need to lift it down on to the floor. I'll have to take the back off and unscrew the rollers manually.'

147

'Oh no, will you? I'm *so* sorry. How incredibly annoying of me. You're in the middle of something and I've made all this fuss and noise and . . . I'm so embarrassed.'

'It's quite heavy. If you take that side I'll take this. Are you strong enough to lift it?'

'Yes,' said Leila, feeling a sudden flare of indignation. 'Of course I am.'

James pulled out the plug.

'On the count of three.'

They heaved it off the cabinet and set it down on the carpet. It was very heavy and for a second Leila was afraid she might drop it after all. But she didn't.

The air was so close and warm that even this brief strain had made her feel sweaty.

The copier sat on the carpet in front of them. James cast his eyes around and then grabbed the paper knife from the pot on Kerry's desk. Using the tip of it he began to unscrew the first bolt on the back panel. Leila watched his tense, pale face, the eyes narrowed in concentration. He was very precise, she noticed. But then of course he was a surgeon.

What a weird job that was, she thought, no matter how important and necessary. You just had to be a bit strange to see the human body that way, to specialise in bits of it and cut into them with knives.

She wished she had broken the copier in front of anyone else. Why him? Why couldn't she have done it in front of Kerry?

The first screw came out in James's fingers and he began to work on the second. He was still silent. Leila felt she should say something but couldn't think what. She searched her mind – and as she did so, gradually she became aware that James's hands were shaking. At first she thought she was imagining it, but it seemed quickly to become more pronounced and the knife tip rattled and jerked out of the groove in the screw so that it fell back into place. He fumbled with the knife for a moment. She looked away.

Did he drink? She had seen this shaking before.

He dropped the knife.

'Hello, hello. What's happened here? Is this A and E?' said Dan. With relief, Leila turned to see him smiling in the doorway. He had a yellow T-shirt on today and jeans and cowboy boots. The yellow clashed with his red hair. He didn't seem to wear his priest's collar all the time.

Kneeling up, James slammed the knife down on the edge of the desk again.

148

'You take over,' he said and without any explanation he left the room.

Dan glanced after him down the corridor. The fingers of his right hand clenched up and released. Then he came over and knelt beside the printer. 'Now, what seems to be the problem,' he said, trying to maintain an air of lightness.

'It's jammed. I jammed it. It's my fault,' said Leila. Dan looked into her face and wondered if she was about to cry.

'Leila, don't stress yourself out. I try not to do it more than twice a week myself.' He smiled at her. 'We're going to buy a new one precisely because of this little problem. Or – well, it'll be nice to buy a new one if we can,' he said, remembering the new facts of their existence.

'I can't believe I've done this,' said Leila. 'I'm quite good at mechanical things normally.' Dan picked up the knife and began to work on the little screw again. 'Thanks so much,' she said.

'Stop. James has nearly done it, anyway.'

Leila looked down as he said this. He levered out the screw and set it on the carpet. He felt intensely conscious of the atmosphere James had left in the room.

'Leila, listen – I may be speaking out of turn, but he's not angry with you, you know?' He noticed her long fingers playing nervously with the hem of her jeans. 'James, I'm talking about – him leaving the room like that. I mean, maybe you didn't think he was angry, but just in case. It's with himself. He gets terribly upset with himself, that's all . . .' Dan trailed off, aware he was being indiscreet – gossiping even. He needed to keep a check on this, he'd found himself having an absurd speculative conversation with Kerry earlier about what Janice's flat might look like.

With what seemed to Leila to be a superhuman amount of strength, Dan heaved the copier back on to the cabinet alone. Then he felt around at the back for the cables.

'Why?' she said. 'Why does James get so upset with himself?'

Dan sighed deeply. It was his own fault for starting it. Now it would be worse to leave it open to speculation.

'It's his hands,' he said.

'His *hands*?'

'Yes. They shake. Didn't you notice? Sometimes it's just a bit and sometimes it's quite pronounced. It started a year ago.'

'But he's a surgeon.'

'It's been very, very upsetting. Well, you can imagine. Initially they thought it was the early stages of MS – but, thank God, it isn't that. *Thank God.*'

'What is it then?'

'The truth is they don't know. He does endless horrible tests but they find nothing. It's a *mystery*, which is not exactly James's natural habitat.'

That's enough now, he told himself. There had been no need at all for the last remark. He plugged in the copier and switched it on again. A sheet of paper came out cleanly from one end. It was satisfying to fix something, he thought. It was broken – and then it worked again. He wished his life contained more of this kind of satisfaction. There was always so much grey area with the charity, with priesthood in general. 'There we are,' he said, 'that seems to have done the trick.'

'You're wonderful.'

'Don't you mention it.'

He watched her picking up the pile of pages again. She began to order them nervously, plainly still embarrassed. Something about Leila suddenly struck Dan as being very like himself.

'I know I've said it before, but it's been great for us, you being here to help out,' he said. 'I bet you don't know how much you're appreciated. You've done such a lot dealing with that filing. And now you've slotted in so easily on reception. Anyway, thank you,' he said.

Leila smiled. Dan noticed the clock.

'Wow, is it six thirty?' he said. 'You should go! You really don't have to work late, you know?' It was impossible not to notice a flicker across her face at this. It occurred to him that perhaps she didn't want to go. Why? he thought. 'So you're . . . you're still staying with Kate, are you?' he said, as she began to pack away her things.

'Just for a little bit longer. She's been incredible.'

'You know Catriona?'

'Who? Oh, the girl who owns the flat? No. Do you?' She still found it impossible to imagine Dan having a social life. The idea that he and James played poker together was bizarre.

'Catriona was unlucky enough to be my first girlfriend.'

'*Not really?*'

He laughed: it was such innocent amazement.

'Sorry,' said Leila.

'Don't be silly.'

'It's just I've never met a priest before. What I mean is a young person who . . . I mean . . .' Dan made himself cross-eyed and then swung the left eye back towards her. Leila smiled.

'What about you?' she said. 'Did you know Kate before she worked here – through Catriona?'

'Mmm? Oh no, we never met. No, it must have been Catriona who told her about the job. I . . . forget now. All the details get fuzzy.' Dan straightened up. He checked there was sufficient paper in the tray for the copier.

'Strange that, isn't it?' Leila said. 'All the details, I mean – the way you end up somewhere. Me, coming to work here.'

'Yes. Innocently wandering in and getting stranded in the middle of that filing.'

'I wasn't stranded. I enjoyed it – it's satisfying doing something like that.'

'No, I know what you mean.'

'But it is strange because all I knew was I wanted to see Kate again. Then this all just happened by accident.'

Dan smiled. 'I don't think I believe in those any more.' Then, having thought for a moment, his expression changed and he rubbed his hands on his jeans a few times. 'Leila, listen – I shouldn't have said any of that stuff to you about James, OK? It's his private business and I feel I've betrayed his trust. It's not that I think you'd tell anyone, but he's such a private person and I'm not sure the others even know.'

Leila studied his face: the freckled skin, the reddish hair, the wrinkles around the eyes, which increased the force of his smile so much. His brow was furrowed anxiously.

'I won't say anything.'

'No, of course you won't. Of *course* you won't,' he said, glancing at her.

'Dan, I promise.'

'Oh no, don't do that! No, no, you don't have to promise me anything, Leila. I just have to stop *talking* so much. Did you know the Bible says that most of the damage we do in this life we do with our tongues?'

'No, I . . . didn't know that.'

Suddenly, Dan felt self-conscious. He felt self-conscious in just the way he had in the early days at the monastery, when what his wonderful Father Simon had referred to so realistically as 'the honeymoon period' had worn off and he found himself reluctant to put on his robes. 'I'm loitering. And I'm keeping you,' he said hurriedly. 'You're probably going out, it's Friday night. I must go and do the kitchen order for tomorrow. Kerry didn't have time to do it and I've got a million and one other bits to finish before I can leave.' He turned to go, thinking perhaps he might try to ring Anne in Munich. Or would it be smack bang in the middle of dinner over there?

'Dan?'

'Mmm?'

'Is Kate still here?'

'Yes, she's upstairs with Kerry. We've had a bit of bad . . . I suspect she may have to work late this evening. So you'll probably have Catriona's whole flat to yourself, won't you? That'll be nice. You can throw open all the windows. Just what you want in this stuffy heat, isn't it? Bit of space to yourself.'

'Yes,' Leila said. 'Exactly.'

She leant down for her bag and put it over her shoulder.

Chapter 24

Once she had reached the Bayswater Road, Leila went through the gate into Hyde Park. This was not a short cut to Kate's flat – in fact the path simply ran parallel to the pavement for a while and then wound off towards the trees and the pond. By the time it led to the next gate, she had to walk halfway back along on the pavement, past the caricaturists and the people selling stolen watches and sunglasses by the railings. But it was worth it: it was good to be among the tall trees and the peonies were starting to come out now.

It had become a sunny evening. She hadn't wanted to go back to the flat alone. Not again. She had a book in her bag and on the way up Ladbroke Grove she had stopped at a shop and bought some cold beer. Now she sat down on the grass and untucked her blouse from her jeans. Then she pulled off her boots and socks and took out the book. But she did not open it yet. The grass felt moist and springy beneath her feet. The beer was cold and delicious, she could smell hydrangeas nearby and the sunlight was warm on her eyelids. The noise of the Bayswater Road was softened by the plane trees.

A man shot past on rollerblades: a graceful surprise, knife sharp, precise as a dancer. Two schoolgirls stood out of his way and he spun a slow circle in front of them, feet turned out to each side, bowing like a courtier. They laughed and he moved off again along the path and Leila gazed after him, back the way she had walked. More figures moved in and out of the dappled light.

Her eyes tightened. Among them was James.

She bit her lip. He would inevitably see her, she thought. Or would he? Perhaps she could just get up quickly and walk on ahead as if she had never seen him. But she had taken off her boots! *Why* had she taken off her boots?

She put down her beer. No, she decided, this was crazy. She was going to make an effort to get on with him. She stood up and waved and after a second or two he saw her. She waited for him to approach.

'Hi, James,' she said. 'I was just sitting here enjoying the sunshine and reading my book. It's such a nice evening, isn't it? Here – d'you want one?' She held out her other bottle of beer to him.

'No thanks,' he said – but at the same time he put out his hand to take it.

Leila laughed.

'Sorry,' he muttered, confused and irritated by what he had just done.

'Well, here's the opener.'

There were a few uncomfortable seconds and then as if in resignation to what had been a mistake, he opened the bottle and sat down rather stiffly a little way off.

He was so rude it was almost funny, she decided. That was the way to see it.

He took out a pack of cigarettes and struck a match.

'You smoke,' she said.

'You'd prefer I didn't.'

'No! Sorry. No, I didn't mean that. I just . . . didn't expect you to, that's all.'

He leant over the match and then flicked it away, so that it spun the flame out in the air.

'This is because someone's told you I'm a surgeon.'

'Yes, I suppose it was that,' Leila said.

James exhaled the smoke.

'Didn't you know we're immortal?' For a second, she wasn't sure whether to smile. He took another long drag. 'I haven't for six years,' he went on. 'I only took it up again recently. I've started buying them now – much to Kate's relief, I imagine.'

As he spoke, Leila realised she had not had a strong impression of what his voice was like before now. He said so little usually. It was quite deep and there was a faint accent of some kind – possibly Australian. Her preconceptions about Australians all involved blondeness and vast appetites, not what James represented at all, with his dark hair and his slender frame. It was odd to imagine him sharing cigarettes with Kate. She had never mentioned him once.

'Your sister,' he said, giving away a slight curiosity, though it was not exactly a question.

Leila nodded anyway. Then she turned away from him.

It was too nice an evening to be unsettled by James, she decided. She had given him a beer and now she would sit peacefully with him until he had finished it. That was all that was required. Thankfully it was a small bottle.

On the path a few metres in front of them a stream of people flowed down towards Notting Hill from offices in Mayfair and Marble Arch and from all the shops along Oxford Street. The men wore suits, their jackets slung over their shoulders in the evening warmth; the women wore blouses and skirts and some had trainers for walking in. They talked into phones or ate crisps or drank out of cans. Occasional joggers weaved through.

'Going home from work,' Leila sighed. 'I like watching it. It's a sort of natural migration, isn't it? God, a bit of sunshine seems to have made everyone happy, don't you think?'

Two women went past laughing, arms linked.

'They're glad to escape probably – glad if they haven't lost their jobs.'

Leila's toes pressed into the grass.

'That sounds so awful. Why d'you say that?'

James looked at her in disbelief.

'You're not serious. You are. You don't read newspapers, then?'

'I . . . Not really, no. They're always so depressing.'

'I don't believe it's possible you've managed to avoid knowing we're going into a recession. The whole of the western hemisphere is having a credit crisis. The party is over. No free lunches for all those hedge funds any more.'

He raised his eyebrows at her and she laughed uncomfortably.

'No, I know it's happening, I just don't know the facts, that's all.'

He shook his head – and then, as if they were on far better terms than they were, she thought, he leant over and picked up her book. He flipped it over in his hand, his eyes skimming the reviews, and she felt strangely uncomfortable – almost as if he was evaluating her anatomy.

'It's fiction,' he said. He seemed faintly disapproving.

'Short stories – yes. She's a Chinese writer. It's *beautiful* writing,' Leila insisted. She noticed his eyebrows twitch in some kind of response and she repressed an urge to snatch the book out of his hand. 'It's so vivid,' she went on, despondently. 'She makes you want to be like her sentences: in a clean white room with everything neat and ordered. You know?' James took another swig of his beer and Leila blushed, realising he might have thought she was making some kind of subliminal reference to an operating theatre. 'So, have you been helping out at the centre for long?' she said quickly, to cover it up – though right away this question only seemed like a more overt attempt to extract personal information.

But then why *not*, she thought? Wasn't it normal to want to know about people? Wasn't it normal to say how you felt about things, like books for example? This was the way people got to know each other.

'I haven't calculated it,' James said. 'Vaguely eleven weeks.'

'Oh.' There appeared to be nothing more to come. Giving another sigh, she attempted to lean back casually on her elbows and drink some of her beer, but for some reason the grass was now very ticklish around her ankles. She jerked forwards to brush it off and scratched vigorously. Then she flattened it down with her foot.

Maybe he was right, she thought. Why bother to extract personal information – as if it was teeth? They might as well just sit in silence. Why had she felt the need to stand up and wave anyway? She could have just said hello as he passed.

A large grey dog trotted by. She thought of putting her hand out to it but did not.

'No, it's good I saw you actually,' James said suddenly, narrowing his eyes.

'*Is* it?'

'Because I feel I should . . . apologise,' he went on, 'for behaving like that.' He glanced back at her – as if to check she was paying attention – and for a moment she struggled to think what he was referring to. 'I don't normally storm out,' he said.

'Oh – *that*! God, don't worry. It must have been incredibly annoying, all that beeping and crunching going on when you were trying to concentrate. Enough to drive anyone mad.'

He tensed slightly at this but said nothing and once again it occurred to her that he might have thought she was angling to know more about him. But then he would have no reason to think that, she reassured herself; he couldn't have known Dan had told her about his hands, so there was no reason for him to do anything but take her words at face value. She was being paranoid – and there was no reason in the world for her to be any less calm than he was.

She could see him out of the corner of her right eye: half lying on one side now, one leg straight, one bent with the arm resting on the knee, the other elbow supporting his weight. Like Michelangelo's Adam, she thought. In his fingers was a piece of long grass. He was plainly relaxed – as happy to sit in silence here as he was in the office. Why wasn't she?

But it was no good. There was something about the depth of James's silence that made her want to throw something into it immediately – as if to find the bottom of it and know it didn't go on forever.

'Anyway,' she said, 'it all ended happily because Dan fixed it. So there's nothing to worry about. He's lovely, isn't he? I really like Dan. I love his T-shirts. Don't you? They're always so bright. Like flowers. Every day a new bright colour.' Her voice sounded tinkly.

'I hadn't noticed,' said James.

'How can you not notice bright green and yellow and orange? The one with the sunflower on it, even?' He shrugged. 'I think he does it for the kids,' she said.

'Probably.'

'It's so *grey*, that estate. I can't imagine living there. Not that I'm from some ivory tower or anything though, so don't think that. No, we didn't exactly have a lot when we were little, but it's . . . I think it's different if you aren't in London – or in any big city. We had fields and a wood nearby at least. Also we had my grandfather's house to live in – my dad's father. It was pretty dilapidated, with only five rooms altogether including the bathroom and this sort of tiny little extra bit at the top where my mother used to paint – but we were very, very lucky to have it. I always knew that.'

As she talked, Leila was aware that he would not be in the slightest bit interested in these details, but also that – oddly – this only made her want to speak more. She was beginning to think she'd been silent for years. Why? She couldn't understand it.

Now she wanted to say lots of things. But there was a sort of magnetic field around Kate that prevented you mentioning anything except the current moment. It was as if Kate had accepted her presence at exactly this price. That she shouldn't talk to the others at the centre was obvious. But James – he was different. He wouldn't care enough to gossip, she thought. And yet, as unfriendly as he was, they still spoke the same language and he could still hear her words – and this mattered.

'We weren't always struggling for money,' she went on. 'I mean, my family wasn't. My mother was quite well off when she met my father, but they lost it all. Well, he did. It wasn't his fault – it was his business partner. I don't know what happened exactly. There was a law suit. That was when I was a baby. We moved into my grandfather's place then. I don't remember living anywhere else but I think Kate remembers our house in London. Anyway, we lost that. Also my mother's father was a gambler so I think there were problems when he died – debts and stuff. We used to have a photograph of this amazing house my mother grew up in and we had this one wine glass from it.' Leila laughed. 'One crystal glass, very fragile: that was all that was left of the whole place. Can you imagine? I think my grandfather pawned everything else.'

Had all that happened in just five rooms? she thought.

'Is that what you are, then?' said James.

'Sorry?'

'A painter.'

'*Me?* No. God, no, Kate's the talented one. She can draw, paint – she can do anything: singing, dancing, acting. Anything.' James couldn't help smiling at this adulation. 'I always thought she was going to be famous. She's exactly like our mother – like our mother was, I mean. Not that I knew really. Our mother died when we were little,' she explained quickly. 'Apparently I'm more like she was physically, but Dad always used to say Kate had her personality.'

She wondered why James had thought she was a painter.

She felt breathless now – and stupid for telling him so much. Her eyes strained off in the direction of the pond, the sunlight glinting off its surface so that it appeared to be a bright mirror, reflecting the sky. Around it she could make out some swans and a few people with dogs, their outlines fuzzing into one another.

'It runs in families,' James said.

'Sorry?'

'Alcoholism. Mother – daughter's not unusual.'

'Oh . . . I didn't think Kate talked about that to anyone,' Leila said, astonished. She had even told him about their mother.

'Fellow smokers,' he explained.

Leila nodded, inwardly hurt. Why to 'a fellow smoker' and not her own sister?

'I still can't believe what Kate's been through,' she said, attempting to smile. She took another sip of her beer. 'I didn't know about any of it. We haven't been in touch for six years, you see, and I – well, I still can't get my head round it, I suppose. It doesn't seem possible that one person could just go on walking around and eating and drinking and going to bed – while the other one's been suffering so much. There ought to be more . . . connection or something. People should be able to *feel* it.'

James threw away the piece of long grass. He brushed off his hands.

'She's beaten the statistics,' he said. 'The relapse percentages are extremely high for heroin and for alcohol. And she's apparently done it all alone. No rehab. She's a strong woman.'

'The percentages,' Leila repeated, glancing down at her bottle.

James noticed this. 'You didn't get the gene, then. Lucky you.'

She looked at him blankly for a second. 'Oh, there isn't a gene. It's way too simple there's just some gene.' He smiled sceptically. 'Yes, *simple*,' she said, becoming annoyed. 'It's stupid, this idea that everyone gets a set of instructions and – ooh, lucky me – I just happened to have one line blank on mine. Printing error sort of thing. It doesn't feel right.'

James swirled the beer around in his bottle. He did the smile again. 'Why doesn't it feel right?'

'Because people aren't like flatpack wardrobes!'

He laughed out loud. 'No, they're not. But that's just words. Fiddling about with metaphors and similes is dangerous. People aren't like flat-pack wardrobes, no. But words aren't like science. That's why we need mathematics – or there's just a load of chaos between us and the facts.'

'People *definitely* aren't like mathematics.'

He let out a faint sigh. 'You're misunderstanding me. You're barking up the wrong tree.'

'I'm not *barking*.'

'No. It's a metaphor,' he muttered.

Leila felt a bit dizzy. To her left, there were two dogs running on the grass. The large grey dog had found a friend and they chased in wild circles together, occasionally tumbling and rolling in a heap only to emerge panting and barking at one another until the game started all over again.

She took another sip of her beer. It was a warm, sunny evening, she thought. Why be unfriendly? Why offer him a beer and then be unfriendly to him?

'Dusty! *Dusty!*' a woman called. She ran over to the smaller dog and dragged it away by its collar.

'James, I'm sorry. I was stupid just now,' Leila said. 'It must be very annoying. I don't know anything about science. I haven't studied it – like newspapers. I've just always hated the idea that people come with sets of instructions: "Here's how to construct person *A*." If that was true, then how could they suddenly change in their lives?' she said. 'Or is that evolution?'

James shook his head. 'Evolution takes centuries – *aeons*. Periods of time too large to comprehend.'

'Well, there you go. You see? I just say whatever comes into my head and usually it doesn't make sense. I must stop doing it.'

James was sitting up now, his arms linked round his splayed knees, his ankles pressed together. She noticed with relief that his bottle was almost empty.

'It's funny,' he said.

'Yes – I'm sure it is.'

'No, I mean it's funny because I thought you were . . . I don't know.'

'What?'

'Just . . . different,' he replied without thinking and then he turned quickly towards her to see what she had made of this unruly word.

She was frowning into her bottle. It was only then he realised for the first time that he had been irritating her, that he had possibly been irritating her ever since he sat down. Perhaps she had been wishing he would go away all this time!

'*Different?*' she said. 'From what? A horse? A dustbin?' It was one of the stupid grammatical points their father had always snagged their vitality on. She had no idea what had brought it into her head.

He let go of his knees in surprise – but there was no opportunity to answer her. The grey dog bounded over with a ring in its mouth and Leila jumped up to play with it, leaving him sitting alone.

She had bare feet, he noticed, as she ran away. Her boots and socks were tossed on the grass nearby. Beside them lay her bag – wide open, the wallet exposed to anyone who might want to steal it. Next to this he saw a notebook, half obscured by a flyer for something. There was a lot of handwriting. '*If I can make myself forget all about it then I can . . .*' he read – and then he forced his eyes to move away.

The sunshine burned in the trees now, setting them on fire. The dog leapt up and down at the ring and Leila ran back and forth with it, turning in circles, dodging, her long hair flying out. Every time she turned, the dog turned – almost as if they were dancing, James thought.

Then a boy came over with a lead in his hand. The breeze carried their voices intermittently.

160

'Is he yours? He's gorgeous,' James heard her ask – but the reply was lost. They spoke for a while longer and then the boy began to attach the lead. The dog pulled and darted, still overexcited by the game and Leila helped hold it still, stroking its shaggy coat and scratching its ears.

Her face was vibrant, pink with excitement; she was still laughing when she turned back – and it would have been impossible for James not to see how it all fell away at the sight of him. He stood up.

'I . . . ought to go,' he said as she got back. 'I'm playing poker with Dan tonight.' Leila wondered if she was expected to be impressed by this. She sat down on the grass.

'Well, I expect I'll see you tomorrow, then,' he said.

She nodded, and after he had stood in front of her for a moment, probably lost in his own great thoughts, she saw his trainers move off.

She pressed the cold bottle against her cheek. She had been rude to him, there was no question about it – but then he probably hadn't even noticed. And anyway, *he* had started it, she thought, ashamed to be justifying herself in this way.

But whatever she had or hadn't done, what she couldn't understand was how someone as generous and kind as Dan could have someone as cold as James for a friend.

By the time she turned back in his direction he had already reached the gates of the park. She watched him walk out on to the pavement and put his bottle into a bin. Then he crossed the road and a series of tour coaches obscured him from view.

Chapter 25

The computer threw its moonlight around the room, picking out the shiny surfaces: the ring binder files, the stapler, the brochures. The rest was darkness. Kate hunched forwards and rubbed her neck. From her chair she could see the top five rows of Hillford's biggest high-rise. Lights on, lights off, she thought: a pattern. People eating and arguing and fucking and drinking and crying and sleeping, she thought. She turned the desk lamp on and the view disappeared, lost behind a reflection of the room. She turned it off again and there it was – humanity, concealed but busy as ants in the earth.

She considered for a second the idea of hauling up the window and leaning out for a cigarette – but of course there was a lock on it. She gazed down into the forecourt. Who the hell designed such places? Who put that much grey into one square of existence? Even the little playground was grey somehow with its three swings and its dismally simple climbing frame. There were never children in there anyway. There were human beings under ten, yes – but only the ones who had known too much from birth, who had little BMX bike wheels for legs and their mum's kitchen knife in their pocket. The real children were kept inside by nervous parents; watching DVDs of Winnie the Pooh, making pasta pictures.

It was *unbearably* grey out there. Heartbreak grey. She put her fingers on the ledge. And where in that greyness was she? Where was Stacey? Her eyes ran along the balconies; they scoured the forecourt. She checked her watch: eleven. Had Stacey eaten anything today? Hula Hoops? Or was it just the Red Bull and vodka, just the alcopop bombs she dropped on her young heart.

Where was she?

Kate kicked off the switch at the mains and the computer went black. Bad thing to do, Kate, crazy thing, she told herself. Shut it down nicely. Oh, so what, she thought. The work would be saved automatically. Either that or it wouldn't.

Then it struck her: the *park*. Elevenish – a lot of them hung out in the park around now.

Suddenly feeling convinced she would now see Stacey and almost painfully excited by this, she grabbed her jacket and rucksack and left the room and then there was something delightful about running down the stairs – something which pleased her soul to its depths. Down and down, round and round, on forever she went, all the way to the basement. She locked the kitchen entrance behind her. You could smell Mr Wing's in the garden. Dan ate it sometimes: dreadful slop in foil containers. Soggy beansprouts in MSG. 'Choy is a *sweet* man,' he insisted – as if this changed the quality of the food.

She keyed in the new code on the back gate and checked it was shut, and then she zipped up her jacket and went off towards the forecourt of Hillford. All she would do was see if Stacey was near the park, she thought – near the wolves. That was all. She would simply check she wasn't buying again.

And if she is, Kate asked herself, what then? But she let the question pound away beneath her jogging feet.

All around her the flats towered. She had often thought Hillford must have been designed for crime. Layer after layer of dingy passage-ways; endless staircases; alleys with wheelie bins to crouch behind – and the expanses, those masterpieces in darkness, she thought, set whirring with bikes in an instant.

When she had walked the length of the high-rise, she turned left, into the second parking lot. A car sat at an angle in the entrance, one door open, a spider's web crack across the windscreen. And there ahead of her was the park. She slowed down now, moving in beside the flats on the ground floor. Behind the curtains there were shadows, voices:

'Anita?'

'Uh-huh? What?'

She kept her eyes on the park. One thing was for sure – they would be out there by now, selling. Coke and crack and H, she thought; skunk and E and speed. Out there somewhere: the boys and the men and the pit bulls and the girls hovering here and there, smoking, kicking their heels on the sidelines, in the tenuous refuge of their sex appeal.

She spotted them. There they all were just over to the right – seven or eight of them, not far off. Holding her breath, she moved behind the bins and watched. Her hand gripped the plastic lid: was that Stacey? But no – no, it was another girl, just somebody else in the uniform – the high ponytail, the hoop earrings. Kate's heart raced. On a bench nearby sat a tall Asian boy beside a white man with a belly. They both laughed and one of the dogs barked. The white man flipped open his phone and then a few curiously weighted seconds passed and then from nowhere, snatching the breath out of Kate's body as they went, two BMX's swooped up behind her and sped out into the park.

They stopped by the bench. The two boys laid their bikes on one side. Then came the familiar routine; the handshakes, the pocketings, the nods. One of the men who had been standing on the outskirts with the girls edged away from them now. The white man put out his hand to him, as if in friendship. They spoke for no more than a second, then the white man sat down with the Asian boy again and the other, pulling his hood up over his head, walked away towards the middle block of flats to take whatever he had just bought.

There it is, Kate thought – there was the shame and the exquisite delight. There was the dance of addiction: that slouched figure and those little hurrying feet.

And then suddenly the two boys were back on their bikes, coming back towards the park gate. For a second they seemed to be heading right at her. But they weren't. There in front of them, as if she had materialised from thin air, was Stacey.

They were all less than ten metres away. Again, Kate held her breath. The two boys were both wearing baggy jeans and T-shirts. One wore a hooded top. They were the same height, the same age – maybe they were brothers, Kate thought. The one in the hoody spoke first.

'Why the fuck you out, innit?'

'Wass your problem? I come down for some weed, yeah?' said Stacey.

'Mum know you're out?'

'Leave it, Jamal,' said the other. 'She a *eediat*. She get caught, dass her beef.'

'I ain't leavin' *shit*. Mum know you're out?'

'She don't know jack. She's out of it. Fuckin' TV talkin' at the wall again.'

'Where's Mehmet?'

'Cabs, innit?'

'He'll be back soon. You betta find your ass *home*, girl,' said the one in the T-shirt.

'Don't fucking tell me what to do, Dwayne.'

'If I want to I will.'

'Yeah, but I ain't *listening*, though am I?'

'You wanna watch your mouth,' said Jamal.

'Yeah? Or what? "*Wah yu ah du, Jamal? Bruk mi nek?*"' She laughed. 'Fucking *yardie* talk. Bullshit. You're from West London, mate. Both of you. Just like me.'

Jamal spat on the floor. 'Get back inside before Mum sees you're gone.'

'All right, all right. Chill out.' Her voice softened. 'You gonna give me something then or what?'

Jamal took it out of his pocket. 'Here, take this.'

'Thank you kindly, little brother.'

'Get inside.'

'Watch me walk *all the way back up* if you want to.'

She waved as she walked away from them. They waited to see she had gone into the stairwell and then cycled off towards the forecourt again.

Kate's mouth was dry. She pressed her hand against her throat. What had they given her? Just skunk maybe, she thought. Not crack. Why assume it was crack?

She leant back against the bin. More transactions went on in the corner of her eye. Figures moved in and out of the park in their pantomime of sociability. It was a busy spot. Christ, she'd even been here to score once herself. She had a vague memory – a very vague one. A flat on the fifth floor. Which block? Who knew? Such details belonged to the filthy old river.

She must have gone there with someone, though, she thought. That was right – there was a skinny girl she'd gone round with for a while – Lisa was it? Linda? It had smelt of piss in that flat. There was a little hallway – a seat, like a fucking doctor's waiting room. They had given their money to a boy of five. A boy of five with no shoes on.

She had never told any of this to the Thomas Summerdale, of course. That thin line, she thought. So much thinner than any of them liked to believe.

Her hair blew into her eyes and she pushed it back, fixing her clip in place. What are you doing here, you idiot? she asked herself. Go home. But the thought of home repelled her. Leila would have cooked something again; something all ready and piping hot for eight thirty sharp. And she would have missed it, once more she would have disappointed. Leila would be asleep and she would creep in through the dark sitting room and into the kitchen and there she would find a little plate in the fridge, a helping of this, a helping of that: her kiddie's supper.

'*Why can't you just fucking cook for yourself?*' Kate whispered into the dark air. She didn't want to eat memory lane every night – it made her sick. She felt sick now, in fact. *Everything was making her feel sick.*

Her cigarette pack was empty. She shook it again pointlessly, then she scrunched it up and put it in the bin. How the hell had she already smoked twenty cigarettes? James wasn't even scrounging them any more.

There was a thundery rumble in the sky and the temperature dropped slightly.

It was glaringly obvious what she needed to do, she thought, setting off. She was just being spineless. Tell Leila she had to find somewhere else to sleep for the next couple of weeks, she thought. Admit it was too much of a hassle her being in the flat. OK, they rarely glimpsed one another during the day, but she was still a presence at the centre – there was still the fact that Kerry wanted to come up and say Kate's eyes were bigger, but Leila's were that extraordinary grey colour and so on. It was exhausting. The comparisons, the resemblance, the implied history. *Exhausting.*

Without knowing where her legs were walking her to so fast, she found herself outside the estate, heading towards a little supermarket on the corner of the Harrow Road. Her feet moved quickly, taking large strides, and next thing she knew her arm was out, pushing aside the curtain in the entrance and the beads all thwacked against the tins of cat food.

There was strip lighting in there; the lino was sticky and it undulated slightly underfoot as if something had warped it – a flood, perhaps. A radio, not tuned in properly, fuzzed out something in Arabic. There was no one around. Above her, nestling in the packets of kitty litter, was a CCTV screen. There was her own image in pale grey, in reverse. She looked up at it: *Got you*, she thought. She put her hand on her cheek and the grey figure did the same. Where was the camera? Hidden. The grey figure was also searching.

A minute later, through another bead curtain, a boy of about nineteen came out and stood territorially by the counter. Kate stared at him and he began to fiddle with a pile of magazines. One slid off and slapped down open on to the floor. A blonde man and woman hugged on a windowsill. 'We're very much in love again,' said the title. There was a lake in the background, some mountains, a blue sky. The boy came round to pick it up and Kate went firmly into the first aisle of shelves.

She stopped dead. In the middle of the floor sat an abandoned wire basket. Inside were a pack of cotton wool and a can of tomato soup. She began to feel sick again. Who had left it there? *Why?* What was the meaning of these objects?

Either side of her were shelves from floor to ceiling, stuffed with more things. She started to walk slowly, one finger trailing along the shelf. *No-time noodles*, she read, then *Mama's Kitchen Soup*, then *tasty wholemeal . . . crunchy nut flavour . . . real strawberry . . . vegetarian . . . spicy . . . 100% . . . sweet and sour . . . baking soda . . . low sodium . . . sweetener . . . baker's yeast*. She paused, her hand drawn inexplicably to some packets of cake decorations – *5 today! Sweet Sixteen!* – but she did not want to pick them up after all. Beside them were rows of soap and shampoo and mouthwash and toothpaste. She picked up a bar of Linney's soap: a pink wrapper with curly white writing. There was something familiar about it, something profoundly familiar.

She lifted it to her nose and drew the smell down into her lungs: childhood. And then behind her all along the top shelf she could feel the bottles of wine, the bottles of sherry, the gin, the whisky, the brandy, the rum, the vodka – all leaning, all gently inquiring.

She dropped the soap in the abandoned basket and left.

Chapter 26

Stacey walked along the balcony passage, twelve floors up. She opened the door to the flat.

Inside, the TV was still on in the sitting room. Her mother's large body was slumped on the sofa like a patient under anaesthetic. On the coffee table was the usual arrangement: a bottle of sweet sherry, a glass, a tatty copy of *TV Tonite* and an ashtray full of butts. Stacey's fingertips touched the bag of skunk in her pocket. She didn't have any more Rizla. There were always packs everywhere, though. She went down the hall and nudged open the door into her mother and Mehmet's bedroom. There was a packet sitting on a pile of Sony laptops. She went straight over to it. Next to her was the unmade bed, the pillows piled up on her mother's side and the remote sitting on the sheet. Mehmet's Qu'ran sat on the stool with the lamp on it. Beside it was an envelope of cash. Stacey took half a step towards it – a ten-pound note was just peering out, almost as if it had been left that way deliberately. Next to the envelope were Mehmet's comb, his nail file, and one fingernail cutting – a perfect white crescent on the surface of the stool.

She backed away and shut the door softly behind her – not that there was any danger of waking her mother up. There were people laughing on the TV, she noticed. Her mother's thin red hair hung across her face.

Stacey went to the kitchen and took one of the green plastic glasses out of the cupboard. There was a pizza box on the sideboard; she pushed it out of the way and half filled her cup with vodka, half with Red Bull. Then she carried this back into her bedroom.

It still stank of man in there. She opened the window and took a gulp of her drink. Two used condoms lay slimily in the bin. Probably another two more to go tonight, she thought. Mehmet usually brought a couple of the guys back from work with him.

She kicked off her trainers and sat cross-legged on the bed. Her little fingers worked quickly and expertly on the spliff and while she licked and sealed the paper she looked up at her poster of Angelina Jolie in her Tomb Raider outfit. She was so beautiful and strong with her amazing figure and all the guns and the grenades for any second she needed them. Her brother Jamal had written 'R U a dyke or wot?' across the face in biro.

Stacey plumped up the two pillows behind her, lifted her drink and leant back to smoke, letting her legs hang off the bed and tapping her ash into a deodorant lid. She took regular gulps of her drink. Through her window, she could see the top of the walls around the big car park. On the other side she could see one edge of the middle block where her eldest sister Debbie lived with her boyfriend and their baby. She didn't know the baby's name. They'd never even seen it because Debbie didn't come round any more. There had been a big row over something. Her mother said Debbie was no daughter of hers any more. She said she wouldn't spit on Debbie now even if she was on fire.

In the distance the city lights turned the sky a muddy brown and the aeroplanes were like tiny spaceships coming to carry people away.

Soon Stacey had finished the spliff and the drink and her eyes closed and the deodorant lid tipped sideways spilling ash and cigarette butts across the sheet.

It was a couple of hours later when she woke up. She could hear her stepfather's voice out in the sitting room. One of her brothers was out there too. Her mouth was very dry; she needed a drink of Coke. She saw the spilt ash and butts and tried to rub it all off the sheet a bit and then she stumbled out into the passage.

'Stacey?' said her stepfather.

'Mum's got it,' she said.

Her mother was still asleep or unconscious on the sofa. Mehmet put his hand into her cardigan pocket and pulled out some folded notes. He was smart as usual: white shirt and black trousers, chain round his neck, his hair combed back smooth. He was Lebanese or Turkish or something – Stacey couldn't remember what exactly. He had a heavy accent. He was her mother's third real husband, but there weren't any children with this one.

'So Ken come round,' he said. 'Who else? Danny?'

'Maybe. Fuck knows,' said Stacey, going off into the kitchen. It made her stepfather furious when she couldn't remember his friends' names.

He came into the room after her.

'Danny or not Danny? This my business associate you talking about.'

His accent made everything he said sound angry. Angry and religious, she thought – like the people in the videos with the flag up behind them and the machine gun. She took the bottle of Coke out of the fridge and drank straight from it, dimpling the plastic as she gulped it down.

'Fuck me, girl – how many times I say to you *don't fucking do that?*' he asked her, curling his lips. '*Think where your mouth been.*' She reached into a cupboard for a mug. 'No, no. *Has'siktir!* Keep that bottle now,' he said. 'It's your one now.'

She put the mug back.

He looked at her dirty tracksuit bottoms and her tiny, frail arms.

'What you wearing your brother's clothes for?'

'My jeans are fucked.'

'*New jeans*, Stacey!'

She snorted.

'I *found* them, Mehmet. It cost you nothing.'

He accepted this. Then he shook his head again – at the spindly arms, the waist as small as a child's. Much thinner and no one would want to use her any more except weirdos like Danny.

'You eating food today, Stacey?' he said. 'Did you eat something? Eat that pizza.' He flipped open the box. 'Here, eat this one.' He threw the remaining slice on to a plate and handed it to her.

She peered at it.

'Pepperoni. I don't like pepperoni.'

'Eat that shit up.'

Her brother Dwayne came into the kitchen. His jeans were pulled low around his hips so his boxer shorts showed around the top. His cap was brand new with the metal tag still on it to show it wasn't fake. He had a green bandanna hanging out of his left pocket, so you knew he was W10.

'Mehmet?' he said. 'There was this breer down the park arksing we can cop dem plasmas any more.'

Mehmet's face contracted fiercely. 'What you saying?'

'This . . . this guy,' said Dwayne. 'Wants a TV.'

'This guy? What you think you doing mouthing off some *guy* in the park about business? About *my* business?'

'Nah, nah. Nothing like that, Mehmet. *He* arksed *me.*'

'How the fuck he *know* to asking you, innit? We got no TVs.'

In the hall behind him was a stack of sets – ten, twelve maybe.

They heard Jamal come in through the front door. He stopped in the doorway, unconsciously mirroring his brother's posture. He and Dwayne were twins – sixteen years old, half Jamaican, with their mother's blue eyes. It was impossible for most people to tell them apart, but in fact Dwayne was slightly smaller and finer boned. He had come out after Jamal; five minutes had made him the little brother.

'Oh – hey, *Stacey*, you bitch,' said Jamal, 'that's my fucking pizza! I fucking *ordered* that. Dwayne, what the fuck, blud? That's my *meat feast,*' he said. 'You got me vex now, man.'

Stacey shrugged and held out the plate. 'Have it,' she said. 'It's disgustin' anyway.'

Jamal sucked his teeth. 'Nah. Fuck that. Not now. I don't want it *now.*'

She put the plate down on the sideboard and lit a cigarette.

'Stacey, you eating that like I tell you,' Mehmet said fiercely. 'You too skinny, right? Men don't like it. No tits.' She looked him right in the eye. Then she lifted the plate and started off to her room with it. 'Where you think you going? *In the lounge,*' he called after her.

'What?'

'You gonna sitting down in the lounge and eat that shit in front of me, girl.' The two boys followed him out after her. Their arms and legs moved in unison.

There was no table to eat at. People ate on their knees or standing up in the kitchen.

'There,' said Mehmet, pointing at one of the plastic garden chairs beside the sofa. He sat in the armchair opposite, leaning over to take her cigarette from her and stubbing it out in the ashtray.

On the TV was the national lottery. It was a repeat.

'And this week, there's a rollover of *thirteen point five million pounds,*' the presenter said.

'Fucking win that shit one day,' said Jamal, 'trus' me.'

'How you gonna win the lottery,' said Dwayne, 'when you don't even buy no ticket?'

'Gonna get myself a *phat* car, *crib,*' Jamal went on, '*everyfink.* You think man's gonna rob and shit forever? No way. Man's gonna be spittin' on the mike in some sick club. MTV and shit. VIP list.'

171

'You gonna get *nuff* girls, Jamal. *Believe!*' said Dwayne, grinning. 'Spud me, blud.' They touched fists.

Mehmet switched the TV off. 'You sell what I giving you, or what?'

Dwayne took the roll of money out of his pocket. 'Here it is. And we give her a ten bag.'

'Yeah, yeah, that's OK,' Mehmet said. 'She can have her bit.'

Folding it into five small pieces, Stacey chewed and swallowed the pizza with gulps of Coke.

'Can I go now, yeah?' she said.

Her mother stirred again on the sofa, her arm flopping down against the floor. There was a name and phone number written on the hand. Mehmet lifted it, read the number and dropped it again. It was just some woman's number.

'Yeah, you can go. *Not going out, though.* Terry coming soon. Round three maybe. We got business but maybe he's gonna see you after,' he said. 'OK? So go tidy yourself up. Be ready.'

Stacey leant back on to her hands to push herself off the floor. Then she paused, her mind weighing something delicately. Her pretty mouth opened, closed and then opened again.

'Mehmet,' she said, 'can I . . . have my little rock?'

He did not raise his eyes. He counted the notes in his hand and gave the two boys a fifty each. Then he took out another wad of folded twenties and started to count these.

'Wash yourself, Stacey,' he said. 'Put clean clothes and maybe I give you what you want.'

She stood up quickly and went off to the bathroom.

Chapter 27

Janice opened the door. She was surprised to see it was Kate who had been rattling it about all this time.

'Morning. Forget the code, did you?' she said.

'I didn't forget it. People keep bloody changing it. Why? Utter paranoia. It's not a war out here. What's the point of changing it every five seconds?'

'Not for the past fortnight, love . . .'

'It was *two, six, six, nine*, last time I knew anything about it,' Kate said indignantly, pressing the buttons again even though the door was now open.

'Six, seven. Two, six, six, seven.' Janice flattened her lips. 'Kate, sweetheart, are you all right?'

Kate, who had pushed past and was now sitting on one of the reception chairs emptying out her rucksack, glanced back at Janice. Janice seemed to be dressed for a holiday as usual.

'Of course I'm all right. Why? What are you getting at?'

'People aren't always trying to get at something, love. Sometimes they just want to make sure you're OK in case you . . .'

Kate rummaged in the bits and pieces on the floor. Her phone wasn't there.

'In case I what?'

'In case you need a hand.'

'A hand?'

'Or a shoulder.'

Kate stood up quickly.

'I don't need anything like that. I've got work to do. I must get upstairs. Kerry and Dan are waiting. Aren't you coming anyway?'

'I can't. I've got appointments today.'

'Oh. Oh, yes, that's right,' Kate said. Sometimes she forgot altogether that Janice was a careers adviser. She was always bustling about with boxes of kitchen supplies. Or mending chairs – she was forever mending chairs. You began to think of her as a sort of caretaker.

For a second, she wondered if any of them showed Janice enough respect. Kerry certainly didn't. But the thought quickly went out of her mind as she began to run up the stairs.

'See you later,' she called back.

'Yes, see you later, sweetheart,' said Janice.

She watched Kate's long legs disappear round the corner. Then she tutted in frustration with herself. Why on earth had she gone and said that about a shoulder – about crying? It wasn't like her. But then she was off-guard with Kate at the moment. She couldn't help it. Those skinny legs, she thought, shaking her head. Those dark circles.

And then suddenly Janice felt terribly sad. Her whole body was weighed down with it, her arms hung at her sides. She breathed deeply and pinched the bridge of her nose. She stayed this way for a second or two, but then, as if she had caught herself doing something she shouldn't, she raised her head again sharply. This was a funny thing that happened to her sometimes. It had taken her years to work it out. Other people didn't want their feelings and she ended up having them instead – like carrying their shopping bags for them.

Moving off determinedly, she went downstairs, through the canteen, and opened the kitchen door on to the courtyard. Then she stood outside, her turquoise espadrilles planted firmly on the concrete. She turned her face up at the sky.

All these *feelings*, she thought: up and down, up and down through life. And none of it meant anything, really. It all *hurt*, oh, it stung like hell, yes – and then it made you feel *marvellous*, it had you up all night in excitement thinking it was *happy ever after from now on*!

She watched a whisper of a cloud move slowly towards the sun. But nothing really changes, she thought. And it never will. All we can do is try not to lose our temper, try to be kind to people for the next ten minutes. The next five, really – why go worrying beyond that? It was only a shame she'd had to get to sixty-seven before she'd understood. She retucked her pink T-shirt into her trousers and smiled. It was already a lovely summery day.

On her way back in she checked the temperature gauge on the freezer. There were lots of nice peas in there, which didn't want to go to waste.

'Janice?' a voice called as she came out into the canteen. It was James. He was striding along waving a bit of paper, looking anxious as ever, she thought. 'Janice, I've got this note from Kerry telling me she's going to be busy upstairs in a meeting all morning.'

'That's right, sweetheart. Yes, she is. Dan and Kate and Kerry are sorting out something important. You're all right, though, James love, they'll be around by lunchtime.'

He frowned.

'No, I . . . it's not that. It's just that I was working on some stuff in the upstairs office and now . . .'

'Best not to interrupt them, you mean? Probably right. Goodness me, though, isn't there anything else you could get on with? There *must* be.'

'Yes, obviously there is. There's plenty.'

'Well, that's all right then, isn't it? You can just work in the downstairs office for a change. Oh – with Leila. That'll be nice.'

'Yes,' James said dully.

Janice studied him curiously for a moment. Was *that* it? she thought. She had noticed how he avoided working in the same room as someone else, how he ate his lunch at the far end of the table, how he never once came to the pub with them on a Friday. He was friends with Dan, of course – but Dan was so busy what with the centre and the church, that they could hardly be spending much time together. She got the impression that he was marooned at the centre somehow, or rather that he had marooned himself there on purpose. The details of his life were unclear – even Kerry didn't know them. All they did know was that he was a surgeon and taking some time out and, as Dan had said, that he was plainly bright enough to be of use around the place. He certainly didn't look too healthy, she thought. But then none of the young seemed to, except Kate's sister, Leila, who had her wonderful glow. Mike was all right too – not much would knock his type, she thought – though he was getting a bit portly these days. Even Dan seemed ragged since the news from Ann Summerdale.

'Leila's a sweet girl, James,' she said. 'You might get on.'

James shut his eyes and sat down on the edge of one of the lunch tables. Then before Janice noticed them he shoved his stupid shaky

175

hands in his pockets. They had decided to go wild this morning and the last thing he needed today was the *concerned stare*.

'No, listen, Janice, I've got nothing against her in particular, OK? We're not on the best of terms, that's all.'

Janice found it hard to imagine Leila being on bad terms with anyone.

'Aren't you? That is a shame.'

'It's not a big deal or anything. Just a bit uncomfortable.'

'Oh yes, I know. Not a big deal. Of course.' Janice fiddled with her earring for a moment. They were glass dragonflies today: blue-green and pearlescent. 'Tell you what. Here's an idea.'

'What?'

'How about clearing it all out the way and just starting again? You can, you know? There's no rules against it though you'd think there were the way we all carry on. You could say something like, "Leila, I think we got off to a bad start and I'd like to see if we can make it better." That sort of thing. Sometimes it's ever so simple, what's needed, and then it all changes, like all the bad feeling was a dream.'

James furrowed his brow. Was she right? He glanced back at the staircase.

'I . . . think I'll go out for a cigarette,' he said.

'Yes. You do that, love. Oh – James?'

'Mmm?'

'You can trust me not to say anything to anyone by the way. I don't gossip.'

'Thanks. I . . . appreciate it,' he said, obviously relieved.

Ten minutes later he sat down at the left-hand desk in the reception office, just as Leila came in. She was wearing a white dress today, he noticed. Her hair was loose.

'Hello. We're working in here together all morning,' he said.

She put down her bag and laid her cotton scarf across the chair.

'Oh. Are we?'

'Yes. I had no idea. It's just for this morning, I'm sure. It's because they're having some kind of meeting upstairs.'

'Oh, right. I thought something was going on. Kate got back late again last night. Later than usual, I think. I never know exactly though because I'm always three quarters asleep.'

'Dan didn't make it to poker either,' said James – and then realising that, as if by accident, they were now having a fairly normal exchange, he said impulsively, 'Leila, I think we've got off to a bad start.'

'Yes. We did.'

'I'm sorry.'

'I'm . . . sorry too,' she said, smiling with relief.

And then, incredibly, it was all just as Janice had said, he thought. Everything changed so quickly that it was as if the bad feeling between them had belonged to a dream. They worked quietly as usual, but there was no heaviness in the air; instead there was a sort of sense of good will, he thought – though of course this was all meaningless in real, physical terms. But then it was true that they laughed now when she got up to use the photocopier, and even the weather seemed to have improved, he thought, noticing how the sunlight poured down into the stairwell and filled the waiting room outside. He shook his head at how absurd he was being.

At twelve thirty, Kerry leant round the door.

'Everything all right?'

'Fine,' said James.

'*Is* it? That's a miracle. People been turning up for appointments?'

'Yes,' Leila said.

'On time?'

'Mostly.'

'Wonders will never cease. Who's on today? Someone popular.'

'It's the woman who comes in once a fortnight, Suzie Baxter. She's done a couple of counselling appointments, but actually it's Janice mainly. Janice's been back to back.'

Kerry had assumed Janice was not at their meeting because Dan had not invited her, not because she was too busy to come. It occurred to her that she might now turn up after lunch. 'Is she on this afternoon too, then?' she asked casually. 'Janice?'

'Um – yes, she is. She's got a break from one until two then she's got people coming till five-thirty.'

'Ah.' Kerry nodded briskly and smiled. 'Righty-o,' she said. In her hand was a bag containing three packs of sandwiches, three flapjacks and three apricots. 'Well, I'll get back up there, then.'

The double doors swung back and forth a while after she left.

'They're obviously hard at something. Not even stopping for lunch,' said Leila.

'Must be.'

'I think I might stop.'

'You're tempted by the *delights of the canteen*,' said James, wondering why he was speaking this way.

'Not much, no. I thought I might go for a wander. There's this

Lebanese stall on the Golborne Road where they sell falafel. They're fantastic.' She threw the lilac cotton scarf around her neck and reached for her bag.

'You know, I don't think I can face canteen slop again either,' said James. 'D'you mind showing me where this fantastic place is?'

'No, of course not. Not at all.'

Over the course of the next week, it became obvious that there was some kind of a problem at the centre. Apart from the tense meetings in the office upstairs, there were other little signs. Kerry told Leila to cancel the adverts she'd written for two extra cleaning staff. Then Dan came down and asked her to make a notice saying there would now only be a cooked lunch in the canteen on Mondays and Fridays.

'Cuttin' back, innit? *Crunchin'*,' said Clint as Leila stapled it up. A small group stood behind him in the hall. 'Dat President Bush done fucked up our free *lunch* now. Ain't gonna have no *lights* on up in here soon. No counsellor – *jus' talk to da wall, boy!*'

There was laughter but it was tinged with an understandable bitterness.

The newsstands seemed to be filled with worse headlines by the day, all describing a country in the process of economic collapse in America's wake. As Dan said, they could hardly have picked a worse time to start looking for private funding.

But in spite of all of this, the weather continued to improve. The days were full and warm now, as if stretched out and relaxed after the contortions of winter. For a few hours each afternoon, Dan and Kerry and Kate worked upstairs, with or without Janice, and Leila and James worked peacefully in the reception office downstairs. It was now as if they had always got on, and even their silences were comfortable. At lunch they ate in the canteen with the others or went out for falafel or to the Thai stall nearby. They talked about their lives in a light, joking sort of way, enough to tell each other a few facts, but not going deeply into any one of them.

Chapter 28

'Oh, yes,' James said one evening when they were drinking beer in the park on the way home. He opened a packet of peanuts and set it down between them. 'I know what it is by the way.'

'What?'

'The big secret. All the scuttling about at the centre. It got mentioned at a meeting I was at but I never knew what came of it because I stopped going to them. Anyhow, it turns out they've been ringing round all the grants and trusts for emergency funding.'

'Emergency?'

'Mmm. Now they're trying to find a private patron somewhere. Dan let it slip last night.'

'You're joking.'

'Nope, it's dead serious. Hopeless looking for cash anywhere now, too. Everyone's going bust, not being charitable. No wonder Kate looks so stressed. I wonder what it'll mean for the centre in the long run. Dan's in agonies obviously about letting on, so don't tell anyone.'

'Of course I won't. But I don't understand. I thought whoever-she-is Summerdale was really rich.'

'Lot of really rich people aren't so really rich these days,' said James, taking a swig of his beer. 'The Summerdale investment portfolio took a bit of a nosedive, apparently.'

'Their portfolio? But they're not *poor*, though?'

'No, no. It's all relative, isn't it? I imagine they've still got what they *need*: few houses, various cars, psychotherapists, masseurs, ski holidays and so on.'

Leila screwed her eyes shut.

'But I thought the centre was in her son's memory. I thought she started it in his memory. Doesn't she *need* that?' And as she said these words, without having any control over it, she felt tears welling and she turned her face towards the road so James wouldn't see.

But he had seen. As ever, he noted the change in her complexion immediately. It was one of the things that fascinated him about her. Kate had it too, only it was somehow much more interesting in Leila. Now he saw a flush running from her cheeks, down her neck, pulsing through all the tiny arterioles on the way to her heart. He remembered something:

> 'Her pure and eloquent blood . . .
> Spoke in her cheeks and so distinctly wrought . . .
> That one might almost say her body *thought*.'

Leila wiped the back of her hand across her eyes.

'What's that?'

He shook his head. 'I'm . . . not sure. Something we learnt at school, I think. I can't even remember; it just came into my mind out of nowhere. How weird. It was your face that reminded me – your . . . you know, the way you go a bit red.' He waved his hand in front of his own face. 'You can tell what you're feeling as soon as you feel it, that's all.'

'Great. Read me like a book.'

'Not a book, no,' he said. Their eyes met. 'Whatever. It definitely wasn't meant to be offensive.'

'It's OK, I know.'

'Listen, Leila, I'm disappointed about Ann Summerdale, too. You're quite right – it is repulsive they cut back on that before anything else. You should have seen Mike's reaction. Mind you, he likes being angry. But it's what people do, though, isn't it? When it comes to money. Even normal people. There's a list of non-essentials that gets crossed off. Charity goes first, then cappuccinos probably, then cabs when you're a bit too pissed for the tube.'

Leila's fingers picked at the label on her bottle. It would be so easy to let him think this was why she had been upset, she thought. She watched him move the bag of peanuts off the front page of his newspaper. The headline said 'US Government to bail out ailing banks.'

'James?' she said. 'I am upset by that, you're right, but it's – it's more than that. It was when I said that about them losing their son. I . . . lost my baby,' she said. 'A miscarriage. Not long ago.'

180

James let go of the page in amazement. He was astonished by the idea that she had been pregnant. Her marriage had been a shock in itself, but it had so quickly seemed remote – unreal. She had stopped wearing her ring and then even the pale circle on her skin had faded. Now the pregnancy gave it an overpowering *weight*. Suddenly he felt that he had been living in a daydream for the past two weeks and that the new feeling of interest in life he had developed had no more substance than his idea of who Leila was. She was a friendly stranger, that was all, he told himself, looking at her soft face, her brown hair. All their talking had been entertaining, but superficial – meaningless perhaps – and now here was her real life. He noticed with disgust that his left hand shook even while it held a bottle now.

'It's not as if I was completely naïve before, but it's like you suddenly realise the world isn't safe at all,' she said. 'Not for anyone, no matter how innocent they are. It's terrifying.'

'Yes. Yes, I know what you mean,' James agreed, putting both his hands behind him on the grass.

'You think your life's all there is, don't you, and then suddenly a door opens behind you and then you're outside it in a completely different place and there's no way back in.' She shuddered. 'Not that you'd even want to get back in. God, I'm so glad I'm here. And I'm so glad I met *you*, James,' she said.

And then very simply and naturally she leant over and rested her head on his shoulder – and James was almost frightened by the scale of his happiness.

The next day was Friday and when Leila had finished her work, he was already standing by the staircase.

'Are you waiting?' she laughed. 'Sorry. I had to do a load of photocopying for Janice. Actually the real reason is I was late doing the photocopying because Dan said it was OK for me to do a bit of digging around in that cupboard outside and see what gardening equipment there is. I got carried away – and filthy,' she said, noticing a muddy patch down her T-shirt. 'It is only six thirty, though,' she said.

'I know – but it's Friday.'

'Is it? You're right, it is. Friday night.' She smiled. 'Well, shall we head for the park?'

'Actually, I was thinking – and I mean, please do say no if you loathe and detest the idea, but I was thinking we could always go for a drink near Portobello,' he said uncertainly.

'What? *Not* go to the spot just behind the third bench on the left? Somewhere different? Are you *sure*?'

'Just a suggestion,' he said, not sure if she was making fun of him and not liking the idea that she had thought their habit was comical.

'No, it's a great idea,' she told him. 'Let me fling on a clean top and we'll go.'

There had been several hot days in a row now and the bars on the Portobello Road had opened their doors and some had put tables out on the pavement. Walking from the centre up Ladbroke Grove led to the bottommost end of Portobello, to its grimier section where there was always a strong smell of marijuana. Further up was where the smart shops began and the bars were more popular, but in fact everything was just an expensive imitation of what had been real lower down. Leila and James arrived at the corner. Reggae played out softly into the road from an off-licence with a metal grille. In front were three boys on bikes peering through the window of a Mercedes.

'D'you know this place? Been to any of these bars?'

'Not for years. All of them look great,' said Leila happily. 'Oh, but let's *definitely* go to the red one over there.'

They sat outside a place with a huge red graffiti design on the wall. The tables were metal with bright red legs.

'Shit, I've run out of cash,' said James. 'We passed a machine. I'm going to run back and get some. Will you order something?'

'Sure. What d'you want?'

'Anything. You pick.'

She ordered two gin and tonics. Then she regretted this and called the waitress back. She was given a menu, but she still couldn't think what to ask for – and then out of nowhere she chose two bottles of the Thai lager she had last drunk on her gap year, when she was eighteen. The waitress was an Asian girl a few years younger than Leila. She had on a low-cut pink top and her hair was in pigtails. She brought over the drinks.

'Summer does exist, then,' she said, laying them out.

'Yes,' said Leila.

'Nick of fucking time. It's Carnival soon. Shitter having rain on Carnival.'

James came back and they drank the lager and then a glass of wine and then they moved on up with a stream of people towards Westbourne Grove. The happiness of the crowd, the warmth of the air, the smells of food from all over the world, were all part of a magic spell.

'So many *people*,' Leila called through.

'Yes!'

'The waitress at the red bar was talking about Carnival. I can't imagine what it's like then.'

'Amazing,' James agreed. She smiled at him and he thought he noticed a relaxed expression he had not seen her wear before. She seemed taller tonight than usual, but also more vulnerable. He felt conscious of other men glancing at her as they walked. Her long hair swung at her waist and she walked on ahead of him, checking every so often that he was still there and smiling when she saw that he was. The clean top she had put on was a lovely pale pink blouse, which tied up with a ribbon at the back and showed the curve of her waist. Her skirt clung to her legs and rippled around the tops of her boots as she moved. She was beautiful, he thought.

They moved out of the crowd now and on to Notting Hill Gate and she stopped. He waited for a moment, assuming she had dropped something and was about to search for it on the pavement. But she didn't move.

'Leila? What is it?' he said.

On the other side of the road was a pub theatre with a billboard outside. She was staring at it.

'It's . . . someone I know,' she said. 'It's his play.'

'You can't possibly read that from here. Can you? Oh yes – just. So, what's the problem? D'you want to see it? Actually, it must be finished by now.'

Buses passed and Leila squinted through. '"Sam Saunders",' she read again, '"Only Love"?' And then there, through the traffic, as if the world had now been taken over completely by the laws of magic, she saw Gavin. He was helping someone into a taxi. It was a girl, she couldn't see who.

'Leila?' said James.

Gavin had seen her. She knew he had seen her. She watched him kiss the girl on both cheeks and shut the door behind her. The cab moved off and Gavin stood opposite now, looking directly over. He raised his hand.

'Is that someone you know?' said James. 'I think he's waving at you.'

'Yes, it's someone I know. Listen, James, I'm sorry, but I've got to go and talk to him. I'll . . . see you on Monday,' she said.

She heard him saying goodbye to her and she did her best to speak back and kissed him on the cheek and then she was out in the traffic, crossing Notting Hill Gate.

'*Leila,*' Gavin said. '*Where the hell have you been?*'

He towered over her on the pavement, waiting for her response, his blondish hair blowing about in the breeze.

'Nowhere,' she said.

'What d'you mean *nowhere*? There's no such place.'

'I mean . . . here.'

He cast his eyes around him rather wildly – at the theatre, at the shops along the pavement, the McDonald's, the Tesco, the Boots on the opposite side of the road. 'I've been *so fucking worried about you,*' he said. 'Do you know that? D'you have any idea?'

'I'm sorry,' Leila whispered, lowering her face.

Questions crowded into Gavin's mind. He wanted to ask her where she had been staying, what she had been doing, why she hadn't wanted to be in touch with any of her friends – not even with him! But seeing her sloped shoulders, her body so still that she appeared to be a statue stranded miraculously amongst the moving traffic, the Friday crowds, he found his mind was quietened.

Why was he so angry? She hardly deserved his anger, he thought.

'No, no, no – this is all wrong. You haven't any reason to be sorry, Leila. Come here,' he said, and he put his arms round her and pulled her close into his chest.

She breathed him in: aftershave, clean washing, books. She felt the warmth of his long, thin body, his arms gripped so tightly around her back that it was hard to breathe.

'I've just been so concerned about you. So concerned,' he repeated, shaking her slightly.

When eventually they moved apart, Leila felt exhausted. She felt so exhausted she could have crept behind the bins outside the restaurant beside them and gone to sleep – or simply hidden. She looked up into his eyes and they both knew what she was thinking but did not ask.

'He's OK,' said Gavin. 'Whatever that means. He's back here now, obviously.'

'In *London*? But I thought he was spending the rest of the summer in *Spain.*'

Gavin's head shook slightly. The way Leila had run away and the way Charlie had accepted it was beyond his understanding. It was as if neither of them felt any claim on the other.

'Not now, no. Not with work and, well, not with his dad, obviously.' He drew his eyebrows together. 'But you probably don't know

184

about that though, do you? How could you, I suppose?' He saw her face blanch in anticipation and regretted the pause. He put his hand on her arm. 'It's Gideon, Leila. Charlie's father had a heart attack.'

Chapter 29

Charlie stood on the doorstep of his parents' house once more, only this time it was not late at night but two in the afternoon, in bright sunshine. In his hand was a suitcase. The cab that had brought him from the airport hummed by the gate for a bit and then went off down the road.

He put the suitcase down and stood with his hands at his sides. In the panels of glass set into the doorway he could see his blue shirt, the top of his suitcase by his knee. He raised his arm to the bell, but just as he was about to press it, he saw his mother's shape emerging through his own and rushing towards him. She had obviously been watching.

The door sprang open.

'Charlie! In the airport they said the plane is *delayed* and I thought my God I must wait the whole day or maybe he comes and it's so late we don't eat together or it's *tomorrow* or maybe he changes his mind or—'

'Mum, calm down,' Charlie said and, becoming silent for a second, Daria then burst into tears and threw herself into his arms. He stared blankly over her shoulder at the hallway with its usual vase of lilies and its Persian rug. He could feel her ribs jerking as she cried.

Daria pulled herself back. She sniffed and dabbed self-consciously at her eye make up. Then she took in the sight of her son and her breath caught: deep brown and slim as a film star. And his shirt was wonderful and his jeans were well cut and he was wearing the good Spanish leather belt she had given him last birthday. At the thought of his birthday Daria immediately began to cry again and then, making a noise to signify impatience with herself, she turned around and led him towards the kitchen, snatching tissues from a box on her way.

There were three steps down from the hallway into the kitchen and Charlie stopped on the bottom one. Beneath him the acreage of polished black and white floor stretched off towards the windows. On the table was a Spanish magazine and a glass of something indefinable, though he suspected it was a vodka tonic. Daria picked it up swiftly and gave him a smile.

'*Carlos*,' she sighed. 'What a *time* we have had. What a time. Everything so . . . *strange*. You know? Like a nightmare. Like a curse. Like a *voodoo*,' she said, widening her eyes. He noticed her nails were unpainted. She was wearing almost no make-up.

'So, where is he?' Charlie said.

'Daddy?'

'He wasn't happy with the cardiologist. You said he might be changing hospitals or something.'

Daria regarded him with anxious puzzlement.

'No, no, he's here, darling,' she said.

'*Here?* For God's sake, he's just had a major heart attack. What's he doing at home? He should be in the bloody hospital – being monitored or whatever.'

'They discharge.'

'They *what*? It's *outrageous* – it's medical negligence, surely.'

'No, darling. Daddy discharge *himself*. Two days they observe and then this morning he says it's enough. Enough! *Impossible*.' She threw up her hands, but the gesture was without any of its usual zest.

She looked older, Charlie thought – or perhaps it was just that she was thinner, or without her lipstick. Her eyes jogged about the room.

'Mum, are you OK?'

'Me?' She took a gulp of her drink. 'Yes, darling!' she said vibrantly. He watched her heels click over the floor towards the fridge. She glanced back over her shoulder, smiling now, 'OK, Carlos, did you eat something? Hmm? No – *don't tell me* – you had this *terrible* little thing on the plane and then *nothing*. Am I right? *Si – estaras muerto de hambre*, Carlos – I can tell it. I know you. I know my son. What should I make you? Hmm?' The fridge, which was silver and enormous, suckered open now and banged against the wall, clinking its bottles of milk and fizzy water and juice and wine. Bright light ran over her figure. Behind, Charlie could see the stuffed shelves. There was row after row of neat delicatessen packages, there were varieties of lettuce,

187

of cheeses, of cakes; there were steaks, fish, vegetables, yoghurts, boxes of truffles. A pineapple head stuck out of the glass compartment at the bottom.

Who would eat all these things? Not her. Not his father.

Charlie averted his eyes. There was something embarrassing about it – something frightening. All of a sudden he remembered how as a child he had discovered one of the spare bedrooms was literally stuffed with brand new cashmere cardigans, most still in their packaging, every single one of them an almost identical pale cream. For some reason, knowing full well that it was a betrayal of a very deep kind, he had gone and told his father. The ensuing row had been fierce. He had listened from the landing above. Through the crack in the doorway, he could see his father's shoulder and arm, very still. Beyond, on the bed, lay all the packages and hangers in a soft cream heap. His mother had screamed to the point where her voice faltered.

'*Yes!* Yes, I *waste* the money. Yes! Waste! Waste! Terrible waste! So what now, Gideon? *What?* Should I *die?*'

'I'd . . . like a sandwich,' Charlie said – though he wasn't particularly hungry.

'*Good*, my darling. *Good*,' said Daria, taking out bread and cheese and lettuce and tomatoes and herbs and a chopping board and several knives. 'And for your drink?'

She looked at him expectantly – hopefully.

'Just . . . some of that juice,' he said. There was a flicker of disappointment.

'Which kind of juice, darling?'

'Orange. Apple. Anything, Mum.' Daria set down the peach juice he had loved as a child. 'So, where is he, then? In bed?'

'No, darling, he's outside.'

'*Outside?*'

As if she had been shouted at, Daria cringed a little and reached for her glass. She spoke into it as she raised it to her mouth, 'Uh-huh. Mmm. Yes, darling, in the garden. For fifteen minutes only. Out there in the chair.' She waved the tomato knife in Gideon's direction. She closed her eyes as she drank.

Charlie went over to the window. At the end of the sloping lawn he could see his father in a wheelchair. Thirty metres or so behind was a blonde-haired woman, reading a book.

'Who's she?'

188

'*She*? Ah, this woman. I forget her. It's just the nurse. Berenece, Berenetta – *something* . . .'

Daria clicked back over to the fridge and again the doors suckered open.

Charlie wondered what he ought to do. It was not the way he had imagined it on the plane. This made him angry. He was supposed to go and visit his father in hospital. He was supposed to see his mother first and hear all the details and then go to the hospital alone. Gideon would be in a white room, in a bed – weak but coherent. The setting would be neutral, sterilised, not sodden with the messages of home, and as if by magic he would be able to speak calmly with his father for the first time in his life; he would be able to convey the message that he had been concerned about him, to receive due acknowledgement for this, and then to exit without a row.

But there was Gideon in the garden. As usual it was all insane.

'Mum, listen, there's no rush with the food, OK? I'm going to go out and talk to him. I'll go now. I'll eat the sandwich afterwards.' He turned to face her and for a second Daria stood against the open fridge, almost as if she had been backed against it at gunpoint. Charlie was unable to hold her gaze. 'I'll eat it afterwards, OK?' he repeated softly. Then he opened the door to the garden and went outside.

The nurse glanced up and smiled as he passed and then went back to her book. She had obviously been asked to sit at a tactful distance. Charlie continued to walk out across the lawn.

A little way off, above the back of his chair, Gideon's hair blew about in the breeze. On the table next to him was a jug of something and a newspaper weighted down with a stone. Both the chair and the table were in the shade of the apple tree. Gideon turned as he heard Charlie approach.

'Oh, it is you,' he said. 'Your mother seemed to be under the impression that you might not get here for several days.'

'My plane was delayed – by two hours. There's a strike,' Charlie began, but he stopped short in surprise.

Was it possible for someone to age twenty years in just a few weeks? His father's cheeks were hollow and there was a sickly translucence to his skin. Underneath his cashmere sweater, he was wearing pyjamas. Charlie didn't think he had ever once seen his father in pyjamas in the day. Even with flu, Gideon got dressed and worked in his study.

'Well, you've apparently come all the way from Spain – aren't you going to sit down for a minute? Or are you too busy and important?'

189

said Gideon. This was his idea of a joke. He chuckled softly and Charlie moved a book off the chair beside him and sat down. 'You've come straight from La Campañera?' Gideon asked.

'Yes.'

'That old place.'

'Yes.'

'How is it?'

'Same as ever.'

'Stifling by now, I should imagine.'

'It's hot.'

'I never understood how all of you spent so long out there each summer. I was stir-crazy after forty-eight hours. Couldn't wait to get back.'

'I remember.'

'You couldn't get *newspapers*.'

'No.'

'Endless eating and swimming up and down,' Gideon said, shaking his head. 'Pilar was there, was she? In residence?'

'She's in Barcelona. I don't think they use it all that often.'

'Well, it's a long way up. She's still married to that idiot Rodrigo?'

'Last time I heard,' Charlie said – though surely his father knew about his own sister-in-law through Daria. They couldn't speak that little, he thought.

Beneath the stone, the newspaper fluttered like a butterfly trapped in a glass. Gideon indicated it with his chin.

'Calamitous out there,' he said. 'I've sold all my Dinston shares this morning. Just in time. Your sort have come off dreadfully. All you hedge funds.'

'Yes,' Charlie said.

Gideon nodded at this. Feeling a dismal sense of the inevitable, Charlie clenched his jaw and waited. Well, it had taken less than three minutes, he thought, for it all to begin. He noticed he was digging his fingernail into the wooden table and he snatched his hand away and laid it on the arm of the chair. But right away he jerked it off again and dropped it on to his knee. It was no use, he thought – already it was no use. No matter how much he had rehearsed the scene on the aeroplane, he was always at a loss around his father, always nervous and uncomfortable and – *angry*. Why?

His eyes narrowed as he prepared himself for the rest of it, for the predictable jibe and dodge which so amused Gideon and had always passed for a relationship. But, after a minute or two had gone by, it became clear that nothing more was coming. Charlie raised his eyes again. The sprinklers came on by the flowerbeds.

Gideon shifted in his chair. He was wearing slippers.

'You know, I had a dream last night,' he said. 'Such a funny dream. Your mother turned into a tropical bird and flew away – right out of the window. Red and yellow and orange and green she was; great big feathers. Up and off over Hampstead Heath. I haven't had a dream that vivid for years.' He smiled. 'I don't know what it *means*, of course. It all *means* something, no doubt. Do you know what it means?' He raised his eyebrows at Charlie.

He was apparently serious.

'I'm . . . afraid not.'

'No. No, I imagine Leila would be more the person to ask.'

Charlie looked up in surprise at this and then found himself digging his nail into the table again.

'What do the doctors say about your heart, Dad?' he said.

'The doctors. Oh, the doctors, the doctors . . . They say the sort of things doctors say.'

'Right. Can't you be any clearer?' He was beginning to feel even angrier now. *I've come all the way from Spain*, he wanted to shout – *you never came all the way from anywhere for me*. But it was appalling to want to shout at someone so frail.

'Oh, they said all sorts of gubbins about myocardial function. I'll spare you the details. It's as you can see, essentially. I'm in poor shape, is the short of it. Me and the economy. Not that I feel all that bad. I did for a day or two but not now. Oh yes, I have got the most tremendous bruise from where I fell, though. Hang on, I'll show you . . .' Like an excited little boy, Gideon began to pull at his pyjama top and Charlie caught sight of a wad of gauze, some dried blood before the hand fell away. 'Bit difficult to get at,' Gideon said. His eyelids seemed heavy after the exertion.

'You're tired.'

'No, no – only physically. Mentally I'm . . . I can't *tell* you, Charlie,' he said, his eyes springing open, 'it's as if I can't . . . it's as if I'm suddenly thinking about everything I've . . .' But he broke off again. Behind them the nurse sneezed sharply several times in a row. Gideon's brow furrowed. 'In all seriousness, Charlie,' he said, 'tell me what's happened to your fund.'

Charlie pushed his hand through his hair. So there it was, he thought.

He snorted once, joylessly, before turning to look at the rows of herbs growing near the fence. It was his own fault for getting all worked up on the plane, he told himself, his own stupid fault for imagining they would be able to talk amicably together when they never had before. Why the hell had he dreamed it would be any different today? Hadn't he given all that up years ago? He ought to have given it up once and for all when he was fifteen, when he was expelled from Russington and Gideon's only reaction was to cut off financial support.

Remembering his expulsion had only made Charlie more upset. Now he glanced back at the nurse reading her book and then at the kitchen doorway. He had been stupid to come out alone. It was always better with his mother – or with any woman around.

'You've gone all quiet,' said Gideon. This was one of his accusations.

'I haven't. Look, you've read the paper, haven't you?'

'Yes, I've read the paper but it's not going to tell me about you in particular, is it? You might have been invested elsewhere. You might have taken any number of precautions – if you'd ever listened to my advice, that is.' Gideon leant back weakly into his pillow.

'Your advice. Oh, for Christ's sake, I didn't come here to discuss my *finances* with you, OK? I came back to see how you are because the last time I spoke to Mum she gave me the impression you had nearly . . .'

There was an odd pause.

'Died,' said Gideon. 'That's right.'

'What I'm saying is I didn't come out here for a lecture on how risky and doomed to failure hedge funds always were. Or to hear some long explanation of how you've escaped all this mess without a scratch on you. In fact, why don't we just cut to the part where you tell me how you managed it. How are *you*, unlike almost everyone else in the Western world, managing to come out of this laughing?'

'You're jumping to conclusions, Charlie. You're just like your mother.'

'I'm not.'

'You are: *incredibly* like. But since you ask, I'm OK because I had a good bolster, that's all. Nothing sophisticated – just planning ahead. I've said it to you before. You always need a bolster if you're going to take risks. I made a bit a few years ago, after the planes crashed. After September the eleventh. I just happened to be near a television when the first one went in. My thoughts were very clear. They went as follows: *one*, this is not an accident; *two*, this is aimed directly at the financial world; *three*, there will be unmitigated chaos in the markets

192

and everything that was will now not be. I was on the phone to IG index before the second plane had even hit. Shorted the FTSE 100 immediately and held my position for a week while the prices sailed down like blossom at my feet. Made as much as I've earned in the past five years in less than five days.'

'Hang on. I can't believe I'm hearing this. *You* shorted the market?'

'Yes, I did. And yes, I'm aware that sounds like hypocrisy to you, but again that's the Spanish blood in you, Charlie, carrying you off before you've absorbed the facts of the situation. You've got to see the distinction between taking a beautiful one-off opportunity when it's thrown in your lap and making speculation into a *way of life* as you have – as so many people have. Yes, I have said it before, but it *was* doomed to failure. I mean, companies valued at their own wild estimation, investments made on hearsay, not on analysis of the fundamentals, banks lending as if they're immortals with great pots of gold – all *crazy*. Suddenly the whole world thinks he's a millionaire – or could be, given enough damn credit. Then suddenly it all goes bang. Well, it had to. Simply had to. So, yes, when those planes went in it was an opportunity and yes, I damn well took it. Why shouldn't I? I wasn't the only one.'

'No, apparently Al-Qaeda did it too. And Hugo.'

Gideon's face lit up.

'Did Hugo? *Clever boy.* I've *always* thought Hugo was a clever boy.'

At this, Charlie's whole person contracted and in spite of his desire to disguise it he began instinctively to get up, only stopping himself once he had twisted round very obviously in his chair.

Gideon's eyebrows twitched together, deepening the criss-cross pattern on his forehead.

'You're . . . standing up,' he said. 'Why are you standing up? Hang on. Wait a minute, will you?'

'What for? I didn't come here to discuss fucking money with you, OK? Can't you talk about anything else?'

'No, no – you've missed the *point*, Charlie.'

'Oh, have I? I'm so sorry. How typical of me.'

'Now just calm down. This isn't *about* money. I . . . Look, what I wanted to say was that I'm well aware it's been bloody out there and if you – well if you are in any financial *trouble*, then don't worry. I know it's been my policy not to give you handouts, but—'

'*Handouts?* I don't need a fucking *handout*,' said Charlie, getting up openly now.

'*No!* No, I don't mean you need a . . . Oh God, what's gone wrong? What's happened? Why doesn't anyone ever understand what I mean unless it's on a spreadsheet?' In a rather desperate scrabbling motion, Gideon stretched his fingers out, clasping them round Charlie's forearm. There was a hospital bracelet still on his wrist. Charlie flinched away from it but the grip was tight. 'Gideon Charles Bell', it read, 'Male. 11.04.1943'.

'*No,*' Gideon insisted. 'What I'm trying to tell you is it doesn't *mean* anything any more.'

'What doesn't? What are you talking about?'

'Oh, for God's *sake*, Charlie – the money! My *money*. They say it, oh, people say it, but you don't believe it I suppose until . . . until your heart stops,' he said. His face was elated, strangely radiant now. Charlie's body felt cold, his head felt hot. He pictured putting the keys into the ignition of his car – but then he remembered he didn't have one. His mouth went dry. 'That's why I've made a decision,' Gideon went on, gripping his arm again. 'I've decided I want you to have it *now*. Not after I die. I want to give it all to you now.'

For a moment, they were still. Around them a breeze blew through the garden, swinging the new apples and whipping up the pages of the newspaper again. Gideon's fingers loosened. Charlie looked down at the grass. His heart was still thumping, but there was something else, something new going on inside him. It was a sort of fluttering in his chest, a sort of exhilaration. What was it? he wondered. He felt like . . . he could hardly believe it himself, but he felt like running wildly about the garden like a child. Yes, that was exactly what he wanted to do. Here was Gideon Bell, here was the Old Bastard himself, he thought, suddenly old and possibly mad, too. It was hilarious!

But Charlie did not move. Instead he stared down into his father's face. He had never seen it so closely before. The eyes were blue flecked with grey, slightly bloodshot and watery, the mouth was broad like his own but paler and thin-lipped; there were deep lines across the brow. And there, on the otherwise clean-shaven chin, was a tiny patch of grey stubble, which he had obviously missed while shaving.

'I don't want it, Dad,' said Charlie. 'Thank you, but I don't ever want your money.'

His lips parting slightly in shock, Gideon let go of his son's wrist altogether.

'Hello? Excuse me? Hello-oo?' said a tentative voice. It was the nurse. She came towards them, diplomatically stooped. 'I don't mean to interrupt . . . I'm so sorry, I'm sure you two are having a lovely catch-up – but I'm afraid it's not a good idea for cardiac patients to sit outside for too long. I think they explained in the hospital, Mr Bell, you have to be very careful about your body temperature.'

Gideon assented without argument. They walked back towards the house together – Gideon insisted on walking – and then the nurse pushed the chair inside. On the kitchen table was a sandwich with a glass of peach juice and a folded napkin beside it.

'I must go and find Mum,' Charlie said. 'She's in a bad way.'

'She's been very worried. It's understandable,' said the nurse, helping Gideon back into the chair. 'But that's what happens when you love someone, isn't it?'

Gideon sniffed. He settled his feet on the footrest. 'I expect she'll be in the drawing room,' he said – and though Charlie told himself afterwards that he had imagined it, he was sure he saw the words 'making a drink' in his father's anxious eyes.

They all went out into the hallway together, the nurse pushing Gideon. A temporary bedroom had been made for him in the break-fast room beneath the stairs. Charlie peered through at it.

'Right, well I'll leave you to it,' he said. 'I'll go and see she's OK.'

Gideon muttered a few words of agreement and looked down into his lap. But then, watching his son walk away down the hall, he was suddenly hit by a sensation so strong he initially interpreted it as the beginning of another heart attack. He thought of telling the nurse and even put out his hand.

But it was not the same thing after all. Tears came into his eyes and his fists tightened as if he wanted to squeeze the feeling out of the air somehow – but there it remained, sapping the colour out of the hall, making Daria's awful lilies seem as if they had been bought for his funeral.

'Charlie?' he called out. His voice was louder than he had expected it to be, but still Charlie didn't hear it. For some reason Daria had turned on deafening music.

In the drawing room, a piano concerto boomed so ear-splittingly from the speakers that even the windowpanes rattled. Daria crouched by the stereo frantically pressing buttons. Charlie shouted out to her a couple of times but it was hopeless. At last she spotted the remote on the sofa and dived onto it, turning the volume down. She pressed her hand to her chest in relief.

'I'm *sorry*, my darling. *Madre de Dios.* It's broken. Something happened with it. I must talk to Leonie. It's broken. Did you see Daddy already?'

'Yes.'

'Oh. Finish already?'

'Yes.'

'Oh.'

Daria went over to the drinks tray and poured herself a vodka tonic – openly now. Knowing Charlie was watching her, she puffed her cheeks out and blew up at her brow for an explanation. Charlie sat down on the sofa. Daria reached for a piece of lemon.

'So. So, he told you all this . . .' she waved the lemon slice in a tight circle, '*everything*, then?' she said. 'Did he?'

'I don't know if he told me all of it. He seems a bit unhinged, to tell you the truth. A bit crazy.'

'Daddy decide he wants to *retire*, Carlos.' She waited for this to sink in. 'Like an old man! Like he's an old man now and I'm an old woman. Retire! I say to him, what about your business? It doesn't *matter*, he says.'

There was a smouldering butt in the ashtray. Charlie stubbed it out.

'Well, you must be glad,' he said, 'you've always wanted him to be around more. He'll be at home with you now, won't he?'

Daria gazed at him with tears in her eyes. Then she came over quickly to sit in the chair beside him. She took a fizzy gulp of her drink. The tears rolled down her cheeks and she wiped them off roughly with the back of her hand. Then she put the glass down and leant over towards him, her upper body almost pressed to her knees, as if she was going to tell him a grave secret.

'*Help* me,' she whispered. 'Darling, *help* me.'

Her face was clenched as if wincing in pain and Charlie felt desperate – desperate to make her happy, suddenly desperate to hear her laughing as she once had when he clowned around for her on their holidays in Spain. 'Watch me! Watch me!' he used to shout before he dive-bombed backwards into the pool.

'Mum, I . . . I *want* to help you,' he said. 'But I can't.'

'Why not, darling? Why, Charlie? *Why?*'

The face was terror-stricken.

'Because this is between you and Dad.'

He put his arms out to her now and she sobbed convulsively on to his shoulder. They stayed this way for some time, as the afternoon deepened outside the windows.

Who knew what would happen, he thought. Maybe his father really would retire – though it was hard to imagine what interest he would have in life without his work. His mother was obviously frightened. But why was this? he thought. She had been begging Gideon, screaming at him all their married life to spend more time with her – and now that he might be going to, here she was, crying as if her life was over.

Just then, marriage seemed to Charlie to be a strange landscape in which the exact opposite of what appeared was in fact the real truth.

Chapter 30

The flat still smelt of new paint. There was a vase of silk flowers on the hall table: huge yellow blooms too good to be true. The estate agent had obviously put them there for the purposes of selling the place. Charlie closed the front door behind him. To his right was the empty sitting room. Inside it, stacked discreetly against the wall, was the pile of boxes he and Leila had lugged around with them for the past few years. He nudged one of them with his shoe. The box on the top said 'clothes and photos'. It was Leila's handwriting, the pattern of showering stars she always drew, even when she wrote a shopping list.

What clothes and photos? he thought. He couldn't even remember. But he could barely remember what was in any of the boxes, it had been so long since they were last opened. He looked back at the suit-case in the hall. This case and the suits on the rail upstairs were really all he owned, he thought.

And yet this was his flat. This empty room, with its pile of boxes, the kitchen with its empty cupboards – all of it belonged to him. There were papers to prove it.

He did not like the feeling of the boxes all taped up beside him and he went through into the kitchen. There were no curtains or shutters in there and the late sunshine came dazzlingly through the windows. In the shadows by the sink he could make out a plant of some kind. He moved forwards a bit to see what it was. It was the bonsai tree Leila had bought. The flowering peach tree or quince or whatever she had called it. It looked dead. It was no more than a twig in an elaborate glass box. The tiny leaves broke off as he touched them. They turned to powder in his fingers. The earth was bone dry.

And yet the shadow it threw across the counter was still a tiny illusion: a real, fully grown tree. He remembered Leila coming in with it excitedly under a cover, saying it was a birthday present for Hugo. It had made him angry that this was her idea of a good present for Hugo. Why had it made him so angry?

That had been the same day she had told him she was pregnant, he thought. The same day the article about him in the paper came out – the one his father had ignored altogether.

He went over to the fridge to see if there was anything cold to drink. There was a bottle of fizzy water in there and some coffee and a mouldy piece of cheese. He took the cheese out and threw it into the bin. He opened the water and drank some. It was flat and sour tasting. He spat it into the sink.

Then he went upstairs with his case. On the bedroom floor was their double mattress made up with the pretty covers they had been given as a wedding present by Gavin. These Leila had always unpacked. Opposite the windows was the clothes rail with all his suits and one of her dresses. On the floor were some of his shoes and boots in a line. There were a few T-shirts, a pair of jeans and some jumpers of hers. She had so few clothes, he thought. Some of the women he knew whose husbands made as much as he'd been earning bought themselves new outfits all the time. But she never had. This had also made him angry, he thought.

Now he felt tired and he went over to the bed and lay down on it. His stomach rumbled and he wished he had eaten the sandwich his mother made him after all. It had been forgotten. Leonie would have thrown it away by now. He pictured it – the soft bread, the creamy cheese and the sweet tomatoes and lettuce. And the glass of cool peach juice beside it. And then he thought of all the delicious packages in his mother's fridge: ham, salami, pâté, pastries. Why hadn't he eaten anything when he was there? He could have eaten anything and everything. But he'd had no appetite then. He was hungry now. He was starving *now*.

For a second, he wondered if there was anything to eat in his jacket pocket – the remains of a bar of chocolate maybe. But he knew really that there was nothing.

He was not only hungry but very, very tired. He leant back on the pillows and his eyes wandered back over to Leila's dress. Why had she left this one? It was too hot for it in Spain perhaps. It was a dark blue wool one with three little white buttons up the back of the neck.

It was one he liked on her – though he had always wished she would wear her hair up more dramatically with it and put on some earrings. But she always preferred to go without jewellery. She said she liked the way her hair felt loose. It had all annoyed him terribly but he knew that if he told himself the truth, there were times, when he saw her out among the other women with their jewellery and their highlights, that the sight of her was like a moment of clarity after a long time of confusion.

Charlie closed his eyes. He did not particularly want to look at the dress any longer. He put his arm over his face and, feeling cold suddenly, he pulled the other side of the duvet over him and drew his knees up toward his chest. Seconds later, he fell into a blank sleep.

After less than an hour he was woken by his phone. He fumbled for it, knowing it was somewhere on the bed. At last he found it was under his arm. It was stifling in the duvet now and he threw it off vigorously and answered the phone.

'Hello?'

'Oh, yes – hi there, Charlie, it's Jeremy. From Tenterton Blake,' said the voice.

Charlie sat up and rubbed his eyes.

'Tenterton Blake,' said Charlie. 'Oh, yes – the estate agent.'

'Well, I guess you're having a good holiday, then! That's fantastic, Charlie. Bloody right. Forget about property. Stay well out of London at the moment, it's not pretty. Quite right. How is it out in *sunny Spain* anyway?' he said, emphasising this personal detail.

'Actually, I'm in London at the moment.'

'Aha. Oh. *Are* you? Well, this could all work out rather nicely then, Charlie. I'll tell you why. Now, as you know only too well yourself, the housing market is *dire* at the moment – *everything's* dire at the moment. The whole world's gone mad. We all know this. However, by a total miracle, I've got a *buyer* for you. And here's what's even more incredible: it's at the bloody *asking price*! It's a Belgian couple who basically want a place to sleep occasionally. Not a home – just somewhere to use every once in a while when he's over in London on business. He's in money. The wife came and peeked round the flat yesterday. Said yes right away before she rushed off back to Luxembourg. I get the impression it's not what you call a priority. Being paid for by the company, I think, which is pretty amazing in itself at the moment with the way things are. Anyway, it's great news. I mean, seriously, I'm telling you, Charlie, we can't shift *anything* for *any* money at the moment, even if it's me selling, let alone at the asking price. We were actually laughing at the office about this. It's a great little property, don't get me wrong – particularly with all the design work you've invested in. That's your wife's thing isn't it? But you can't take anything for granted in this climate. So, anyway, long preamble, but like I say: a little surprise for you,' he said. A moment passed. 'Hello? Oh, fuck it. This *fucking* phone . . .'

'No, I'm still here, Jeremy. Don't take it out on your phone.'

'Oh. Shit – sorry. I'm a bit . . . stressed out at the moment. Sorry if I sounded—'

'It's fine.' Charlie sat up.

'Great. Great. So. Well, so we should obviously move on this *asap*. I can get the paperwork round to you by bike this evening?'

'Jeremy, would you mind holding on for a minute?'

'Um . . . You mean you actually want me to stay on the line? God. Scratch that. Sorry. That sounded . . . yes, obviously I can hang on. Go ahead. I mean, please. Take as long as you like.'

He breathed heavily for a moment and then there was the sound of his footsteps and a car door opening and closing. Music came on and was hurriedly switched off again. An engine started up.

Charlie put the phone to his chest and walked out on to the landing. Then he went down the stairs and into the kitchen. The bonsai tree sat on the sideboard surrounded by its little scattering of leaves.

He lifted the phone.

'Hello? Yes – I'm not selling it any more, I'm afraid, Jeremy. No. No, I'm going to keep it myself.'

When the phone call had ended, Charlie went into the drawing room with a knife and began to tear open the boxes.

Chapter 31

It was nearly midday. The windows were open but the air was still outside. A small fan brought in by Kerry whirred away on the bookshelf, doing not much more than disturbing a tissue sticking out of a box beneath it.

'Kate, you don't seem in the mood for this,' said Dan.

'What? No, I am. I want to do it. I have to.'

Dan smiled. He put his rosary down.

'It's not something that should be forced. It's not like fitness – like breaking through a pain barrier or something. It has to be natural.'

Kate pushed her chair back.

'Oh, natural, *natural*,' she said. 'That bloody *word*. What does it mean? What if nothing comes *naturally* to me?'

'Kate, I know for a fact that's not true. You're a wonderful teacher for one. You've got a genuine rapport going in your life skills classes. And if anyone can get us out of our funding muddle, it's you.'

She stood up and went over to the window.

'God, forgive me for saying this, Dan, but you're such a fucking optimist, aren't you?'

Dan laughed. He leant back against the wall with his hands behind his head.

'Am I?'

'I don't know how you can even question it! Take this funding *"muddle"* as you call it. I mean, OK, Janice's all sunny but I don't think that woman's ever frowned once in her life, but there's me and Kerry, all doom and gloom, wondering whether to start sending out our CVs and then there's *you*, quietly confident we'll be OK somehow.

Why the quiet confidence? We've all got the same information. What's the difference?'

'No idea.'

'I think it's God.'

'God?'

'It *must* be. It must be your belief. Your faith.'

'You think faith's like a badge. Stick it on and once it's on it's on forever?'

'Oh, please. Don't go there, Dan. Come on – you don't exactly go off the rails.'

'Maybe I do. Maybe you don't know what it's like in my head.'

'I've always assumed it was much like your T-shirts,' said Kate, looking down into the paved garden.

Dan stretched out the hem of his T-shirt. It was bright orange with a design of little dancing fish. His brother had given it to him after a holiday in Sicily.

'Did you honestly?' he said.

Now it was Kate who laughed.

'Oh no, you look all pissed off now. It wasn't meant to be rude.'

'Teensy dancing fishies?'

'I meant it . . . sweetly.'

'Ah – *sweetly*. Yes, I'm sure you did.'

'I did!'

Her face was transformed when she smiled, he thought. Her light brown hair was not clipped back with the usual severity today. Instead it fell in curves by her cheeks. She looked old-fashioned – 1920s somehow, sepia-tinted. And no matter how fierce her words, she just was elegant, he thought, noticing the way her slim arm draped across the window ledge, the way her two long legs were crossed at the knee and the ankle.

'Fishies aside, Kate,' he said, 'the fact is I struggle as much as anyone else to keep believing.'

'Yeah, yeah, I've heard priests do this number before. It's in your manual somewhere: *how to comfort the flock.*'

'For goodness sake, what fucking century are you living in? You're not the *flock*.'

Kate felt shocked for a second hearing Dan swear. She hadn't ever heard him do it before. She looped her rosary around her wrist.

'Whatever. Enough about you. Let's talk about me again. What am I going to do about this mantra, then?' she said, smiling mischievously.

'You can't help yourself, can you?'

'No.'

'Now, why is that, I wonder?'

'Bad genes?'

'Your sister seems like such a good girl, though.'

'Oh yes, you're right, Leila's perfect,' said Kate. 'Bad stars? Bad karma?'

Dan was cross with himself. He hadn't meant his remark about Leila the way it had sounded – as if he was weighing one against the other. She seemed not to have been annoyed by it, but you never knew with Kate, he thought, she was so complicated.

'Hail Mary, full of grace, the lord is with thee. *Om namah shivayah, Om namah shivaya*,' said Kate. 'What's the earth-wrenching difference?'

Dan rolled his eyes.

'I'm not listening to you.'

'Why not?'

'Because you're being *like that*.'

Kate pressed her hand to her chest. 'Oh, yes. So I am. Thanks for pointing that out.'

'My pleasure. This is what friends are for.'

Again, Kate felt a momentary awkwardness. Then she regretted her joke about his T-shirts. She wondered if Dan's mock-offence had concealed a real one.

'Look, if you really think it'll make a difference I'll come to the church, OK?' she said. 'Though I still can't see why it matters.'

'Well, in one sense it doesn't. I mean, God's everywhere, you're right – you can find Him everywhere, in any situation. I suppose it's more that *everything else* isn't in a church. None of *this* stuff.' Dan laid his hand on the lengthy application form they had filled out that morning.

'You really believe that *God's everywhere* business? You actually think that statement's real, like the taste of salt?'

This struck Dan as a typically Kate-ish formulation.

'Yep. Yes, I do,' he said smiling.

'He's even down there, is He – out in that park at night when they sell drugs to kids of twelve?'

'Even there.'

'Funny kind of God you believe in.'

'It's us that's funny, not God.'

'Oh yes, I'm hilarious. I crack myself up. Honestly, it's a laugh a minute being me.' Kate's face was red now.

'You're angry,' Dan said.

'Yes, I am angry.'

'Why?'

'Because I'm . . . Because I'm in need of a little fucking assistance.'

'And what if this is what a little fucking assistance looks like?' Dan said.

Kate shut her eyes.

'A man in a silly T-shirt?'

'Come to the church.'

'All right, all right, stop banging on about it.' She checked the clock. 'Well, would you look at that, tea break's over. How time flies. I shall have to see the light some other time.'

There was still work to be done before lunch. Kate and Dan went down the stairs together and then Kate went off towards the life skills room at the back. Dan went down to the basement office.

'Morning, you lot,' Kate said, pushing open the door. There was a smell of polish. It had been cleaned in there at long last. Five had turned up today, which was a surprise, Kate thought, what with there never being a free lunch on offer afterwards now. Right away she saw there was no sign of Stacey. She put her files down on the desk and picked up the register. 'Right, who's in, who's out?' she said. They checked the names off. 'No big surprises there, then. Anyone seen the incredible vanishing Aditya these past few weeks?'

'He don't live on Hillford,' said a boy at the front.

'No, I know that, Matt, but you do *sometimes* see people who aren't from Hillford.'

'Not that guy, though. He a loser.'

Apparently this was such a statement of fact it didn't even warrant laughter.

'Right. We've got no Clint, which is a shame.'

'Your favourite,' said Matt.

'How can you say that? *You're* my favourite, Matt,' said Kate, tutting. There was a general titter. 'No Tyrone, but I know about him actually. And . . .' she paused breathlessly, 'anyone got any idea where Stacey Clark is?'

There was a palpable change in the atmosphere. Yes, there was no question about it, she thought. Matt leant his elbows on the table as if to imply complete innocence. Tanya began searching for something in her bag. Even the quiet boy, Dean, scribbled anxiously on the front page of his jotter.

They knew something, Kate thought. They all knew something and they were withholding it. She felt her palms becoming sweaty. She made a sudden odd movement with her left hand and her pencil skidded across the floor. Matt leant down and picked it up for her and she muttered a thank you. *Calm down*, she told herself. But this was impossible without a few facts.

'I must just go and check something,' she told them. Then she hurried back out and down the corridor and through the swing doors, and then having momentarily forgotten that the old girl Jenny had left, the sight of her own sister at reception was a great shock to her system.

'*Kate*. Hey . . . I missed you again last night,' Leila said. 'Did you find the soup and the Greek salad and everything?'

'Um – oh, yes, yes, I found it all.' She had wrapped the salad in newspaper and thrown it into the bin. She had poured the soup down the sink.

'I burnt the pine nuts a bit,' Leila said. She stood up rather nervously as if she was going to walk over, but instead she edged round the desk, sitting down on the corner of it with her hands pressed beneath her.

'It was all – great. Thanks,' said Kate.

'Good. I . . . I just wanted you to have something nice to come back to. You're working so hard. You're never at home.'

Kate wondered if this was the moment. Just say it: you have to go – out of the flat, out of my space, out of my line of vision. But then this hardly mattered now! Next to Leila's left hand was the appointments book. In this book would be a record of whether Stacey had been at her appointment with Mike yesterday. If she had at least been to that, Kate thought, then all was not lost. There was still some structure in her life. There was still a faint belief in sobriety.

'*Kate*. Just the person,' said Janice, coming in behind her. Kate turned round with a start and backed against the filing cabinets, knocking over an empty mug. Janice put up her hands. 'Oh, sorry, love. Kerry always says I do that. I must walk very softly or something. I'll try and walk more noisily. Sorry, sweetheart.'

Kate picked the mug up and set it upright. 'It's fine, it's fine,' she said.

'Now, Leila,' said Janice, her lavender smell already sweetening the room, 'I must get you to do some more copying in a minute, but while I've got your big sister here . . . I just wondered if you'd seen Sean this morning, Kate?'

'No, I haven't,' Kate answered stiffly. Then she exhaled, letting her shoulders sink down into place. There was no way of finding out now, she thought. Not in front of Janice. She could forget it. If she had been alone with Leila she could have made it seem like she was searching through other people's appointments for some official reason. In fact she had been stupid when she first came in: Leila was the ideal person to be confronted by because she had no real idea of how the place worked. And anyway, she had always believed anything Kate told her.

'Well,' said Janice, 'I'm afraid we've had a little burglary. Frozen peas and chips. Three whole boxes. You can only assume there was real need. Must have been. Anyway, there's no money to get any more in so Sean's been very upset. I was thinking you'd probably be the best person to sort it out, to be honest.'

Kate felt as if she was being asked to take part in a very faint, long-distance phone call.

'Did you?' she said.

'He takes you *seriously*, is the thing. He thinks I'm a batty old woman. Well, I am a batty old woman. Maybe you could have a word, love. When you're free, obviously. I thought you were doing your classes this morning . . .' Janice said, checking her watch.

'I am. I'm in the middle of one, actually. I must get back out there,' said Kate. 'Excuse me.'

Janice stood aside to let Kate pass. Kate went away quickly down the corridor.

'Dear me. She's a bit rundown, your sister. A bit on edge, isn't she?' said Janice. Leila smiled sadly. 'What are we going to do about it?'

'I'm the last person she'd want to help her.'

'Now why d'you say a thing like that? You're her sister. Hey, what's the matter?'

She smiled at Leila. Janice's thick grey hair shone under the lights. Her eyes glistened; their brown colour was live somehow, like an otter turning in water.

'I said it because . . . it's not as simple as it might look between the two of us. Maybe you don't know about us. I'm sure you don't actually. We hadn't seen each other for six years – before a few weeks ago that is.'

'Oh. No, I – I didn't know that.'

'Well, I don't think she was planning on seeing me ever again, Janice. I just turned up on her front step. Now she regrets opening the door. Now she wishes she'd pretended she was out and I'd just gone away forever.'

'She *doesn't*, sweetheart.'

'Maybe she's right. I mean, just because you spent lots of time with someone, even if it was your childhood, why assume there's this big connection which never goes away?'

'Oh, but there is. There *is*.'

'As far as she's concerned I turned up out of the blue one day – like a stranger. She's only given me a place to sleep out of charity. No different to doing free overtime here. I should have left her alone. I should have left her in peace. Kate's life is none of my business.'

'What nonsense,' said Janice. 'And I had you pegged as someone with a lot of good sense. We're *all* each other's business. We *can't* leave each other alone. When you think about it, that's what's so painful *and* what's so wonderful, isn't it? No escape! But no lonely desert island either.'

Leila fiddled with the box of paperclips, turning it in her hand so that the clips rattled from one end to the other and then back again.

'I don't know,' she said.

The photocopying was a welcome distraction. Janice had given her a large pile to do and because the copier was now even more temperamental than it had been, each sheet had to be fed in manually. Every so often, Leila found her eyes wandering towards the clock. James would be in soon, she thought. When she remembered the way she had rushed off like a lunatic when Gavin had waved at her, she couldn't help assuming James would have thought she was rude. She hoped this hadn't hurt his feelings.

But then this was impossible: James was so admirably rational. She wished she could be more like that. She thought of the way she had reacted to the idea of his being a surgeon when she was first told it. It had made her shudder. She had thought it was disgusting – sacrilegious almost, to be able to put your hands on to a human being, to locate the kidney and press in a knife. Now she thought it was beautiful. Now she felt conscious that beside James, who could illuminate every opinion with scientific fact, she was just a pale, flickering image.

Chapter 32

James drained the contents of his espresso cup and began to feel his pockets for money. He found two pound coins in his jeans, dropped one on the pavement, picked it up again and laid them both on the table. Then he put his book away, folded the café newspaper and pushed back his chair.

'*James*,' said Dan, arriving breathlessly at the table. He put his hand on his friend's shoulder. 'I'm *so sorry*. I've run all the way here.' He was pink in the face and a bit sweaty. 'I'm a physical wreck. You've been waiting for ages, haven't you? The truth is I forgot. I forgot and then I . . . remembered.' They both laughed gently at this explanation. 'Anyhow, the long and the short of it is I'm an utter bastard and can we just say lunch is on me?'

James feigned serious deliberation.

'Yes, I suppose we could say that,' he said.

'You're not furious?'

'No. Just starving.'

'Uh-oh. Is this going to be an expensive apology?'

'*Bankrupting*,' said James, and Dan laughed and thumped him on the back.

But James never ate much. They went back into the café together and ordered from the bowls of salad and pasta and fish cakes behind the glass. Then they went outside again and sat down with their plates. The first table had been taken now so they sat at one a little closer to the road. It wobbled slightly and James wedged a napkin under it, testing it with both hands until it was perfectly steady. Seeing their two plates beside one another Dan felt embarrassed that his had twice as much on it and began to eat quickly as if to dispose of the evidence. He had been upset that morning about the graffiti on the back gate and that kind of thing always made him hungry.

'What's this all about, then?' said James, straightening up.

'What?'

'Lunch à deux?'

'You don't have to sound all French and sinister. I wanted to see you, that's all. You know, catch up a bit – hear how it's going. It's not that easy to talk at poker what with all the noise and the general bollocks being spouted and anyway I've missed it the last couple of times.'

'You don't need to remind me about that. It's been a free-for-all without you there. Josh has been on a disgusting roll.'

'Has he? He's a shameless bluffer, that one.' Dan watched James chew a forkful of raw fennel. His food seemed somehow penitential. There had been so many more delicious things – most of which were on Dan's plate. 'Well,' he said, after a few seconds had passed. He felt his body tensing incrementally. 'So, how are the old hands, then?' For all his concern about it, the question had come out more artificially than he could possibly have imagined. It rolled like a bright marble across the table.

James took another mouthful of fennel.

'On the end of my old arms. Where I left them.'

Dan flattened his mouth.

'Well, that's reassuring,' he said, reluctantly taking part in the game. There was always a game.

'Yes, reassuring. And let's face it, you've got to take your reassurance wherever you can get it in times like these,' James went on, reaching for the mustard. 'Seen the papers today? Dale-Hogan and Huylers are going bust. This is two of the biggest banks in Europe and they're going bust. Iceland has gone bankrupt, more to the point. Forget the banks, Iceland is a country. What's the world coming to?'

Dan put down his fork.

'You know, it's no good, I can't help it – all this just does annoy me a bit. Not to do down the suffering of the individuals involved at all, but this way of talking about it all the time. The world's not coming to anything for goodness sake. It never went anywhere in the first place.'

James raised an eyebrow. 'Explain?'

'History. These things are patterns. Take dinosaurs. Or – no, look

210

at the Roman Empire. Things get big, then they get small again. Always have; always will. This is another instance. I don't imagine all that much has changed since, oh, I don't know, since—'

'The Garden of Eden?'

Dan exhaled. 'Well, exactly. Yes, that's *exactly* how I was going to put it, James,' he said, rolling his eyes sarcastically. 'You're not a scientist, you're a *mind reader*.'

'I specialise in priests.'

'Do you,' Dan said. 'I know. How about we don't talk about the credit crisis and instead you tell me something about your hands?'

James leant back slightly. His blue eyes and very clear skin were striking in the shade of the café awning and Dan wondered if women thought James was beautiful. He had never been particularly aware of other men's looks before.

'They're unpredictable, Dan. OK? That's the constant.'

There seemed no reason not to continue now.

'Well, I'm sorry to hear that. And what do they say about it at work?'

'They say nothing. I'm not in touch. They've given me another three weeks, so I may as well take them before I start thinking about . . . Anyway, there are still some tests to come back.'

'*More* tests? You must have done every test known to man. You must be like a walking pincushion by now.'

'What's your purpose here, Dan? To depress me?'

'No, of *course* not. I'm your friend. I feel frustrated, that's all. You're not getting any *answers*.'

'Which is why I keep going for tests. You see the logical connection.'

'Yes,' Dan said, suddenly feeling depressed himself, 'I do.'

James pushed his knife and fork together and took out his cigarettes, but there was a large no-smoking sign just over their heads. A woman with a baby glanced at him suspiciously. He shoved the cigarettes back in his shirt pocket. He didn't particularly want to smoke anyway. He checked his watch.

'Well, what with your talent for timekeeping it's pretty late. We should be getting to the centre.' Dan groaned and rested his head in his hands. 'What's the matter with you?'

'I'm reluctant to go back to work, James.'

'Yes, I can see that.'

'No need to sound so superior. It's all right for you, writing eloquent emails all day, having Kerry tell you you're a genius. It's another grim round of phone calling for me. Another grizzly afternoon trying to drum up cash.'

'Poor old Dan.'

'Yes.'

'Ann fucking Summerdale,' James muttered, getting up.

Dan was surprised by the vehemence.

'That's a shame. You liked her when you met. They've lost a lot of money, you know?'

'How terrible for them.'

'Ann's life is not an easy one. No, don't do that face, James. It's no good hating the rich – as if their pain isn't *real* in some way. *We're* the rich to plenty of people, after all. Is your pain real? Mine sure as hell is.'

They went back inside towards the till. The girl began to ring up their total.

'I also took an apple juice, which I don't think was on our bill,' Dan told her.

'Oh, Dan,' said James, shaking his head gently.

'What?'

'It's nothing. I'm sorry. It's just . . . I don't mean to be rude, but sometimes I do wonder what there is for you to be in pain about. I mean, you're not like the rest of us mortals. You don't have to worry about a mortgage, you don't have to insure your car, you don't even have to think about . . .' he trailed off. He never approached the subject of Dan's celibacy. 'About so many things the rest of us lose sleep over. Maybe you have got it right after all. Perhaps the joke's on me. D'you think there's a church somewhere that doesn't require you to believe in anything at all that'll have *me* as a priest? Hey, now put your money away, you don't have to buy me lunch really; it was a joke. Come on, it's on me.'

But Dan moved rather forcefully ahead of him.

'No, I want to get it,' he said. 'I've got the money and I said I'd buy you lunch, so I will.' He thrust out his large hand with a twenty-pound note in it and the girl behind the counter was visibly startled.

Chapter 33

Propping the tray of geraniums on her hip, Leila pushed the kitchen door open with her knee and went out into the courtyard. She had already taken out the valerian and the scented rosemary and the lovely purple aubretia, which she hoped would encourage the butterflies. Half of the courtyard lay in shade, half in bright sunlight, with the shadow of the wall dividing it neatly in two. She looked at the empty frame of flowerbeds round the edge. There was soil in them; there were neat rows of tiles in front marking them out. Obviously someone had intended there to be a garden out there, but somehow it had never materialised. The idea of a garden had always had to come behind the need for cleaning products and marker pens and frozen peas.

She put the geraniums down on the ground beside the three other trays of plants. It was irrational to be planting flowers when there was no way of knowing if the centre would even exist in a few weeks' time. But it might, she thought – and if they weren't planted, then they would never grow and the beds would never be full and lively and the garden would never be more than a flat paved space like all the other flat paved spaces outside the gate.

The plants had all come from a shop on the Harrow Road. She had gone off and bought them by herself during her lunch break. She had bought them with money she had earned at the centre. This had been satisfying. It had felt good to contribute to the place in some small way. What else had she contributed to in the last few years? Nothing, she thought. Her work on the flats had made *money*, yes, but in the end she and Charlie had only put money into – money.

That was what the fund had been about, what their life had been about: making money out of money and investing it in the fund again to make more money. It made her feel dizzy and sick to think about it.

She cut open the bag of soil. She had a pleasant sensation of doing something good, something for others.

It was deserted inside again now that the appointments had finished. Kate was out as usual and she hadn't even had a chance to speak to James before he was called upstairs by Kerry to help with something. She glanced back up at the window where the meeting was going on. She couldn't help feeling left out – she even felt jealous, though she knew this was all unreasonable. She was very much the newcomer. But even that was overstating it, she thought; she was the outsider. This was Kate's place, not hers and it was becoming increasingly difficult to remember why she was there at all. Why was she sleeping on Kate's sofa? Why was she sharing a flat with an invisible person who never wanted to eat with her, who came and left while she was asleep? Perhaps everyone at the centre wondered what she was doing there too, she thought. Even if they had still been looking for a replacement secretary, which they weren't any more now that money was short, she was not qualified to do the real job.

The geraniums sat in rows, waiting to be planted and Leila put the old towel down on the ground and sank on to her knees on top of it. It was a lovely, familiar feeling. She put her hands into the bag of soil and even lifted it to her nose. It smelt damp and sweet and immediately brought to her mind the taste of hot tea, the feeling of her nose turned numb after a day spent working in the wind. She hadn't done any gardening for a long time. One of the flats they'd done up had had a tiny space outside and she'd put in palms and ferns and the estate agent had called it a 'Tropical Roof Terrace'. But it hadn't been much really. Those were just words – just an illusion conjured up to make money. The last time she had genuinely worked on a garden had been years ago, when she and Jules had thought they were going to fill London offices with leaves and flowers. African daisies, not anti-depressants, Jules used to say. Peonies, not Prozac. Verbena, not Valium. People laughed as they bought the bouquets.

Leila began to fork through the soil. It was dry and hard and needed to be broken up. She reached for the small trowel.

Where was Jules? she thought. Somewhere in America still, maybe. He had never written back to her. But then she had only tried once and it was possible he hadn't even got the card. She hadn't been certain of the address when she wrote it. Why hadn't she tried writing again – or checked if any of his many ex-girlfriends had a new number for him or an email, or if he'd called one of the guys at the flower market?

It was so easy to lose touch with people, she thought. How could it be so easy? They filled the horizon one minute – and then they were gone.

Or was it you that went?

It had been *six years* since she had seen Kate. At one time this would have seemed as unimaginable as . . . the idea of her mother dying, she thought, surprising herself with the comparison. Unconsciously, she laid down the trowel and put her hand on her forehead as if she was checking whether she had a temperature. Then she thought of her father. When was the last time she had spoken to him? Had it been last winter? No, it had been longer. It was several years, now, she decided. It was several *years*, if she told herself the truth.

Where had the time gone?

All these ideas and questions arrived in Leila's mind in a strange watery rush. She had turned her face up at the sun while she thought, narrowing her eyes to protect them until its glare became a wild shimmering between her eyelashes. Her eyes began to water and now she looked down again, at the aubretia and then at the geraniums, their petals shivering slightly like wings.

Cupping her hand beneath its roots, she picked one of them up. Then she dug out a little place for it and laid it gently into the bed. Upstairs, behind the window, the meeting went on – but she felt better about this now. She was glad to be outside after all and a part of her couldn't help picturing how surprised and pleased they would all be. Even Kate, she thought. Especially Kate. Kate would see the flowers every time she came out for a cigarette.

Now Leila threw back all her hair and twisted it into a heavy bun; she found a pencil in her pocket and pushed this through to hold it up. Then she continued to work, digging out little holes for the roots to fill, carefully putting the geraniums into them and patting the earth down around their stems.

About half an hour later there was a knocking at the back gate and she sat up in curiosity. No one really used this entrance except delivery people who needed to unload in the car park outside. But deliveries were never scheduled for the afternoon – and anyway, she thought, there was a bell out there, so there was no need to knock. Perhaps the bell wasn't working, though. Given the general state of the electrics, this was possible. There was another knock, firmer this time, and Leila brushed off her hands. As she stood up, the pencil came out of her hair and it all fell in waves around her shoulders again.

She went over to the wooden gate with its huge, slightly insulting lock, which kept Hillford out on the other side. Above her the new CCTV camera blinked uselessly. It had worked for less than a week and now it was too expensive to fix. Kerry still maintained it had been worth buying, that she had not been wrong to suggest it.

Leila tugged the gate open and outside was a small figure in a hooded top. It was Stacey Clark. Even though they had only met once, Leila remembered her immediately. She was leaning against the wall to the right of the entrance. After the effort of knocking, it was a second or two before she opened her eyes. She was almost too drunk to stand. There was also a strong chemical smell on her. Her pink leggings were inside out and the washing label brushed against the wall at the back.

Stacey turned her face towards Leila and made an attempt to lean forwards. Her eyelids blinked heavily.

'Kate,' she said. 'Wansee Kate Raine.'

Leila was taken aback. No one had ever asked her for Kate before.

'Oh, I'm sorry, Stacey, but she's not here,' she said. 'The centre's actually closed now and I'm afraid she's out.'

The small brow furrowed.

'My name,' she said. '*Stacey . . .*'

'Yes,' Leila said cautiously, unsure what this had meant.

'Why sayin' my name? I dunnowyou.'

'I . . . Oh, because I remember it. I've been working out on reception so I've read it a lot and I remember it. Also we met briefly. You came for an appointment.'

Stacey wrinkled her nose up and shook her head contemptuously at this.

'Fuckin' *'pointments*,' she said. 'Wassapoint? Sameoleshit. "'Snot a *slooshun*, Stacey. 'Snot the way to deal wi' the *'motions*, the *feelin's*. Jus' make it *worse*." 'Snottrue though! You getme? I'm . . . I'm like wasser-name. Like wasserface—' she attempted to pull an imaginary gun out of an imaginary thigh holster, though the mime would have been un-intelligible to any observer. 'You getme?' she said again, sinking back against the wall. 'Yeah, you getme . . . Pretty girl . . . hair all longan-brown . . . but I *dunnowyou* though, doowi? Sayin' my *name*. Whathefuck?'

216

she scowled and spread her little fingers out on the air, 'Kate Raine,' she repeated, more adamantly now. The knuckles were grazed, as if she had fallen and scraped them – or even hit something deliberately. Leila wondered for a moment if Stacey was drunk after all. What she saw in front of her could easily be the effect of any number of drugs. Or of alcohol and drugs together.

But why on earth did she want to see Kate? The part-time woman Suzie and Mike were the addiction counsellors. As far as she knew, Kate only gave some kind of cooking class.

'Listen, Stacey,' she said. 'Mike's here. He's upstairs. You could come and sit in the canteen while I go and get him.'

'*Kate*,' Stacey said quietly, 'Only wansee Kate.'

Leila put her hand against the wall. She was beginning to feel exasperated and frightened. Now she saw for the first time the graffiti across the outside of the gate and wall, which Janice had mentioned that morning. Scrawled red letters – she couldn't make out the words with the gate open. Ahead of her, vast and grey, were Hillford's three main towers.

'She's out at a *meeting*. She's *not here*,' she said.

'Made chicken forme 'gain. Mightof. Chicken forme an' I din' come.'

'What can I do? What can I *do*?'

'Get Kate.'

'I *can't*, Stacey. I wish I could, but I can't help you!'

At last receiving some element of this message, Stacey flapped her hand contemptuously and launched herself away from the wall. But then, as if the push had come from someone else and she was now resisting its force, she stopped herself on her toes, skidding forwards a few steps in her little high-heeled sandals. She turned back unsteadily towards Leila.

Her eyes were red. Her pretty mouth was cracked and dry. She tilted her head back and shoved her hands in the pockets of her hoody.

'Knowhatchewcando?' she said. 'You can *fuck* y'self. Wassa fuckin' pointa this place anyway?' she slurred, peering through the gate, past Leila. She laughed harshly. 'Fuckin' *flowers*.' Then she reeled away between the parked cars and on towards the forecourt.

Leila closed the gate. Then she locked it and leant her forehead against it. Her face was burning. Stacey shouldn't talk to her that way, she thought – she had never done her any harm. But when she turned around and saw all the little plants, so prim and genteel somehow in their trays, her indignation was replaced with a deep sense of shame.

Through the canteen window she could make out the remains of the cake that Kerry had brought in to celebrate Mike's birthday. It was a huge white chocolate cake with a pile of strawberries and around it were cards and dirty glasses and the remains of a bottle of wine.

Without knowing why, she felt as if she was going to cry.

'Wow. What's happening out here?' said James coming out of the kitchen doorway.

'Oh, it's nothing,' Leila said quickly, feeling even more embarrassed now to have been found out there with all the bags spread so dramatically around her. Why had she spread them all out like that? she thought. She could easily have come in over the weekend and done it without anyone knowing. Had she deliberately chosen to do it when they were all around, when she was likely to be *seen* doing it? It was horrible!

'It doesn't look like nothing,' James said.

'Well, it is. It is. It's just a few little plants. Really.'

James watched her rush about gathering all the various strewn bags, stuffing them all into the largest one in her hand and then screwing this up and putting it in the bin. Then she hauled the bag of earth into the outdoor cupboard and locked it.

'Are you . . . in a hurry?' he said.

She sat down on the bench and put her hands in her lap. 'No. No, far from it. I've done everything Kerry wanted me to do already, that's all. There's less for me to do now with this whole funding thing. I know everyone else is busier than ever, but it's all stuff I can't help with.'

He glanced up at the window three floors up, where the meeting was still going on.

'Yes, it's all quite involved, I think.'

'You must know. You help with it.'

'Barely. Only with the numbers.'

'They're probably the most important thing!' Leila said. 'At least you can do something useful.'

Neither of them spoke for a moment after this. The one remaining tray of plants sat discreetly in the shade of the bin now. James said, 'You were in a hurry on Friday, though,' and then he turned away and took out his cigarettes.

Leila remembered again the shock of seeing Gavin. It had been as if the centre and the whole of the new little existence she had made for herself had scattered in pieces on the road.

'Yes, I was slightly crazy, wasn't I? It was someone I wasn't expecting to see. An old friend. You know when you see someone in completely the wrong context and it makes you feel like you've got lost – as if you've wandered into the wrong room, sort of thing? Like when you were at school and you saw your teacher coming out of the super-market or something.'

James turned back to her.

'It was an old friend?' he said.

'Yes.'

Not the husband, he thought. He threw away the cigarette.

'You were disoriented. No, that makes perfect sense.'

'Yes, I was . . . disoriented,' Leila repeated.

James sat down on the arm of the bench. He smiled.

'I've brought something to show you.' He took a book out of his pocket. 'I marked a page for you. We had a conversation once – the first time we had a drink in the park together. You probably don't remember what you said. It was about genetics.'

'Oh God, no, I don't remember. What did I say? I'm sure it was idiotic. I can't believe you've even thought about it again.'

'I was reading something over the weekend and I came across this passage and it made me . . . think of you.'

He handed her the book. Leila laughed.

'Charles Darwin's letters made you think of *me*?'

'I've folded down the page.'

She opened the book. James had underlined the relevant sentences with neat pencil lines. There was something touching about their neatness.

'In my opinion, the greatest error which I have committed has been not allowing sufficient weight to the direct action of the environments, i.e. food, climate, etc., independently of natural selection . . . When I wrote the "Origin", and for some years afterwards, I could find little evidence of the direct action of the environment; now there is a large body of evidence.'

She looked up at him.

'James, I'm sorry, but I don't understand. I think you must have thought I was saying something more complicated than I was.'

'We were talking about alcoholism. You said you thought it was "way too simple there was just some gene". You said . . . let's see if I remember this correctly, you said we don't come with sets of instructions "like flatpack wardrobes".'

'Oh, God. How embarrassing.'

'Well, obviously no one thinks there's just *one* gene responsible for anything – or for very few things, just a few diseases—'

'James, please don't. Please. I really don't know anything about this stuff.'

'But you said something else. You said you didn't see how, if we do come with these sets of instructions, how people could suddenly change in their lives. Anyhow, I read that letter and, well, it got me thinking.'

Leila shook her head. 'About *what* exactly?'

James laughed. 'About the idea that our genes control us. Or whether there really are other possibilities, other external forces that might . . . control *them* in some way.'

Leila stared down into the open book.

'Like "food and climate", you mean?' she said.

'Yes, those – and other things. What about "*etc.*"? What does that "*etc.*" mean? That's what's interesting. There've been articles on this stuff – mainly by biologists with beards in California – but I've never taken it seriously before. And the thing is it wouldn't only be genes. You'd have to consider . . . well, all the systems in the body.'

Leila furrowed her brow. 'You started thinking all that because of something I said?'

'Yes.'

'But I don't know what I'm *talking* about, James.' She handed the book back to him. 'You don't want to waste your time thinking about some rubbish I said in the park. Read Charles Darwin obviously, but not because of something I've said.'

He gazed at her silky brown hair, the curve of her cheek, the whiteness of her neck. Her arms were full and soft. She was entirely . . . feminine, he thought.

'Why are you always saying that, Leila?'

'What?'

'That you don't know what you're talking about.'

'Because I'm not like you, James, I haven't studied anything.'

'You can still have an opinion.'

She shook her head, 'Not a *scientific* one.'

James opened the book and closed it again. He had meant her to have it but now he couldn't think how to bring that about. He felt awkward holding it still – but then perhaps she would have thought it was a weird present anyway. He pictured himself buying the new

220

copy for her that morning and underlining the words while he waited for Dan.

No, it was ludicrous. What had he been thinking?

He raised his eyes to Leila's face again and seeing her mouth he knew there was nothing on earth that could stop him from leaning over right then and there to kiss it.

And then he dropped the book on the ground.

Chapter 34

Kerry picked up a strawberry, dragged it through the thick icing and popped it into her mouth. She made a faint sighing sound. It was the best cake she'd made in a long time. Sometimes, she had to admit it, she made them too sweet, but this one was bang on.

'Oi, you – that's *my* birthday cake,' laughed Mike, coming into the staff canteen.

'Caught red-handed,' said Kerry with her mouth full.

'Sticky-fingered more like it.'

'*Don't*. I've eaten that much cake I won't need any dinner tonight,' she said, patting her flat little stomach.

'It's not you that needs to worry. Get a loada *this* big boy,' Mike said, pushing out his belly and rubbing it.

'It's twins,' said Kerry.

Mike continued to gaze down at his stomach. Then James came out of the kitchen with a mug of tea. He was surprised to see the others in there; it was not a usual tea-break time.

'Do you do deliveries, doctor?' said Mike.

Kerry snapped out a sheet of cling film.

'I'll wrap it up nicely,' she said. 'Nice and tidy for you to take home.'

'You're not that kind of doc, though – are you, doc?' Mike went on.

'No,' James said, picking up a crumpled paper.

'Hang on, Kerry – before you mummify it. James here didn't get any. He might like a bit with his tea.'

'Would you, love?' said Kerry, continuing to wrap it up. James never wanted anything.

'Um . . . OK. Thanks.'

'I shall get you a plate,' she replied in amazement.

James sat down by the window with his tea and his slice of cake. It was a good cake − a little too sweet for his taste − but the strawberries went well with the white chocolate. He couldn't think when he had last eaten cake. He never told anyone at the hospital when it was his birthday. Behind him the other two continued to clear up the mess they had all made earlier. He was thankful that he and Dan had been at the café while it all went on. Dan would no doubt be beside himself for forgetting about it.

James pulled the paper towards him and opened it, though he didn't particularly want to read. He had a desire simply to sit and think. He'd worked hard in the upstairs office all afternoon and this was his first break. He had expected to find himself alone down there and was disappointed. Still, an open paper or book was always a good cover and he pretended to read for a moment. Then he wondered if this was really necessary. It was now accepted that he 'wasn't much of a talker'. It was always a relief when this point was at last reached and people moved about him without feeling the need to make fake conversation. He looked out of the window at Leila's flowers.

'Honestly, I don't know how we made so much *mess*,' Kerry laughed. 'Nice that Sean and Pat made it. Perked Sean up a bit.'

Mike hauled the two long tables apart.

'You call *this* mess? You want to see my place at the moment.'

'Suzanne still away is she?'

'She's back tomorrow. And she'll take one look at the flat and go right back out again if I don't sort it out.'

'It's been a long one for you both this time, hasn't it, love?'

'Three weeks. It's me and the hoover tonight. I might ask the marigolds to join in if they're lucky.'

'Aah, bless. Slice of cake as a reward, then.'

'Too bloody right,' said Mike. 'Bit of birthday curry too,' he said, rubbing his hands.

'Aah. Shame doing the hoovering on your birthday, though.'

'Don't you worry, I'll do my birthday properly tomorrow − when Suze is back. I've had my work do today, thanks to your good self, so that'll keep me going.'

Kerry lifted the tray of glasses and carried it off into the kitchen.

Mike went about the room gathering up the paper napkins. Every so often he saw a nice bit of leftover cake on one of the plates and put it into his mouth. Out of the corner of his eye, James watched this for a minute or two. Mike was probably the person he had spoken to least since he had been at the centre. Not that he had spoken to anyone much – but he felt particularly distant from Mike with his blunt way of talking and his red face. There had seemed to be an ocean of differences between them.

But James was beginning to have a sense that such differences were not really as important as he had thought. And even if Mike was some kind of counsellor, he was actually quite a solid, straight-talking man. He cleared his throat.

'I hear there's some graffiti on the back gate,' he said.

Mike bowled a clump of napkins into the bin.

'How*zat*?' He raised his arms to an imaginary crowd. 'Graffiti? Oh yeah, our new spray-can decorating job. It's a bugger getting it off, that stuff.'

'It's happened before?'

'Not like this. We've had tags before, but this is different.'

Kerry came back out with a soapy dishcloth.

'What's this?' she said. 'What did I miss?'

'Nothing. Just the charming message on the back gate,' said Mike.

'Oh – that.'

'D'you hear they nicked some boxes of food, too? Chips and peas.'

'They *didn't*. What the hell did Sean say?'

'I won't repeat it to you, Kerry,' said Mike.

'Explains the long face on him. I tell you, though, it was never this bad when I lived there. *Never*. I know I always say it, but it's the drugs. It's the drugs, the drugs, the *drugs*!'

'You don't need to convince me, Kerry,' said Mike.

'I know. Sorry. I get fired up about it, that's all. You need to let off steam sometimes.'

'Nothing wrong with that. Doesn't bode well for Carnival though, does it? If it's like this now.'

'No, it does not. *Gawd* – I'd forgotten all about that palaver. When is it?

'This coming Sunday and Monday.'

'It's not, is it? Phewee. It'll be Christmas before we know it.'

'Kerry, it's August,' Mike laughed. 'Give us a chance.'

'Who is it nicking *chips and peas*, for crying out loud? Same lot as make these prank calls, I should think.'

Mike adjusted his trousers, pulling them up and tucking in his shirt. 'Is that what we're saying they are? Christ.'

Kerry continued to wipe the table, scrubbing at a sticky patch, her mouth setting a little.

Mike said, 'They're not *prank* calls and you know it. I'm sorry, Kerry, but I can't pretend on this. You know what I'm saying is right.'

Kerry stopped wiping.

'I don't know anything,' she said.

'*She's been seen out there at night.*'

'She has not.'

'She's been seen out there at night, *wandering around*. Two – not one, but two of my kids have seen her. They actually mentioned it in their appointments. At night. Doing *what* for Pete's sake?'

'Oh, Mike. Doing nothing at all, I'm sure.'

'This is why they wrote it: "KEEP OUT."'

'They wrote it to stop the kids coming in, was what I thought.'

'No.' Mike shook his head. 'To stop *her* going *out*.'

With a start, Kerry remembered that James was sitting in the window. Even if he was reading the paper as closely as he seemed to be, he still had ears.

'Love, I . . . *don't think this is the time,*' she told Mike, swinging her eyes in James's direction. But as frenzied as the signal was, Mike didn't pick up on it. He was too worked up.

'It's *never* the time,' he said. 'Is it? Not for anyone. Not Dan or Janice, or you. But this is an *important issue*. Mark my words. There's graffiti now – and they smashed the intercom off and those calls are not friendly, they're not '*prank*'. And to tell you the truth, I'm not surprised, Kerry. We're here on trust. That's the deal, that's the way it works or we're just more of the same old shit. This isn't just a transgression of boundaries – it's so far beyond that! It's . . . it's disgusting.'

'Oh, it's not *that*. It's not *that*,' Kerry gasped, pressing her hand to her chest and letting the dishcloth fall out of it. She knelt down to pick the cloth up again.

'Kerry, you do make me smile sometimes. You know she's that way – it's obvious.'

Crouched, Kerry paused a heartbeat longer than necessary beneath the table.

'Not to me it isn't,' she said quietly. She touched her little crucifix. Then she stood up again. 'All right, all right now. Enough's enough, Mike,' she said, sweeping the cake crumbs into the palm of her hand.

'Anyway, you get my drift,' he said.

'Oh, for goodness sake, of course I do. And yes, I agree something's got to be done or said or . . . God only knows what, though. *Right*. Now, let's get these plates in the dishwasher,' she said briskly, lifting the tray.

'Hold your horses,' Mike said. 'Come on; give me and my belly a bit of a workout. There's two of us and only one of you.' He took the tray from her, nudged her with his elbow and winked. She rolled her eyes at him and peace was made. They went through into the kitchen together.

James continued to eat his cake in puzzled silence. And then, as if a butterfly had come in quietly through the window, he remembered overhearing a conversation a few weeks before.

Was that who they were talking about? How could Kate possibly be connected with the graffiti? It seemed unlikely. No, it seemed impossible. He liked Kate. She knew how to leave people alone.

What the hell was it that Mike had called '*disgusting*'?

Just then he felt a resurgence of his initial aversion to Mike. There was something aggressive about his clowning after all – and then there was the fact that he was always making comments about peoples' accents, dividing them up into 'posh' and 'normal', which was pure snobbery. It deserved no better name. But then this was the same kind of snobbery he himself had been accused of earlier by Dan, when he had suggested that Ann Summerdale's pain was not real in some way – because she was rich.

And he had made light of Dan's pain, too. How patronising that had been. It was hard not to think of Dan as protected, as exonerated from pain in some way because of the weird get-out clause of being a priest – but James felt ashamed to have spoken to his friend in that way. What had given him the right? When he thought about it he knew it was not the first time, either.

He ate the last mouthful of cake without tasting it. Then he put down his fork and as he did so his elbow brushed his jacket pocket. He could feel its weight against his hip. Somehow, even though he hadn't given it to her in the end, this book was hers. He felt a kind of stillness come over him. He need only put his hand in his pocket, he thought, and his fingers would be in contact with one of her possessions.

Closing his eyes, he did this now.

Chapter 35

It was never completely dark in London, even at night. This had been one of the things she had first noticed when they arrived at La Campañera: the dense blackness at the back of the house, when the moon was on the other side. There was nothing like it in London. It was the darkness she had known in winter time in the country, aged four or five, when her mother sat on the step after supper.

'Mind Mummy's *wine*, darling. *Mind out*. I know, why don't you see if you're brave enough to walk all the way to the bottom of the garden? Both of you. Go on, I'll watch.'

They had both suspected even then that it was only so she could be left alone, wrapped in her old leather coat, with her wine and her cigarettes. But there was just the chance she had asked them to do this odd scary thing out of – love. There was just a chance she truly was watching. So, she and Kate would set off. They didn't hold hands; there had been a sense that this would diminish the achievement, but they walked close together, Kate first. 'Go on, I'm not going anywhere,' she would call after them. When she thought about it, this sentence was really all Leila remembered her mother saying. And it had turned out to be a lie.

The end of the garden had been a terrible place, filled with odd silky trails across the face, clumps of wet leaves, sludgy and ankle deep – and sometimes a snail crunched in its shell underfoot.

There were dark gardens, Leila thought – and then there were jasmine-scented moonlit ones.

She turned on the sofa jerkily, twisting the sheet around her ankles and kicking them free again. It was hot. The balcony doors were propped open with a book. For a couple of hours there had been a faint sound of calypso music from an event down the road connected with the Carnival, but after a lot of cheering, this had all stopped. Now there was just the usual soft jumble of TVs from all the other flats.

In the kitchen sat Kate's untouched dinner. Leila had not bothered to put it on a plate this time. Earlier that evening when she changed the bin bag, she had found the Greek salad wrapped in newspaper. Even so, it would not have been possible to cook without making enough for Kate.

But she had not come back and then the news had ended and then it was suddenly past eleven. Leila had got ready for bed and now, sitting at the foot of the sofa, was her packed bag. It was incredible how quickly possessions multiplied, she thought. The bag had been almost empty when she came and yet it was now so full she had had to squeeze her new skirt into one of the pockets. But it had all gone in – every last thing. When she left in the morning there would be no sign that she had been there at all, except for the ferns on the balcony, which Kate had noticed once and which would now die just as the other ones had.

There was no escaping the fact that all Kate wanted was to be left alone. Well, then that was what she would do, Leila thought. She would find another sofa to stay on for the next week and finish the time she had agreed to work at the centre. And then she would have to decide what to do.

Her fingers tightened over the edge of the sheet. It was so late. Where was she? What was she doing so late every night? She wasn't out with friends. And where did she go in the morning? She ran, yes – but where to? And why? Why was she always running?

Leila tugged the sheet up over her shoulder and threw her head on to the pillow again and precisely then there was the sound of a key in the lock. Light came in as the door opened and then it went dark again. There was a rustling sound – a plastic bag dropped and picked up – and then a loud crash as the bowl of loose change skidded off the dresser and on to the floor. There was a shower of coins.

'Fuck it,' Kate whispered. There was more rustling and then there was another bang, possibly the two books or the bike helmet which also lived on the dresser. '*Fuck it*,' Kate said, slipping on the coins as she walked through them.

There was no point in pretending to be asleep.

'You OK?' Leila called out.

'Fine. Fine. Everything's fine. Go to sleep.'

Leila sat up and peered over the back of the sofa. Kate ran her hands along the wall like a blind person.

'You can turn the light on, I'm not sleeping,' Leila said.

Kate gave a great sigh. '*Right*,' she said. She fumbled for the switch.

The lights came on very brightly and Leila blinked and shaded her eyes. Kate slumped at the table. She rested her forehead on her arms. She was wearing jeans and a white T-shirt. The T-shirt had marks all over it. Her hair was in a mess.

'Are you all right, Kate?'

Kate laughed. 'Why d'you ask?'

Leila was not sure how to answer. It seemed unwise to joke.

'Kerry said you were out with Ann Summerdale and the Bentingdon people all afternoon. How did it go?'

'Money, money, money,' Kate said, talking at the wall. 'Money, money, money, money, money, money, *money*.'

There was something terrible about this chant. A moment passed.

Leila said, 'Mike's little party was a success, wasn't it? I'd never spoken to Suzie before. Good to meet all the other people who work at the centre – Pat and Sean and so on. Nice for you to get everyone in the same room.'

'Heavenly.'

'It was sweet of Kerry to do it.'

'She'd do it even if we begged her not to. Any opportunity to be Mummy. That's one hell of a frustrated woman.'

'I . . . thought you liked Kerry.'

'I do.'

Leila drew her knees up towards her chest.

'Christ, I'm cold,' Kate said. 'But before you offer: *no, I do not want a cardigan*.' Then she put her face in her hands.

Leila bit her lip. She did not want to cry. It would be the worst possible thing to do. But she couldn't think of a single thing to say.

Then her face brightened.

'Oh yes, someone was looking for you today.'

'Really. Not that idiot Julian whoever-he-is about setting up a *drama group*. Who are these people with their born-again AA bullshit and their Jesus complexes? Who the fuck do they think they are?'

'It wasn't him. It was one of your students.'

Kate looked up.

'Who?'

Something in the tone of the question made Leila's throat clench. It was in the same way as her whole body clenched and she started dropping things when Charlie made her hurry. For a split second she couldn't remember the name. Kate glared at her and it crossed Leila's mind that she was holding her breath.

'Stacey Clark,' she said.

'When? *Where?*'

'She came to the back gate. This afternoon.'

'The back gate? What back gate? *Here?*'

'No, at the centre,' Leila said, wondering why on earth Kate imagined Stacey would have come to her flat.

'But the bell's not working. They smashed the bell off.'

'I know. She knocked.'

'But . . . how did you hear? I mean, was everyone outside or something? You don't smoke. Who was out there with you?'

'No one. It was just me outside.'

Kate stood up. She shook her head to clear it.

'What day is it? What *day* is it?' she said, searching the flat as if it would give her an answer to this. 'Have I . . . been to bed?'

'It's Monday. It's still Monday, Kate.'

'Oh, all these fucking *days* blurring into each other. I thought it was Friday.'

'You took your class today. You do your class on a Monday.'

'Yes, all right, all right, I forgot that was today, OK? You're perfect, aren't you, Leila? A perfect little treasure in a glass box. Oh look – I can't talk, I've got to *go*,' Kate said and, leaving all her possessions in a pile by the table, she ran out of the flat, letting the door slam shut behind her.

After a minute or two had passed Leila pulled the sheet off and stood up and at once she knew what she had been trying to ignore since Kate came in. It was the smell of wine.

For the first time since she had come back to London, she felt desperately lonely and frightened. She went out to the balcony and leant over it. The ferns brushed against her bare legs. The sky was a brownish purple above the opposite block. Just as she herself had at La Campañera, Kate had run off into the night. Suddenly the feeling of the ferns was like the feeling of the grass on the ledge overlooking the wind farm, and she flinched away from it and went back inside.

Without questioning what she was doing, she pulled on underwear and jeans and socks and boots and a T-shirt. Then she folded the sheet and duvet and put them back in their place above the wardrobe in Kate's room. Then she went into the kitchen and threw the leftover pasta into the bin and washed the saucepan and the spoon. She wiped down the sink.

And then biting her lip and hurling the dishcloth on to the table, she ran out into the sitting room again and stood there staring at the front door. Where had Kate gone? She checked the clock. It was 1 a.m. – not Monday after all, but Tuesday morning. Where had she gone to at one in the morning?

Just as it had been before Leila arrived, Kate's life was an impenetrable mystery. In some ways she knew no more about it than she had done when she sat at the bus stop holding the little bit of paper with Kate's address on it. What did she know? She knew where Kate worked, she knew where she lived. But these were just buildings.

On the floor by the door the little light flashed on the top of Kate's hated work phone and Leila went over to it and picked it up. Feeling as if she was reading Kate's diary, she opened the list of contacts and scrolled down them and there was James's number. It might easily not have been in there because he was not an employee – but it was. It was.

She pressed 'call' and then there was ringing and a moment of great relief and then it went to voicemail. 'James Lawson. Leave a message and any contact details.' Leila hung up and began to cry. She looked at the sofa with the freshly plumped cushions. What was she doing? Why had she dismantled her bed? She could hardly find somewhere else to stay tonight – and she was not going to sleep on the street.

But then how could she even think of sleeping when Kate had run off in that way? The flat felt brutalised somehow by her exit. Was this how the others had felt when she ran off at La Campañera?

What had Charlie felt?

And then, very gradually, she became conscious that the phone was ringing. She watched it for a second or two. It vibrated on the table, turning itself in a small glowing circle. Its ring had been turned off.

Perhaps it was Kate, she thought suddenly. Perhaps Kate was sorry she had gone off like that after all. She ran towards it and answered.

'Hello?'

'Kate?' said the voice.

'No. No, it's Leila. Her sister, Leila.' She felt huge disappointment. It was a strange man's voice. Of course it wasn't Kate, she told herself. Why would Kate call her own phone? She would have called the land line if she wanted to ring the flat.

'Leila? Is everything OK? I had a missed call from Kate.'

'*James?* Oh, I'm so glad it's you. Your voice was funny.'

'I've been asleep.'

'Yes, it's so late. I'm sorry. Look, it wasn't Kate who called you. I did.'

'What's happened?' he said. 'Has something happened to you?'

Leila sat down. 'No.'

He adjusted the receiver. 'Then . . . what?'

'Oh God, I don't know, James. Maybe it's *nothing*. She makes it so hard to tell, that's the problem. You feel like you're going crazy! It might be nothing. But . . . she came in here and knocked everything over and then she was all sort of confused and I think – I don't know for certain – but I think she's been drinking again—'

'This is Kate we're talking about?'

'Yes, Kate – of course.'

'Sorry.'

'Where does she *go*, James? That's what I want to know. Every night she's out late. Every morning she's gone before I even get up. She doesn't sleep – she doesn't seem to eat anything, I think she just throws it all away and—'

'Leila, what's actually happened? Have you had an argument?'

'No. It's not that, it was just she . . . she came in and she was all . . . strange and then I told her about one of her students, about this girl who came looking for her, and then she suddenly ran out again for no reason.'

There was a pause.

'D'you know where she's gone? Did she say?'

'No. She just ran out. Why? Why's your voice gone all serious? Is there something going on?'

James took a breath.

'I think there might be.'

'Oh my God, *what?*'

'I don't know exactly.'

'What? Oh, what d'you *mean?* Is it bad? Is it *dangerous?*'

'Where do you think she's gone, Leila? If you had to guess.'

But she did not have to guess. There was no question in her mind.

'To find that girl.'

Chapter 36

On one level, there was no way of justifying this response, James thought, as he pulled on his old khaki shorts. There was no crime being committed. There was simply the possibility that Kate was putting herself in danger. What business was that of anyone else's? What gave anyone the right to chase after someone else in the dark? It was Kate's business. It was not Leila's – still less his. But he couldn't let Leila go off in search of Kate alone. He couldn't. And he had had to tell her the truth when she asked him directly – and she was not the kind of person who would have been able to do nothing and go back to sleep.

So there it was. When it came to human relationships, there were apparently two choices: negligence or invasion.

He put his shoes on and pulled a clean shirt off a hanger, buttoning it up over his long slim body as he walked. In his sitting room the desk lamp was still on and the computer came to life as he clicked past it over the parquet floor. He must remember to turn it off, he thought. He never turned the computer off and the monitor often lit up because of a vibration from the road and then he was tempted to work in the early hours of the morning. If he turned it off properly this would not happen.

But then who was he if he didn't research the medical journals online? This fragment of his former self was all he had. This dim snapshot.

Photographs, he thought, noticing the empty space beside the keyboard. The desk was the standard place. There were none anywhere in the flat, though – not one. But then in the past he had hardly had time for that kind of thing.

No, it was absurd – it was laughable: there were people out there who still believed success involved luck or chance. And what was the great big mystical secret? It didn't. You just had to work ten thousand times harder than anyone else.

So you called home at Christmas. And there was poker. You saw women, obviously, but you didn't get into . . . How could you? *There wasn't time.*

If he turned the computer off now, he thought, it was as if he might cease to exist.

James frowned. Now he sounded mad on top of everything else. He lifted his right hand and there it was: his new friend, his laser hand magicked into a trembly little leaf. Well, fine, he thought – it would get no rise out of him tonight.

He drank half a glass of water, grabbed his car keys and went out.

Leila was waiting on the road as he arrived. He pulled up beside her and she got into the car.

'James, is this crazy?' she said, shaken by the reality of the engine and by the strangeness of his being there beside her late at night.

'Possibly.'

'Oh, God. How are you meant to tell?'

'Why don't we just go to the centre?' he said. 'She might be there.'

'Yes, you're right. Let's just go.'

James moved the car out again and they drove off.

But there was not a single light on at the Thomas Summerfield Centre. Neither of them said anything about this; instead they ran down the steps, Leila first.

'You have got keys, haven't you?' she said. 'I've not been given any.'

'No keys but I know the code, don't worry. You type it in, though – you're ahead of me,' he said.

It was airless inside and filled with the carpety smell of an empty building. They went through the swing doors and then James went up while Leila went down. Then they met in the hallway again. Leila sat on the stairs.

'I don't even know why we thought she would be here. If Kate went looking for Stacey, then she's out there, not in here. Why would she be *here*?'

'There was a chance,' James said. 'You said the girl came to find her here earlier.'

'Because she knew Kate was at work.'

'Well, I suppose it's possible they . . . met here regularly,' he said, 'when Kate did early shifts or something.'

Leila shook her head in bewilderment.

'Yes. Maybe they did.'

Chapter 37

Out in the park, in the pool of lamplight, stood the usual-sized group. Behind them their long shadows slid over the grass and danced on the wall at the back. On the bench a few metres off sat the white man with his belly sticking over his tracksuit bottoms. Not far off his dog trotted and sniffed about in the dark. The Asian boy was not with him tonight, Kate noticed. She reached her usual place by the bins and continued, walking out openly up the tarmac path. There was a waft of marijuana, there was some laughter but no one paid her any attention. Ahead of her the man on the bench raised his head momentarily; then continued to eat from his carton.

She arrived at the bench. He was a large man, his T-shirt strained over the muscles in his arms and his thighs were broad. On his left eyebrow was a scar from an old piercing. His mouth chewed, giving little flashes of his tongue and teeth. His skin was worn, though he was probably no more than forty, she thought. In his hand was a polystyrene box smeared with ketchup and a few chips.

'I'm looking for someone,' Kate said. It was hard not to slur.

The dog came over and sat at his feet. It was a Staffie, bullish and thick.

'Can't say I know him.'

'It's a girl. A young girl, about fifteen. Very pretty.' The man blew out his cheeks and laughed. 'I'm not police,' Kate told him. 'I'm . . . I work at the Thomas Summerdale Centre. Over there.'

'You're pissed.'

'Yes.'

The man laughed again. He put down his chips.

236

'That's nice for them, isn't it?'

'You care about kids do you?'

'I have an interest.'

'Have you seen her?' said Kate.

He went into his pocket and took out a phone.

'I've seen everyone, mate,' he said, beginning to text.

Kate put a hand over her eyes. She was unsteady and nauseous. It had been a long time since she had drunk. Three years now. She had bought herself a bottle of wine. Why wine? It had never been wine before, always gin or vodka. Get straight to the point, as she had once used to say in bars – in the days when she was immortal.

Perhaps buying wine had been avoiding the point. But then drinking was avoiding the point, wasn't it? Was it?

What was the fucking point anyway?

She turned away from him, walked off a few steps and stared out into the park. It was all blurry. By the fence she could see there were two or three girls the right age. There were boys too; she recognised some of them – and they would be recognising her right back. The dog came over to her and rubbed itself against her leg. Then the man snapped his fingers and it went back to him. From the block behind, music echoed out anonymously from various balconies, each tune lost in the other. Kate ran her eyes along the windows. The block where she lived was tiny by comparison. Here were hundreds and hundreds of lives, she thought, all in a great big pile beneath the moon.

It was a new moon, she noticed; just a little sliver. And then behind her she saw two bikes coming up the path.

It was Jamal who pulled up first, then Dwayne. The man on the bench accepted something Dwayne handed to him then he lit a cigarette, reaching both arms along the back of the bench and blowing his smoke at the sky. The dog cocked its leg against the dustbin. Jamal walked round in front of Kate. He touched the brim of his cap and narrowed his eyes. Then Dwayne came round the other side and stood next to his brother.

'What the fuck you want my sister for?' he said. Jamal sucked his teeth at this eruption. 'You ain't family,' Dwayne went on, 'you ain't social services. What the fuck you want?'

Kate turned to him directly.

'Why-are-you-here-in-my-face, yeah? What *do you want?*'

Her hair hung over one eye.

'I want nothing,' she said.

Jamal smiled. He shook his head.

'Everyone want *somethin'*,' he told her. Off behind the wall there was a faint sound of dogs barking. A boy wandered up to the bench and handed over a note. Something was passed back to him in a downward-facing palm. 'Everyone want somethin',' Jamal went on softly. 'And I know – *I* know what *she* want.'

Dwayne put up his hands, 'Nah, blud. Nah, nah – don't *say* that shit to me. Jus' don't *say* it to me. *Serious.*'

'Comin' round here nights. Walkin', scopin',' Jamal went on. He still had the smile on. They spoke differently, Kate noticed; it was a *pas de deux.*

Dwayne hopped about a bit now, as if on hot coals.

'Nah, nah, I'm tellin' you, I don't wanna *hear* it, blud. That shit gonna make me *sick.* Trus' me, my stomach gonna empty out right here on the floor.'

Jamal laughed. Then he leant in towards her.

'I think she a *filthy dyke*,' he said.

Kate held her breath. The face was tense as a knuckle, unreal in the extremity of its expression. She found herself wanting to laugh into it, to laugh at its fabricated value system, its shadow play of trespasses and vindications. The pale eyes shone against the dark skin. He was beautiful, she thought. She could see the resemblance to Stacey; the delicate curve of the jawline, the cheekbones. Then a flicker of movement caught her attention.

There at the fence was Stacey with her hand on the railing.

Without a second's thought, Kate dodged out of Jamal's way and began to run towards her. Stacey backed up a few steps and then setting her mouth tightly, began to walk off towards the forecourt.

Kate called after her but got no reply and as she got closer she slowed to a walk, remaining a few paces behind.

'Stacey, just stop and talk to me for a minute,' she said. 'They're not even following. They're still over by the bench, OK? They've done their bit now.'

Stacey continued to walk out into the forecourt. She spun round.

'Kate, what the *fuck*?' she whispered. 'Oh my God, go *home*. What the fuck you doin' here? What you *doin'?*' Her eyes searched the darkness behind Kate's back. 'Fuck's sake! The centre ain't even open nights no more . . .' she said, staring at her in confusion. 'Someone . . . seen you, Kate. They said you was standing down by . . . Was you here the other night?'

'Yes,' Kate said.

Stacey gazed at her in shocked silence.

'You come looking for me?'

'Yes. And today you came to the centre looking for me and I *wasn't there*.'

Stacey pushed her hands through her hair.

'This is my fault,' she said. 'I should never of told you all that shit about my life. I should never of put your number in my phone.'

'What? Why not? Why shouldn't you talk to me – and why shouldn't I listen to you? Can't anyone care about you?' Stacey lowered her face. 'Well, I do care about you, Stacey – and I wanted you to call me if you needed to.'

'You ain't here for Clint or Dean or Nate . . .'

'No, I'm here for you. Is that so terrible?'

Stacey lifted her face.

'No,' she said. And then letting her eyes close, very gently, she put her arm out to Kate and took her hand.

'Kate, *they will hurt you*,' she said.

'You don't have to worry about me. I can handle myself.'

Stacey gripped Kate's fingers. She shook her head vehemently.

'You ain't hearin' me! They think you're in their business now, you get me? You seen that shit on the gate round the Summerdale? They ain't gonna touch me cos I gotta be able to . . . cos my stepdad won't let them. But *you* – I ain't jokin', Kate.'

'It's OK. Really. I'm not afraid of them.'

'But . . . *why*?' Stacey stared into Kate's eyes for a moment, searching for an answer to this, half terrified of what it might be. 'You have to . . . go home,' she muttered.

Kate felt another wave of nausea. She let go of Stacey's hand. And then, with its quiet inevitability, there was the sound of bike wheels behind them, first the whirring and then the rubbery scrape on the tarmac as they stopped.

Dwayne laid his bike on the ground first. He shoved Stacey's shoulder.

'Clint tellin' me lies is it?' he said angrily. 'Clint tellin' me lies 'bout this bitch, you said. What's that about then, Stacey? You fuckin' diss your brother?' Stacey gritted her teeth. 'You diss your brother, gel?'

Ignoring him, she turned stiffly towards Jamal. Her face was white.

'Jamal, please. *Please just leave her*,' she begged. 'What's she done to you?'

He sucked his teeth.

'Wha' she here for, Stacey?' he asked. Stacey's heart sank: he was doing the yardie voice. Jamal laid his own bike on the ground. 'Wah she here for? Tha's my question.'

'It's about my *appointment*. She come round to see why I weren't at my appointment, yeah? That's all.'

'She your mother now, is it?'

'No, Jamal. She's just a woman from the Thomas Summerdale.'

He pursed his lips. He frowned in curiosity.

'Tha' place. What they wan'? You tell me?' he said, turning towards Kate. 'Some silly lickle white boy die an' they start all that. Wah for? Wah you think you ah do for us? *We don' want it.*'

'I didn't come for you. I came here for Stacey.'

At this Dwayne spat on the floor, then he checked his brother's face.

'Stacey my property,' Jamal said.

'She's a *human being*. No one can own a human being.'

'I cyan,' said Jamal. His sinewy arm hung at his side. The other hand was in his pocket. Dwayne stood behind him, his posture an exact replica of his brother's now.

And then, without any warning, Jamal reached out and grabbed Kate's hair. He tore some out and flicked it off his hand in disgust, letting it catch on the air. Then he grabbed again and used it to pull her towards him. Her arm thudded against his bony hip.

'*Jamal*,' Stacey cried out. It was almost a whimper.

'Gimme your phone,' Jamal said.

'I haven't got it on me. I've got no money, either.' She could smell the sweat on him. He smelt excited. He laughed at her.

'I don' wan' your fuckin' pennies, slag. I jus' don't want you callin' no feds.'

Stacey began to cry.

'What are you gonna do? She's a nice person, Jamal, you piece a *shit*. You piece a fucking *shit*.'

Now he reached into his sister's pocket, took out her phone and dropped it into his jeans.

Dwayne watched all of this and then, with an awed horror, which threatened at any second to dissolve him into hysterical laughter, he followed Jamal across the forecourt. His brother's right fist gripped the woman's hair as he walked her beside him. She put up no resistance at all. Where was he going? Dwayne thought. What was he going to do?

This woman wasn't like a teacher – she was more like social services, closer to a policewoman, even. But there was Jamal pulling her hair and dragging her up the ramp into the car park, like he didn't care. It was good and dark in there now that they'd smashed in the lights, he noticed. They would probably smash in the last few now.

He never had cared, though, Dwayne thought as they walked out among the cars all shining softly in the blackness. No one was anyone to Jamal. That was why he was going to be famous.

With the two bikes splayed at her feet, Stacey watched the figures disappear into the car park. Then she ran away.

She ran all the way across the forecourt, past the wheelie bins, past the park and into a staircase in the middle block. She was breathing fast. She could hear her own breath – her own breath was like another person who wouldn't leave her alone. Having checked the stairs for a third time, she put her hands in her pockets, rummaging frantically. She checked one last time to see if anyone was coming and then she took out the little rock of crack Mehmet had given her. She sat down and took out her pipe and her lighter. She put the rock in the pipe, lit it up and inhaled.

When it was not too beautiful any more she opened her eyes. She could see the staircase winding up and up and up above her. Six floors up, she thought, her sister's little baby would be asleep in its cot. It was a little girl. Dwayne had seen it once in the corner shop. He said it was butters like its dad, but it wouldn't be. It would be like Debbie, too. Debbie was so beautiful. It might be called Jessica, Stacey thought suddenly, because Debbie had always loved that actress with the red hair.

Moving herself up a few steps, she lay down on the ground on her side. Someone had pissed in the corner as usual but it didn't matter. It was all good now. All good. She wasn't really there.

She drew her knees up to her chest. She loved babies – not to have one, just to watch them sleep. She could watch them sleeping for hours. You wondered what there was to see, really, she thought. But there was something. It was almost like they were the baby Jesus out of the story and you were one of the animals come to see if something amazing had happened.

Chapter 38

It was a little past three when the mobile rang. It was James who answered it; Leila was asleep against his arm. Neither of them had known why they were staying at the centre; what it was they were waiting for. But they had not felt able to leave.

As it turned out, they had been waiting for a phone call.

'Hello?' James said. The line had an external quality to it; it was not a mobile. There was a faint beep and the sound of a coin. When he thought about it afterwards, he was intensely relieved that it had been he that answered. It could so easily have been Leila and the thought of that voice lodging like a thorn in her consciousness was too much to bear.

'If you want your filthy dyke slag friend to live you best get her off the floor of Hillford car park,' it said. Then the phone went dead.

As if woken by an electric shock, Leila sat up.

'What?' she said. 'Something's happened.'

James called the ambulance as they ran. In his hand was the little first-aid kit from the kitchen. In what felt like a horrifying cartoon, they ran up the ramp of the car park and out into the darkness.

'Kate? *Kate?*' Leila shouted. Her voice was raw with terror; it bounced off the surface of the cars. But there was no reply. 'Oh my God, where is she? Where is she? Why aren't there any lights? *James?*'

'I'm here; I'm right behind you. The lights have been smashed in. There was one hanging off the wall outside.'

'What if she's unconscious?' Leila said. 'We won't find her. She won't hear us and *we can't see her.*' They were both silent for a second. 'We aren't going to find her,' she said softly.

Then she put her hands over her face in desolation and in her mind's eye she saw – Charlie. He pulled Camellia out of the pool.

Leila brought her hands down sharply to her sides.

'James, stay here,' she said. 'I'll be back in a second.'

With her hair flying out behind her she ran back down the ramp and across the edge of the forecourt toward the back entrance to the centre. There was the shocking scrawl: 'KEEP OUT.' She had forgotten it was there. She keyed in the code and pushed open the gate. Then she went over to the outdoor cupboard, undid the lock and grabbed the small hand trowel she had been using earlier that day. Then she ran back out once more, through the forecourt, up the ramp and into the darkness again.

'James?'

'Yes, I'm here. Here.' He put out his hand. 'There's still no answer. I can't see a thing. How can it be this dark? Not one single light.'

Guided by the gleam on a bonnet, Leila made her way off to one side. She felt the edge of a bumper against her shins and she ran her hand over the bonnet and up to the windscreen. She found the door. Then with all of the strength in her body she slammed the metal trowel in against the side window. On impact the glass shattered, breaking into a shower of little squares over her legs and feet. Then there was the screeching alarm. She leant in and switched on the headlights and immediately the place was illuminated. It was much smaller than it had felt – just two floors of cars, the floor they were on holding less than sixty of them. And there, just metres away behind a pillar, were Kate's legs, stretched out across the concrete.

Leila arrived beside her first. She was lying on her side, one arm stretched under her head, and Leila found herself remembering Kate once sleeping that way on the grass in the garden when they were little. It was a sunny day – there was a feeling of peace. Their mother must have been asleep, she thought – or perhaps she had already died. In her own fingers was a piece of long grass. She had tickled Kate's cheek with it, giggling to see it brushed off like a fly.

Some of Kate's hair had been torn out. There was blood on her forehead. One eye was beginning to swell.

'Oh my God, where's the ambulance, where's the *ambulance*?' Leila said, feeling her mouth go dry.

'Some of the roads are blocked off.'

'What? *Why?*'

243

'That bridge they've been fixing forever near Barlby Road. They must be trying to do it in a hurry before the carnival this weekend.'

Even in the limited light from the headlamps James could see that Kate's face was turning blue. On her white T-shirt, among a multitude of other marks, there was a growing bloodstain. He knelt beside her and lifted the T-shirt. Beneath it there was a small stab wound probably made with a kitchen knife, he thought. He leant down towards her mouth and he could feel short breaths against his cheek. He laid the first two fingers of his left hand along the furrow in her ribs and between the whirs of the alarm he tapped on them and listened to the sound. He did this on the left first and then he did the same on the right. The right side sounded different. It sounded hollow, he thought, but then the alarm was so loud he might be wrong. There were barely two seconds of quiet between the screeches – he might so easily be wrong.

Could he trust his judgement anyway? He forgot things; he lost things now. And then there were his hands.

At this split second of doubt James felt his body ignite with fear and, clenching his teeth as if to crush it out again before the flames could spread, he put his ear right down against the wound itself. The alarm screeched and paused, screeched and paused, and then there it was: an unmistakeable sucking sound.

Moving quickly now he tore open the first-aid kit and four plasters and some cotton wool fell out. Even the scissors were missing. He patted his pockets; they were empty.

'What do you have in your pockets?'

Leila emptied them: there were a couple of sweets and a tube ticket. A pound coin rolled across the ground.

James shut his eyes. Then he got to his feet and ran over to the open car. Sweeping the glass off the doorframe he leant in and wrenched open the glove compartment. It was empty. 'Let there be something,' he whispered, '*something.*' And then his eyes closed again in gratitude. On the back seat, beside a magazine, there was a yellow plastic biro. He grabbed it and ran back over. Then he tugged Kate's T-shirt up further, to her armpit. Her thin body, her small breasts and the whiteness of her ribcage were all so . . . *vulnerable* against the concrete, he thought. The body never looked this way in an operating room, where there was simply a relevant section exposed between cloths. Here were worn-out trainers, one toe pointing in; here were wine stains on a pale mouth; here were bitten-down nails and cuticles picked raw. Here it was – a whole person, in all of its heart-wrenching irrelevance.

His hands moved over her ribs again. The wound was small but it was obviously deep; there had obviously been force. It was not far from her heart. Moving his hand further up he touched a new spot, in the way he always did – as if naming it to himself – and then, without any further thought, he lifted his arm back and stabbed the biro down hard between Kate's ribs. He heard Leila shout. Then he pulled the biro out again, tore off the end, tugged out the nib and the ink cartridge and pushed the empty yellow case back into Kate's chest. He leant down to it and immediately the trapped air began quietly hissing out.

He sank back on his heels in relief.

Chapter 39

The hospital was made up of three brick buildings with another one round the corner. Having arrived at A & E, Kate had soon been transferred to a private room and Leila and James had been allowed to sit with her while she slept.

Morning came and James went down to the cafeteria for coffee. Leila wanted nothing. As he went back up in the lift again, eating his sandwich, he experienced a familiar sensation: the exciting complexity of a hospital, its network of corridors and wards revealed in glimpses each time the doors opened.

It was another hour before Kate woke up. 'You're still here,' she said. James smiled. He had not been certain she had seen him when she first woke a few hours before. Leila had been sitting at the bedside and had leapt up crying the second she opened her eyes. Then the nurse had come in and, feeling self-conscious about his place there, he had stayed over by the door.

There had been no rape apparently. Only the stabbing.

'Where's my sister?' Kate said.

'Getting something to eat. I made her go.'

She turned her head on the pillow. The slatted blinds were hitched up wonkily at one end. It was a bright day – with the kind of deep yellow sunshine that contains the sound of bees. She blinked a few times.

'My eye hurts,' she said, 'My head feels twice human size. Elephant woman. Is it?'

'There's some superficial swelling over your right eye.'

'Ooh,' she said, 'don't we sound all medical?' James smiled. Even

246

now she was mischievous, he thought. 'So is this your hospital, then?'

'No, it's not *my* hospital.'

'How disappointing. When I went to such trouble.' She stared up at the ceiling for a bit. 'James, I assume I owe you an apology,' she said, 'unless you're here on a sunny afternoon for kicks.'

'You don't owe me an apology.'

Kate adjusted herself on her pillows, sitting up a bit. She noticed she was wearing a blue hospital gown. It ballooned stiffly in front of her and she patted it down. There was a tube running from her chest into a bottle on the floor beside her. The bottle was half full of water.

'What's all this caboodle?' she said.

'Your lung was punctured. Don't worry; they repair themselves quickly. That caboodle's draining the air out of the chest cavity so the other lung isn't compromised. The water stops the wound sucking any more air in. The bubbles you can see are the air coming out. It's an effective system, but it doesn't work if the bottle is raised. It must stay beneath the patient.'

'What d'you mean, doesn't work?'

'The water would go into the cavity.'

'Oh. What would happen then? Would I die?'

'Yes.'

Kate took this in.

'I thought that's what the nurse said – about my lung collapsing – but then I also thought I dreamt it. There's less of a distinction all of a sudden.' Kate watched the bubbles of air rise to the surface for a bit. 'How did you find me?'

'Someone rang your mobile. They told us where you were.'

Kate met James's eyes.

'How considerate of him. But how the hell did they have my—' she blinked slowly. 'Oh, yes, I remember,' she said.

Then, making them both jump a little, the ward doctor opened the door and came in. He was a man in his late thirties with thinning hair and kind blue eyes. James stood up and moved back against the wall again while the doctor examined Kate and took her pulse. Then he shone a little torch in her eyes. When he had finished doing this he glanced over at James.

'D'you mind me asking . . . are you the one who found her? The surgeon?' James nodded. 'That must have been quite some moment. Not that this is *any* of my business.'

'This sounds interesting,' said Kate.

'No, I'm sorry. I was overstepping the mark,' said the doctor. 'I apologise.'

'I haven't got any marks left – except grubby ones. Overstep at will.'

He smiled. 'It was just how your friend over there saved your life.'

'Saved my life?' Kate turned to James again. 'Did you?'

'No.'

Kate raised an eyebrow. 'He says you did.'

'The paramedics arrived very shortly afterwards. It's not even worth talking about,' James said. 'The fact you're here has far more to do with Leila managing to find you in the first place.'

The doctor fiddled with the chart, slotting it back on to the end of the bed again.

'Well, I . . . Again, not to interfere, but I think that's what you call self-effacement.'

'James, stop being boring. *How did you save my life?*'

There was silence.

'With a ballpoint pen,' said the doctor, grinning.

'What?' Kate laughed. Then her chest hurt and she laid her hand over it. 'Did you write me a stern letter? Bring me to my senses?'

'I used it to release the pressure in your chest. There's a place in the upper portion of the ribs – if someone has a collapsed lung like you did, it's where you're taught to do it.'

'Well, yes, but with a syringe though, usually,' said the doctor, still smiling. 'It's here,' he said, drawing it out on his own chest. 'The idea is you can't puncture anything vital there – the heart, for example. It's called The Safe Triangle.'

'The Safe Triangle,' Kate said. She nodded, then she muttered thanks to James and then she sank down lower into the bed, pulling the sheet and the blanket up to her chin again, as if she was suddenly cold and tired.

'OK, well, you should take it very easy,' said the doctor, observing this. 'Not too much talking. Her temperature's up again,' he said to James. 'The lung should heal in a day or two but there's the psychological element. I tend to think that's the biggest factor in recovery. But you know all this.'

Kate had closed her eyes and was apparently asleep now and James followed the doctor out into the hall. Leila was just coming from the lifts. She winced with anxiety to see them together.

'Nothing's happened, has it? Is everything OK?' she said, walking up to them quickly.

'It's fine,' James told her. 'Nothing's changed.'

The doctor said hello and goodbye briefly to Leila and then nodded to James. They watched him go into the next-door room.

'She's asleep again,' James said. 'She's been talking a bit. Laughing – amazing as it sounds.'

Leila's face broke into a smile.

'Really?'

'Yes. It's good to see.' James put his hands in his pockets. 'Listen, I think I should go now. I'm going to leave you both to it, OK?'

Her smile faded. 'You're tired,' she said. 'You must be longing for your bed.' She tried smiling again, but the truth was she didn't want James to go. She was frightened of him going, frightened of being alone with Kate. Even though he had done nothing but sit silently in the room behind her all morning, his presence had been a deep comfort. You were alone but not alone with James, she thought.

'She's going to be OK,' he said. 'I mean it. You can stop panicking. The human body is extraordinarily resilient.'

'I know. It's just so hard to believe it when we saw her lying on the ground unconscious like that. It's as if she was turned to stone and now she's . . . come back to life.'

'Yes, it's like a miracle sometimes,' James said, 'which is a lesser-known medical term.' He smiled. 'Well. Maybe you'll call me later and let me know how she's getting on.'

'You don't honestly think I wouldn't?' Then Leila remembered the drink she had brought up for him. 'Oh yes, I got you this. It's that horrible fizzy orange stuff I've seen you drinking. They didn't have it in cans.' James looked at the cup, the hazardous meniscus just waiting to slop over the edge the moment his hands made contact. There was no way he could allow her to see this.

'I . . . I'm not thirsty,' he said, tortured that he might seem ungrateful.

'Oh. OK, well, I'll just leave it here.' She laughed inwardly. He was so direct, she thought – so truthful. Like a scalpel. 'Well, I'll call you later then,' she said. She put her arms round him and held on for a moment. He was very stiff and she wondered if he was in shock – it was possible; he was more sensitive than she had imagined, there was no doubting that now. She had been moved by his concern for Kate. 'James, you've got to promise to sleep really well,' she said. 'OK?'

'OK.'

Then she kissed him goodbye and went into the room alone.

Kate woke up again ten minutes later.

'Hello,' Leila said softly. 'I hope I didn't give you a jump.'

'You shocked the hell out of me,' Kate sighed. 'But then what did you expect, turning up on my doorstep like that?'

Leila looked down at her hands.

'Kate, I haven't meant to cause you any upset, but I know I have.' Then she raised her eyes again questioningly but said nothing, and Kate turned over in the bed so she was lying on her back again, staring at the ceiling.

'You don't have to *gaze* at me like that, Leila, I know what you want now. You want to know what I was doing there. You expect an *explanation.*'

'I don't expect anything.'

'Yes you do. People always expect things, that's how it works. You've got me all wired up in a hospital and now you want an explanation in return. You want a little story.'

'Kate, stop it,' Leila said. 'A story? Sometimes it's as if you think I'm a child or something – still five years old and you still making our suppers. I'm an adult, you know? And I do actually know what it means to love someone.' She leant forwards, her hands on the edge of the bed. 'I know what it means and I know it doesn't always make sense to other people, OK? I wish you'd felt able to talk to me about it, obviously I do . . . but then I suppose I've never talked to you about Charlie. I did want to, though. I wanted us to talk about *everything*, but . . . oh, it's so stupid saying that kind of stuff now. Just forget it.'

Kate frowned.

'Hang on. Forget what? Sorry, I think you might have to help me out here, Leila? What the fuck exactly are you talking about?'

'I'm not talking about anything. I'm not trying to draw you into some kind of a debate. I'm just saying people fall in love, Kate. I'm saying I understand that; *I'm not a child.*'

Kate laughed. 'No, you're not a child – but I think you might be completely insane. Who the hell d'you think I'm in love with?'

'Kate, please.'

Kate pushed herself up.

'No, I can't actually believe this. Is this possible? Do you mean *Stacey Clark*? Are you talking about *Stacey*?'

'Kate, don't do this.'

'Oh my God, I certainly fucking will do this. *She's barely fifteen years old!* What the hell makes you think I'm in love with her?'

Leila gritted her teeth. It was unbearable to say these things aloud. These were the most private details of Kate's most private life. It was more painful still to see her lie about them.

'Well, for fuck's sake, don't stop now,' said Kate. 'You may as well just say it all now. Where the hell has this screwed-up theory come from?'

'It's not a theory.'

'Oh, it's fact is it? There's evidence.'

'People see things. It's like you think you're invisible, Kate. You're not invisible.'

'What *things*?'

Leila found it impossible to meet her eyes.

'You've been following her. You've been watching her at night out at Hillford. It's the reason for the threatening calls, Kate, and then the graffiti and now . . . this.'

Kate sat up fully now. Her face was gaunt but her grey eyes were large and more beautiful, Leila thought, than ever before. She shook her head. She laughed joylessly.

'It never ceases to amaze me. Never. We all speak the same language, don't we?'

'I don't think I can bear this.'

'What can't *you* bear? I don't think *I* can bear what *you're* saying! Did I have to be *in love* with her to care about her? Did it have to be *sexual*? That's what those little bastards thought. You're as bad as the fuckers who stabbed me. You and all my so-called colleagues. They did the front, you lot did the back.'

'Kate, don't say that! And please lie down again – you're meant to be resting.'

'Shit, I mean if it wasn't so unbelievably offensive I'd think it was funny. No, it is funny. It's hilarious. To think I've been convinced it was glaringly obvious to everyone – to think I was sure the whole centre was gossiping about it. I'm not in love with Stacey, for fuck's sake, I'm in . . . it's *Dan*, OK?'

'Dan?'

'A Catholic priest. In this day and age. I like to think only I could have managed this. I always did have an ear for the absurd,' said Kate, 'a talent for composition.' She shrugged. 'Anyhow, it's going nowhere, for obvious reasons. He's got God, I've got Catriona's three-legged cat, so we really wouldn't have had time for the relationship.'

There was quiet for a few seconds. Leila felt a deep heat spreading over her body. She felt sick.

251

'Kate, I . . . I don't know what to say. I'm *so sorry*,' she said.

'Are you? What for? Mortally fucking offending me? Or saving my life? Or are we talking about my poor achey heart? Well, you can forget about my heart,' Kate tucked her hair behind her ears, 'but I can't *believe* you thought I was chasing after a *child*. You can apologise for that. My God, you really do think I'm fucked up. Everyone I work with does, apparently.' She turned slightly towards the window and then she appeared to wince in pain so violently that Leila was afraid she had torn her stitches somehow. But when she stood up and caught sight of Kate's face, she saw that she had been mistaken.

'*Kate*,' she said. The tears ran down her sister's cheeks.

'No. Leila, do not get me a fucking cardigan. I don't want to be *rescued*. Why are you constantly trying to rescue me?'

'I'm not trying to rescue you!'

'You are. Look at me – you already have! *Here*: a fucking drip or whatever this thing is. Good enough for you?' She pinched the bridge of her nose. 'Everyone I work with thinks I'm some kind of *sexual predator*.'

'No, that's not how it was. Please lie back, Kate. Please? They haven't known what to think, that's all.'

'You knew what to think.'

'Only last night. Only when you ran out like that when I mentioned her name. And that's just me, Kate. Don't hate them – not Kerry and Janice.'

'Oh, I don't *hate* them, Leila. Don't be so black and white. Maybe you do need to grow up after all.' Kate pulled out a tissue and blew her nose a few times. She settled back against the pillows. 'I can only blame myself, I suppose,' she said. 'As usual. They've been right to be suspicious of me. Even that wanker Mike.'

Leila frowned. 'I don't know about him. He's an angry person.'

'He's an *addictions counsellor*, Leila. He could probably smell me a mile off.'

'What d'you mean "smell" you, like you're rotten.'

'I am.'

'You are not.'

Kate smoothed her hair back. Outside the window there was the sound of a large van or lorry reversing. Then it drove away.

'You know what?' she said. 'It's just dawned on me. We're both escape artists. The pair of us. One very unconvincingly reformed addict

252

and one . . . what are *you*, though, Leila?' she said. 'You're obviously better at it, I don't even know what to call you.'

Leila felt her face getting hot again.

'You knew what to call me yesterday night,' she said. Then she stood up and went over to the table by the wall. She poured herself a glass of water.

Kate snorted.

'If you're expecting me to repeat it, you'll be disappointed. I'm afraid I can't recall my observations of yesterday evening; I was off my face.'

The water was warm and stale-tasting.

'You said I was "a perfect little treasure in a glass box".'

Kate folded the sheet over the edge of the blanket, pulling it straight.

'Like I say, I was drunk. And there's also the fact that I'm a bitch. Both things should be taken into account.'

Leila put down the glass.

'Now who's rescuing who?' she said. Kate flattened her mouth. Leila drank some more of the water, then she pulled apart two of the slats in the blind. There were ambulances parked beneath the window. Two elderly women were walking up the driveway, the sun in their white hair. On the opposite side of the road a street cleaner emptied the bin into his cart. 'When I found out I was pregnant,' she said, 'I didn't tell Charlie for almost two weeks.'

'Oh,' said Kate. 'Didn't you?'

'Things had been bad between us for a while, but we'd somehow avoided talking about it. I don't even know how that was possible any more. Where was I? Anyway, then I got pregnant. I went around in this sort of daze of fear, too scared to tell him and too scared not to. It was a strange time.'

'It sounds shit.'

'It reminded me of going home sometimes, when we didn't know if Dad was going to be drunk or not. D'you remember?'

'Yes,' said Kate. 'I remember.'

'Anyhow, the night I did tell him, it was his business partner's birthday. He's called Hugo – he's very brash and obsessed with money. He's like a great big bull.'

'Sounds delightful.'

'Yes, you'd hate him. Anyway, I'd got him this present. It was a bonsai, a flowering quince tree. Very delicate, in a little glass box.'

'Sounds ideal. Did he sit on it?' But Leila didn't answer. Instead she continued to stare out of the window.

'Leila, I'm sorry, but I don't think I get you,' said Kate.

'No, no, don't be sorry. I'm not even sure what I'm saying myself.' She drained the glass of water and put it down. Then she turned back into the room. 'Why follow her, Kate?' she said. 'She had counselling at the centre, she had your classes. That's what all the others have, isn't it? If you aren't in love with her, then why trail about after her in the dark?'

Kate's cheeks were suddenly red, passionate.

'Isn't it obvious? Because she's *desperate*. She's *lost*, Leila. She's terribly lost and in danger and *not one single fucking person in the world cares for her.*'

Leila unhitched the blind and set it straight.

'Who cares for you, Kate?' she said.

'What?'

'How can they though when they don't know anything about you? They don't know who you are. You said it yourself – they've been right to be suspicious. Why haven't you told them about your history? I thought that's what recovering addicts were meant to do. And why won't you ever let me say a single word about Mum?'

'Christ,' Kate said. 'There's no stopping you now, is there?'

'Oh, stop *joking*. *Why can't you take anything seriously?*'

'Why can't you stop shouting and give me some of that water?' Kate said. Leila poured a glass and handed it over. Kate drank a little and put it on the bedside table. 'What is there to say about her, Leila? What is it you want to talk about so much?'

'About . . . what happened.'

'*You know what happened.* She swallowed enough paracetamol and gin to kill a horse, then to make absolutely sure she cut her wrists too. She died. She died and . . . and you found her. Didn't you? Well did you?' Kate's eyes were fierce.

'Yes.'

'Yes. You were my responsibility and you found her. And then good old Dad refilled her glass and he's still drinking out of it now. End of story. OK?'

'What do you mean I was your responsibility?'

'Well, I think I mean you were my responsibility.'

'You weren't my mother, Kate – she was. You were a child.'

'That fucking ballet class. It's ridiculous. If I hadn't gone, if I'd just stayed at home like I usually did you would never have had to see it. I could have kept you away. I should have found her, not you.'

'*Why?*'

'Because you were innocent.'

'So were you!'

'No, not me. I was never innocent.'

Leila wiped away the tears which were now streaming down her cheeks.

'Why did she do it, Kate?' she whispered.

'Why? God. Who knows? Because she was too fucking *delicate* for this world, I suppose.'

Leila ran her finger along the window ledge. A few moments passed and she felt her breathing begin to slow.

'Yes, it's funny,' she said. 'I can't remember much about her but when I do I always think of a delicate flower. An orchid. I see her standing at the bathroom mirror, doing her lipstick . . . pink lipstick.'

'Sounds right.'

'And she had these . . . these big billowy white sleeves sort of flopping down her arms, as if they were petals and her arms grew out of them. She was an orchid really.'

'Yes, she was an orchid,' said Kate, 'and orchids always die.'

Leila went back to her chair and sat down again.

'You're so angry.'

'Oh, and you're not?'

'Yes, I am. But I'm not as angry as you are. And you're almost more angry with *him*.'

Kate adjusted herself on the pillow again. 'I have reason to be.'

'Yes, you do. But he won't ever change. I've left messages, I've written, but he's not interested. He never noticed us and he won't start to now.'

'No, he won't. And I have actually given up on that no matter what it may sound like. I did go back and see him once, though – when I was still drinking.'

'Did you? My God.'

'There was a scene – somewhat predictably. He slapped me. I slapped the bastard back.'

'You didn't.'

'Yes, I fucking did. Then he stormed out. Back to the pub I should think. I went upstairs and looked through all Mum's things. It was all still there – all of it. Moth-eaten dresses. The leather coat. That floppy hat. I even found one of her paintings.'

'I thought you said he burnt them all.'

'It was in the back of her wardrobe. He must have missed it. Anyway I took it with me.' Kate closed her eyes. 'Yes, I think that was the second worst day of my life. I stopped drinking the week after.'

Leila shook her head. Her fingers gripped the arms of the chair so that her knuckles were white.

'I wish I could make it up to you,' she said. 'You do know that?

'Make what up to me?'

'I wish I could give you your childhood back. I still got to have one somehow – but only because of you, only because yours was . . . sacrificed. I wish I could give it back to you.'

'Oh – *that*. Well, you can't. It was trampled on and lost, trampled on with everyone's filthy shoes – just like Stacey's,' Kate said. Then she burst into tears again. She did not stop herself crying this time and Leila did not get up and the tears stung on her swollen cheekbone and she wiped them off very gently.

Out in the hallway a trolley went past the door. A voice said, 'Over at Douglas ward, I think. Give them a call if you're worried.'

Kate looked down at the bottle on the ground. She took a breath, let it out and did the same again. The bubbles rose to the surface of the water and popped.

'What do we mean, Leila?' she said. 'What do we actually *mean* when we say we love someone? Do any of us know?'

'Yes. I know what I mean.'

'Do you? Are you sure? I don't think I do. I haven't seen you for six years, right? I haven't seen you for six whole years and yet the truth . . . the truth is I love you more than anyone else on this earth and I always will.' Kate's eyes filled with tears again; they fell on her hands as she spoke. 'And Stacey – what about her? It wasn't the kind of love you thought it was—'

'Kate, I'm *sorry*.'

'No, no, it's OK, you can stop apologising now. As I say, it wasn't that kind of love – but it was love. At least I think it was love. But then all I wanted was for her life to be *safer* and instead I caused all this . . . confusion.'

'Confusion?'

'Yes.'

'They stabbed you, Kate.'

'Oh yes, but me, not her,' she said. Then her face softened. She smiled. 'And then there's Dan. Then there's the intriguing fact I've fallen for a man who can't ever love me back. I've found the one man who would have to destroy his whole identity before he could be with me. And I wouldn't even want him to do that – it's his identity I'm in love with!' She laughed out loud. Then she turned to face Leila, her eyes strangely luminous again. 'But it's not just me, though, is it? I mean, you're married, Leila, right?'

'Yes.'

'So where the fuck is your husband, anyway?'

Leila studied her boots.

'It's complicated,' she said.

'Is it?' Kate smiled to herself again. She touched the padded gauze on her chest, over the place where Jamal had stabbed her. Then she smiled at Leila and for the first time Kate noticed how tired she looked. 'Leila, you're exhausted.'

'I'm not.'

'Of course you are, you've been up all night chasing after your crazy sister.'

'No, I'm OK. Really. You're the one that needs to rest, not me. I'm fine.'

'Go back to the flat and sleep. Will you please? Go back to the flat and get in my bed, not on the bloody sofa. Go on, leave me alone for a bit, I've got thinking to do.'

Leila stood up. She picked up her bag. Kate watched her; the silky brown hair, which was so like their mother's, the long fingers, the wide mouth, the profile which might actually have been their mother sometimes. She went over to the door and as she was about to open it Kate's throat contracted slightly in fear.

'Leila? You will come back, won't you? Later?' she said.

Chapter 40

Kerry chewed her lip and drummed her neat fingernails on the desk.

'You've been through a lot, poppet,' she said. 'You're a nervous wreck. Who wouldn't be? Hmm?' She neatened a pile of papers. She was sitting behind the desk where Leila usually sat. Leila stood by the door holding her bag and cotton scarf. She had just arrived. 'To be honest, there's not a lot for you to do, anyway. I've told James not to come in either – he'd only be twiddling his thumbs now the Bentingdon thing's in. Now we've sealed our fate one way or the other. Listen, you made all that headway with the filing was the main thing, and then when all this nightmare started with the funding – well, you've handled all the calls and the appointments. But there's so little on now. If the phone rings I can manage it myself, to tell you the truth.'

Noiselessly, Janice put the hole puncher back in the drawer of the other desk. She tried not to feel dishonest for this little act of discretion – but the fact remained that she was listening in. What could she do, though? She wasn't going to go anywhere. Who knew what Kerry might say to Leila? She had upset Magarida, the cleaning lady, earlier by telling her to go home and then, when Magarida hadn't understood the English and was afraid she was being fired, Kerry had made matters worse by doing a crazed mime of the Thomas Summerfield Centre blowing up. It had taken Dan to calm the situation down.

'But you've already paid me till the end of the week, Kerry,' said Leila. Janice had noticed Leila's habit of letting her hair fall across her face when she was uncomfortable. She was such a shy girl in some ways – it was unexpected, given the way she smiled at you. Kerry leant her forehead on all ten of her fingertips. It looked precarious and uncomfortable. It seemed designed to look precarious and uncomfortable.

'Sweetheart, it doesn't *matter*. OK? I tell you, we're going under anyway. We're *drowning*, choking to death. We've got no appointments; we can't even do the two lunches this week because half the food's been nicked!' She started to cry, but this was not an event in itself because Kerry had in fact been crying on and off all week.

There was silence. Then Janice dropped some pens into the desk-tidy.

'I know,' she said, as if she had remembered the answer to a crossword clue. 'The garden.'

Kerry blew her nose vigorously. She dabbed her eyes.

'What? What are you on about now?'

'Leila bought all those plants for the garden. Didn't you? Haven't you noticed them out there, Kerry? You must have. It's looking fantastic. Really fantastic, you should check it out if you haven't already. Anyway, there are still some plants in trays. I've seen them. She can finish putting them in. Can't you, love?'

Kerry sighed, lips tensed over her front teeth.

'The garden,' she said. 'Janice, I know we've never really seen eye to eye but this time you've got me completely flummoxed. What on earth's the *point*?'

Janice pushed a hand through her thatch of grey hair. Her dragonflies bobbed.

'Does there always have to be one, Kerry?' she said.

Leila was grateful to have something to do – something which at least had the enthusiasm of Janice behind it. She planted the rest of the helianthum and this was an improvement. But it was still not a garden, she thought. There was still one bed completely empty and the other two were hardly overflowing as it was. She wondered what her old friend Jules would have done – but then she had often found his taste a bit garish. Not that she had ever told him this.

She herself had always felt that a garden was a sort of conversation. What was important was not only the colours, but also the way the textures and shapes and even the lightness or heaviness of the plants got on with each other. It was as if they each needed a fair say, though some said a lot in few words and some needed to talk for longer. She had never studied garden design – she had simply learnt on the job with Jules. She had read a little about Japanese gardens, though. Hadn't it been Kate who had given her the book? Where was it? In one of the taped-up boxes no doubt.

She remembered the page: a photograph and a diagram. If you were to stand in a Japanese garden and draw imaginary lines between the rocks and the trees, the book said, the shape you would invariably draw would not be a rectangle or a square, but a triangle. It was a guiding principle. It represented the forces of heaven, earth and man.

Jules had no time for Japanese gardens – he thought they were empty. But they weren't. He had missed the point. They had everything in them – if you paid close attention. It was just that the Japanese knew what to leave out, they knew how little you needed. Sometimes one rock was the concept of mountains. Jules thought that was funny. But why not? she thought.

She looked down at her knees, spread out a little at each side, her body upright. She herself made a triangle. She glanced up at the sky. It was a fierce blue.

Then she turned to the empty beds again. Perhaps she should ask Janice or Dan what they thought the garden needed. But they were so busy. She could hardly ask Kerry and no one else was in.

She would have to finish it by herself. It had been such a long time since she had thought about gardens, though. But then perhaps, she thought, this was not knowledge that could be forgotten. She leant back on her heels and laid her hands on her legs. It struck her that even though she knew very little about the world, the things she did know were all things you couldn't learn, and because you couldn't learn them, perhaps you couldn't forget them either. There was something safe about this.

She walked over to the florists on the Harrow Road. The owner had been to the flower market in Covent Garden early that morning and he insisted on selling to her with no mark-up. She was his only customer who really knew her flowers, he said – and anyway his mad daughter had bought double the quantity they needed for the posh Maida Vale place they were supplying and it wasn't stuff most people were going to buy.

There was pure white alyssum and trailing ivy and rosemary and lavender.

She carried the bags back in two trips. She had used all but twenty pounds of her money.

It did not seem shameful to be working out there now – not as it had after Stacey knocked at the gate. She couldn't think why it had seemed so shameful then. She had bought the plants herself, hadn't she? And now she was putting them in the earth. Nothing could be simpler. In fact, whether it was useful to have a garden or not seemed as insignificant now as the flowers themselves had in the face of Stacey's desperation. It was as if everything had turned on its head since what had happened to Kate.

A strong smell wafted in and Leila wasn't sure what it was for a second. Then she remembered Magarida had used some kind of solvent to scrub the graffiti off the back gate.

While she worked, Leila could hear the faint sound of music being sound-checked from the end of Ladbroke Grove. Speakers blasted and the occasional truck passed. It was the start of the preparations for the Carnival. The signs were going up now with directions to the various sections: Jazz zone, Reggae, Soca. Outside the pubs and bars there were placards for cheap beers and rum punch and burgers and spiced rotis.

There were bees around the geraniums. Janice tapped on the window and smiled – and even Kerry came out once to see how she was getting on, peering into the remaining bags, curious to know what was in them and where Leila was going to put each plant.

A while later, Dan brought out a cold drink.

'Hello. This is all very pretty. I like those ones,' he said. Leila gulped the water.

'Helianthum,' she told him. 'Very fragile. They only last a day.'

'Only one day? How terrible!'

'Well . . . new ones keep opening.'

'Do they? Oh. Well, I suppose that's all right then. Helianthum,' Dan said. 'I didn't know you knew about plants.'

'A bit. It was my job once.' He seemed nervous, she thought. 'Yeah, I used to sort of help run a little business. This was years ago, though.'

'It can't have been *that* many years ago, you're not so terribly old, Leila.'

She smiled and brushed the earth off her hands.

'Sometimes it feels like I've had a few different lives,' she said.

'Oh – yes. Yes, I know what you mean,' Dan agreed – though she could see his mind was elsewhere. He walked a few paces. Then he put his shoe out and scuffed its sole against the leg of the bench a few times, as if he was trying to scrape it clean.

'So,' he said. 'I'm just off to see your sister in a bit. At the hospital.' His freckly face was vigilant, she noticed, the stare narrowed on a

point above the fence. He cleared his throat. 'You think she'll . . .
D'you think she'll want a visitor?'

'Oh, yes.'

'Me, I mean?'

'Yes, Dan, I do.'

He nodded.

'She might have been tired, that's all. Some people might prefer to
be left in . . . peace.' He leant down to one of the geraniums and
fiddled with a petal, feeling it between his fingers. It was thin as a
moth's wing, slightly rubbery. Before he had noticed what was
happening it had torn in half and rolled into a ball. He was shocked
by what he had done. Then he knocked the pot over and as he lunged
forwards to pick it up again, he managed somehow to kick it across
the ground instead and the earth scattered out spectacularly over the
paving stones. Beads of sweat broke out on his forehead and he threw
himself on to his knees, scrabbling his fingers, trying to cram the earth
back into the pot.

'Oh, what is the *matter* with me? What is the *matter* with me?' he
said. 'I must stop *touching* things. Stick to matters of the spirit,' he said,
'or something.'

'Dan. Hey, Dan, it's not a big deal.'

He tried to pat the soil down, but the flower was now bent over
at the stem, its head hanging down on one side of the pot. He handed
it back to Leila. 'I'm so sorry,' he said, unable to meet her eyes.

Chapter 41

That evening, Leila walked alone in the park. She had called James again to let him know Kate was still all right and she had been quietly relieved to get his voicemail. It was not that she didn't want to speak to him – it was that she didn't want to speak. She wanted to be alone. Even though she had been exhausted after leaving Kate at the hospital, she had slept badly, dreaming and waking all night. She was too tired for human company now.

She had dreamt of the baby. This was the first time it had happened. In the dream, the violence Kate had suffered was somehow related to the baby's death. This made no sense, but the feeling of it had not left her all day.

Leila began to cry now, her mind leaping from one subject to the other. Why had she and Charlie moved house so many times? she thought. They had gone on long after they needed the money and this unspoken fact had simply lived alongside them in its own taped-up box. She felt sick at the thought of this, sick at the thought of their whole existence. They had never had anywhere to rest! They had never made a home at all, not in six years.

She walked on down the path and all around her the evening went on beautifully and there were people having picnics on the grass.

The flat was darker and emptier without the possibility of Kate. After her visit to the hospital on Saturday morning, Leila lay on Kate's, bed and tried to read most of the day. She tried her novel and then a few of Kate's but it was hard to concentrate on words and at last she threw the book on to the floor.

She watered the ferns instead. It was a punishingly hot day for plants. She decided she would go to the centre and water the garden there too.

It felt good to walk out into the courtyard at the centre and to find all the work she had done. The lavender smelt delicious and the trailing ivy went beautifully with the alyssum. She hauled out the hosepipe. When the water splashed on the paving stones it dried instantly. It was a simple pleasure to see this. Like sweeping, she thought.

It was very quiet. The centre was empty for the weekend. She sat for a while and ate half a sandwich, then she found herself pressing her fingers to her chest. She could feel her heart beating. She could almost hear it. It was as quiet as night, she thought. Why? She felt afraid for a second and then she remembered the roads had been blocked off now. It was carnival the next day.

She swept up one last time and pulled some dead twigs off the rosemary. And then she walked back through the empty roads, up to the flat, locked the front door behind her, went straight into Kate's bedroom and flung open the wardrobe.

She had a sense of danger – or rather of superstition, just like she'd had when she ran to the end of the drive at La Campañera and saw the little shrine with its flowers and candles on the road into the village. She had run into the hills instead.

There were not many clothes in there – just some shirts and a couple of dresses, a winter coat; some long cardigans. She crouched down and her mouth went dry. She shoved her arm through.

It was smaller than she had imagined, much smaller. But she had known Kate would keep it there. She took it out into the sitting room and sat it on the table. It was a still life: a glass. Nothing else. There seemed to be a dark joke in this, which she did not want to think about.

It was not a particularly good painting. This fact was a surprise in a dull and rather terrible way. She stared at it for a while, then she carried it to the bedroom, put it back in the wardrobe and lay down on the bed.

Later that evening, as she sat down to eat, there was a knock at the door. It was the Taiwanese woman from along the corridor. Her little boy clung to her leg. Leila waved at him and he ducked behind his mother, peering out with one eye.

'Can I help you?' Leila said.

'Oh hi, yeah. Looking for Kate.'

'She's away at the moment. Can I do anything?'

'You her friend is it?'

'No, I'm her sister.'

'Oh, OK, her sister, is it. OK, yeah, she didn't say she had a sister here. You don't look nothing like her. She so skinny, that girl. I wanna make her lunch! You know?' The woman giggled and the little boy pulled her trouser leg and she put a hand on his head. 'Yeah, so I got my partner coming. He moving in this weekend and he got his kid, too, so just needing Kate take that big table top out now, yeah? She say end of week and I got no space for it no more. Sorry. So you gonna come take that now, yeah?'

'Oh. Sure, OK,' Leila said. Swallowing the remains of her mouthful, she left the door on the latch and followed the woman to her flat. The little boy ran out into the room, confident now, diving across the floor to a pile of plastic figures. Leila watched him making them fight.

'*Peow-peow! Peow-peow!*' they went.

'*Kate sister?* You wanna come help me?' The woman called. 'It too *heavy.*'

'Oh yes, I'm so sorry. Just coming,' Leila shouted back. She went into the woman's bedroom. There was a double bed with two bedside tables, one empty – cleared for the partner's things. She stared at it for a second.

The woman was tugging something from behind the curtains. Only her back and her legs were in view. She called out again and Leila went over and pulled back the curtain. Behind it was the table top covered in bubble wrap. Leila hauled it out single-handed.

'Oh, you so *strong*!' said the woman, laughing – but in fact it was much less heavy than she had made it seem. Leila dragged it out through the sitting room and into the hall. The woman followed to the door,

'OK, then. OK, thank you very much!'

'You're the one who stored it. Thank *you.*'

'Hey, no problem. I don't care. I'm too happy,' she giggled, giving Leila a wink. 'See how long it last, right?'

'Good luck,' Leila said, meaning it.

'Cheers!'

The woman shut the door. It was quiet in the hall. The timed light clicked off. Then Leila dragged the table top back into the flat and propped it against the sofa. She went back into the hall, double-locked the front door and felt better for doing this.

She threw the keys into the fruit bowl. In the kitchen, the three-legged cat was eating from its bowl, crunching its fishy biscuits. You never knew when it was going to turn up.

265

Leila's own plate lay waiting for her on the table. She sat down to continue eating. It was just an omelette, but it was the first food she had taken any pleasure in for two days. Even so, she had only taken a few mouthfuls when her curiosity became too great. She laid down the fork. What on earth did Kate need a huge table top for? she thought. It wasn't as if she had loads of people over for supper. There was no room for it in the flat anyway. She wouldn't even be able to store it on the balcony.

Leila stood up and tried to peer through the bubble wrap. There was some kind of a pattern on its surface – but it was hard to see. Then something touched her leg and she jumped back. But it was only the cat. She laughed at herself: what else could it have been?

She sat down again and lifted her fork. Then, struck by an impulse and not allowing herself time to feel ashamed of it, she ran to the kitchen, took a pair of scissors from the drawer, ran back out again, sliced open the bubble wrap and tugged it down to the floor.

It was not a table top – it was a wooden panel. One side was plain. On the other was an oil painting. It was a garden: a woman on a doorstep with a lighted doorway behind and two smaller figures; two children walking into a darkness tangled with plants.

She sank to the floor in front of it. It was dizzying. Every colour was dark almost to blackness – and yet, as the eye rested, as the eye adjusted to its new world, they were not black at all. In fact they were the deepest possible greens and reds and browns and blues and greys and purples, each one almost but not quite swallowed by its own depth. At one end of the picture, the plants writhed and curled, unknowable as a seabed and all was vague, all was suggested in wild brushstrokes. And at the other end there was the sharp light from the doorway and within it, the etched figure, one arm raised to drink. And in the midst of all of this, pale as a dream or a hallucination, were the children.

It was magical; it was her own most secret memory brought to life. And yet of course it was Kate's memory too. It belonged to Kate, too.

It was live as a real garden, she thought. The picture was live in every way their mother's picture was dead. It sounded terrible to put it that way, but it was true. She touched it and the brushstrokes were rough beneath her fingertips.

Who knew what people did at night, she thought? Who knew where they went to and why? It was true: no one had much idea about anyone else and never really could. You simply had to take what you could on— trust. She pictured the empty bedside table next door again and felt a mixture of jealousy and of terror.

Then she thought of Kate again in the hospital. They might have killed her, she thought. Kate might now have been dead. The kitchen knife had been centimetres from her heart.

She wanted to call James. Yes, that was exactly what she wanted to do, she decided. Perhaps he would come over for a drink. This seemed such a good idea, such a relief; she wondered why she hadn't thought of it before.

But before she got up for the phone she found that quite suddenly she was too exhausted to keep her eyes open. Leaving the plate on the table and the painting propped against the sofa, she got into Kate's bed, pulled the sheet over her and went to sleep.

Chapter 42

The buzzer gave a short burst and Leila's eyes sprang open. Something about the abruptness of the sound suggested this was a final attempt. She sat up and retrieved her T-shirt from the floor, pulled it on and picked her way through the mess in the sitting room and out to the entryphone. She caught sight of the clock: it was past twelve.

'Hello?'

'Oh, you are in. I was about to give up.'

Sounds of music drifted up from the street. The procession went right past the end of the road this year. Leila's fingers tightened on the receiver. A long whistle screech sounded and was answered by a series of horns.

It was Charlie. She couldn't think what to say and so she just pressed the buzzer to let him in. Then she looked down at her bare legs and ran back into the bedroom for her skirt. She splashed water on her face and went back out again. There was a knock at the door. 'Coming,' she shouted, but as she reached the door and tried to open it she remembered she had locked it from the inside after she dragged in the painting. She had thrown her keys down somewhere. *Where?* It seemed somehow typical that this should have happened now. She searched the mess on top of the dresser but they were not there. He would probably be rolling his eyes out there, she thought. She ran back into the kitchen and there they were, draped over an orange in the fruit bowl. She grabbed them, took them back out and opened the door.

He was leaning against the banister, a few feet back from the door – as if he was ready to be photographed, she found herself thinking, as if he had arranged himself for maximum impact. He certainly did look well. He was wearing a white T-shirt and he was even browner than when she last saw him. His hair had been cut.

Neither of them spoke. Then Leila said, 'So Gavin told you where I was.'

'Yes.'

'But how did he know the address? I only mentioned I was staying with Kate.'

'Christina. He knows Christina from somewhere. He's actually been over here once. He met Kate.'

'Gavin met Kate?' This seemed too enormous a concept to take in − as if two planets had been forced together in the night sky.

'He only worked out she was your sister afterwards.'

Leila was suddenly uncomfortable with the idea that this had all been discussed.

'*Catriona*,' she said.

'Sorry?'

'The girl who owns the flat. Her name's Catriona, not Christina.'

'Oh. Right − sorry. Catriona.' Charlie narrowed his eyes and leant forward slightly, as if she had spoken very quietly and might continue to do so. She was irritated by this. She could feel him waiting for something to happen. For what? What did he expect?

She bent over and picked up a few flyers from the floor. 'Pizza! Pizza! *Pizza!*' she read. The next one was for the local curry house. Kate was right, it was a waste of paper and it was amazing no one made a law against it.

Charlie watched her. She was healthy again, he thought. She had become quite thin out in Spain. He noticed her hair was incredibly shiny and something about this made him want to smile. It fell almost to her waist now in beautiful waves. He thought of telling her this, but could not think how and instead he watched her fold up the flyers, pressing her nail along the crease, and putting them in the waste-paper basket.

She seemed very calm. He smoothed the front of his T-shirt. 'Well, I picked the craziest possible day to come,' he said. 'It's chaos out there. It took me forty-five minutes to walk from Marble Arch. Everyone's covered in mud. Why *mud*?'

'It's to do with the emancipation of slaves. It's a sign of freedom. The colonials used to think they were dirty so when they were freed they made themselves even dirtier and danced.'

'Oh.' Now she seemed angry, he thought. Her eyes flashed at him. 'You know a lot about it,' he said.

'Hardly. I saw a thing on TV, that's all.'

They could hear the music again. Charlie said, 'When there was no answer I thought maybe you were out there with them.'

'No, I was just sleeping.'

He put his fingers on the door handle.

'Late night?'

She stepped back a little. She frowned.

'Well, I suppose we can't just stand in the hall, can we? D'you want something to drink, Charlie? Shall I make you a cup of tea?' This seemed a bizarre thing to be saying. Leila glanced down at her bare feet. In her boredom yesterday she had painted her nails bright pink. She felt obscurely ashamed of this now. 'Or there's coffee. You prefer coffee.'

'Yes, I do prefer coffee,' he said. 'But tea's fine. Whatever.' He put his hands into his pockets.

Leila sighed.

'Right, well, come in then. It's a total mess, OK?' He followed her and stood in the sitting room over at the far end of the sofa, by the bookcase. Seeing him there, his T-shirt TV bright against his tan, Leila thought the room had never looked so small. Small and dingy. She saw the dirty plate and glass on the table and rushed them away with her into the kitchen.

Charlie found he was curious to see Kate's flat. There were a lot of books with heavy, political-sounding titles, he noticed. This didn't surprise him. Then he saw the painting. He lifted the bubble wrap hanging down the front.

'God. What's this?'

Leila leant back on one foot. She didn't like him touching it.

'It's a painting.'

'Well – yes.'

'It's better if you leave it alone, OK? It's Kate's.'

She watched him go out to the balcony. He leant over. No doubt he was thinking how cramped it all was, she thought – how much in need of renovation.

Why had he come in person? she thought. Could he not have called? Obviously they needed to speak at some point, but why now, without warning? It was like being crept up on in the dark.

She set the coffee pot firmly on the ring and brought two cups out into the sitting room.

'There's no milk left. Kate only has soya,' she said. 'You can have that if you like.'

'No, I . . . I'll let Kate have that all to herself, I think.' Leila turned away. 'She's still vegetarian?' he asked politely.

'Yes. She's passionate about it.'

'Good for her. I mean it. There aren't many people who live up to their principles.'

Leila regarded him sceptically.

'No, there aren't,' she said. He was still standing over by the balcony doorway. Was he too disgusted by Kate's place even to sit down in it? she thought. 'Has the flat sold?' she said, taken aback by her own bluntness.

He met her eyes.

'No.'

'Well, it's not surprising, I suppose. No one's buying anything until the market settles.'

'Yes, you're right.'

She frowned again.

'Charlie, aren't you going to sit down?'

He cast his eyes about the room. The sofa was covered in Leila's clothes. On one of the chairs was the spare duvet and on the other was a skirt and a few of Kate's T-shirts, which Leila had planned to take in to the hospital for her later. She hadn't noticed all this until now. 'Um, where should I go?' he said, smiling.

Feeling her face redden, Leila swept the clothes off the sofa and threw them into Kate's room.

'I warned you it was a mess. That's how I am. Shocking, isn't it?'

'It couldn't matter less,' he muttered, but she didn't hear him. She had forgotten to turn the ring on and she hurried back into the kitchen, irritated with herself.

Outside there was a round of cheering and shouting. It was good to have this reminder of the outside world, she thought, switching the ring on. It sounded like a revolution. This thought excited her. She rested her fingers on the sideboard.

'It's loud out there,' she called through.

'Loud is not the word. You can barely tell up here. This is an ivory tower, I promise you. You feel like your head's going to explode on Westbourne Grove. This goes on for two days, doesn't it?'

She came back out.

'Yes. They call this Jouvert. It's the opening day.'

'Most people are wasted already. Except the ones with children. Some of them, even.'

'They won't stop drinking until Monday night.'

'Christ,' he said. Leila snorted and he looked up at her. Her knee jogged on the arm of the sofa; her face had an expression he had never seen it wear before.

'You disapprove of drunkenness, do you?' she said. He sat down. This struck her as a predictable response. 'Make yourself comfortable,' she told him. 'The coffee will be ready in a second.'

Charlie fiddled with his cigarettes and put them back in his pocket. He barely wanted to smoke any more. Neither of them could think what to say and then, at the same moment, they both became aware of a smell of burning.

'What the hell's that?' Leila said. The smoke alarm went off. They both went into the kitchen. '*What have I done now?*'

She had turned on the wrong ring and the tea towel sitting on top of it had caught fire. It blazed dramatically and Charlie grabbed it between two wooden spoons and plunged it into the sink. The flames went out in a cloud of black smoke. He tugged open the window to let this out, but it was a tiny window. Their eyes watered.

'We can't let it get into the rest of the flat – it'll make the place stink,' Leila said, shutting the kitchen door. They flapped the smoke out together with a tea tray and a magazine. They coughed, but it began to clear. Above them, the alarm continued to beep.

'Oh, shut up, *shut up*. I've *got* to shut this thing up!' Leila said. Grabbing the broom, she stood on a chair and began to jab at the button on the sensor.

'Are you meant to do that?' asked Charlie, amused by this sight.

'Yes. It's what Kate does.'

At last the noise stopped. Leila got off the chair. She picked up the coffee pot and peered into it. The powder sat there intact.

'You know what?' Charlie said. 'May I make a suggestion? Shall we have something else instead?'

She looked at him with her eyebrows drawn together and then for the first time her face relaxed. 'Yes, OK. All right, yes we can. I've got a bottle of wine. We can have that.'

'Perfect.'

'It might not be up to your standards.'

'You know perfectly well you always chose the nicest stuff.'

'I don't know anything about wine, Charlie.'

'Yes, I always found that extremely irritating.' He smiled at her and she turned away quickly and took the bottle out of the fridge. He noticed the strawberry yoghurts she liked and a melon. The things she always bought. She shut the door.

'I heard about Gideon,' she said. 'I'm sorry. Is he OK?'

'Yes, he's at home now. He'll have to take medication for a while. He'll have to take it easy – but he's fine. There was a lot of talk about him giving up his work, but he's decided not to after all. Huge surprise.'

'It would have been like turning out the lights. It's the only thing that interests him. He's only alive when he's working.'

'Yes, you're right. You always understood him. I think he knows that.' Leila rummaged noisily for the corkscrew and then found it was right in front of her on the sideboard. 'Anyway,' Charlie went on, 'one rather big thing though, is that my mother's decided to leave him. She wants to go and live in Barcelona.'

'My God. How do you feel about that?'

'I think she's . . . made the right decision.'

Leila's eyes lowered.

'So do I,' she said. 'But I hope he's OK.'

'He's OK. He asked after you.'

'Did he?'

'You sound amazed. He is your father-in-law. He does care – in his own very peculiar way.'

She went back out quickly into the sitting room to see if there were any more glasses out there, but there were only the five dirty ones in the sink. She wondered why she had bothered doing this when she knew there were only five glasses. 'Charlie, why don't you try sitting down again?' she told him. 'I'll wash up some glasses.'

'Can I help?'

She rolled her eyes.

'You're not doing my washing up. I'm going to get a clean T-shirt on and then I'll do the glasses.'

'Fine,' he said. He sat down as she had told him to and, shaking her head, she gave him a wry smile over her shoulder as she walked off, and as she did so he remembered her walking off and smiling in just the same way shortly after they met. It had been at someone's barbecue, he thought. They had been kissing for days, too fascinated to sleep. Gavin had arrived – it was the first time she met his friends – and they all chatted for a bit on the grass and then she went off to get them some drinks. And as she walked away, her plait swinging at her slim waist, Gavin saying how lovely she was, Charlie remembered thinking very clearly to himself: this can't last. This is too good for you. You don't deserve it.

But it's here *now*, he had told himself – and this realisation: that this precise moment, with his best friend and the warm evening and the incredible girl, contained everything he had ever wanted, had made him so happy he threw himself back against the grass with his arms over his head. Gavin had laughed at him and mussed up his hair.

Why wasn't it possible to go on living in those early moments forever? Charlie thought. Why?

The buzzer went. He waited a few seconds, thinking it might have been the one for the next-door flat – the walls were paper-thin. But it went again.

'Leila?'

'D'you mind answering it?' she called from the bathroom. 'It's just people selling stuff. They ring and ring if you don't answer.'

She heard him go off across the sitting room.

Having tried and failed to hear anything on the entryphone, Charlie leant over the banister to see who it was.

'Sorry, I could hardly hear you,' he called out, 'with the music.'

'I couldn't hear you either,' replied a man coming up the stairs. It was not someone selling something. He came to a stop opposite Charlie, in front of the door. He was a young man about the same age.

Charlie had a strong sense that his own person was not what had been expected.

'Are you a friend of Kate's?' he asked.

'No,' said James. He was tall and pale, very slim. 'I'm a friend of Leila's.'

'Oh, right.'

'Is she in?'

'Yes, she is.' Charlie leant forwards, peering at something. 'You do know your shirt's ripped, don't you?' He pointed at a flap of cotton on the left of James's shirt. James lifted it and tried to tuck it back into place. But this was pointless: with nothing to hold it, the strip of cotton fell away instantly and the shirt gaped again.

'It must have happened just now,' he said. 'There was a bit of panic at the station. Someone threw a bottle or something. I got shoved through the barrier by a bunch of kids.'

'Why the hell did you come by tube? You're mad.'

'You can't exactly drive anywhere today,' James said, taken aback.

'I walked.'

'I don't like crowds.'

274

'Hey, it's not a crowd, it's a *carnival*.'

'It's very slow walking through it.'

'Well, yes, that's true. If you were in a hurry.'

James ran a hand through his hair.

'So are you . . . are you Catriona's boyfriend?'

'Who?' said Charlie – and it would have been impossible for him not to see the pain: just one pulse of it, deftly controlled. 'Oh, *Catriona*,' he said. 'No, I've . . . I've never met her, I'm afraid.'

He was holding something, Charlie noticed. It was wrapped up, but it seemed to be a book. There was a ribbon round it. James shoved it roughly into his pocket. Their eyes met. Charlie moved back a little into the corridor and stretched his arm out so the palm rested on the opposite wall. He gave a broad smile – and as he did so he knew with a dismal, sickening feeling that there had been few moments in his life in which he had been so dishonest.

Behind him, Leila came into the sitting room.

'Oh, hi, James, is that you?' she ducked to see him.

In her hands were two glasses, a bottle of wine – and their attendant bundle of false implications. Charlie let his arm fall.

'Yes, I dropped by stupidly,' James said. 'I'm sorry, I had no idea you were . . .' But he was interrupted by the smoke alarm.

Leila put the glasses down. She threw up her hands at the ceiling.

'Oh, for God's sake! I can't hear. I'm going to chuck that thing out the window!' But she paused for a second, covering her ears. 'James, I was going to call you,' she shouted. 'I was going to call yesterday evening – but I passed out cold. I've slept for *twelve hours*. Can you believe it? I only woke up because Charlie rang the bell. Lucky, or I'd probably have gone on sleeping all day. Oh, that thing!' She screwed her face up at the smoke alarm and went into the kitchen.

'It got set off earlier,' said Charlie. 'Something burnt.'

'I see,' James replied, but he had not really heard. He was only aware of the fact that he had spent two whole days convincing himself to do something; to say something, that he had not slept all night for the excitement; that he had conjured up feelings, which had previously seemed as unreal as spirits or primitive gods and now there was nowhere to put them. It was too late. Or it had always been too late.

'You're not going to believe this,' he said. 'I've arranged to meet someone and I completely forgot. Will you say I had to go?'

'Of course,' said Charlie. 'I'll tell her you had to . . . rush off.'

James took in the jaw, the rich brown eyes. It was the face of a leader, he thought – of a man who took people into battle. It won your confidence.

'Thank you,' he said.

Charlie closed the door behind him. Then he rubbed his hands over his face and went back into the sitting room.

'Oh. Where's James?' Leila said.

'He had to rush off.'

She let the broom fall against the table.

'How come? That's so strange.' She couldn't help being relieved, though. She would call him later and explain.

She poured the wine and held out a glass to Charlie.

'Well, here you are, then. At last,' she said. But for some reason he did not put out his hand to take it. Her brow furrowed. 'Don't tell me you don't want it now.'

'*It only happened once,*' he told her.

'What?'

'Once was enough; I'm not saying once wasn't enough. But it was just that one kiss.' In the jasmine bushes above the swimming pool, he had found her footprints in the dust. He had not been certain until that moment. Camellia was sick when he told her. 'It's the only time I've ever been unfaithful to you, Leila. But I know I've been a bad husband in other ways. So many other ways.' Leila lowered the glass to her side in amazement. 'I know what I did wrong,' he said. 'I must know *most* of it anyway. I've thought it all through this whole time. I don't want to repeat my father's mistakes, Leila.'

He looked at her beautiful face, the grey-blue eyes, the soft mouth. She might have been anyone's wife, he thought. Why on earth was she his? They had been so young when they got married – that was the only reason. It must be. She hadn't known any better. It had all been a joke, all a game for her and then she was stuck. She might have walked away for those drinks at the barbecue, her plait swinging, and just never come back. It would have made more sense. 'I should never have let you stop doing your gardening,' he said. 'Your plants. I should never have made you.'

'You didn't . . . you didn't *make* me. I chose to.'

'Did you really have a choice? I made it seem like a fire. We all did. Me and Hugo and all of us. We saw all these ways to make money and that was all that mattered. You gave up everything you cared about – for me. In the end it *was* a fire I suppose, just not the way we thought.'

The music thumped in the window frames. People were dancing next door.

'I . . . don't know what to say to you,' Leila said. Her voice was very quiet.

Charlie lowered his head.

'Leila, I did something just now.'

'What?' But he did not know how to explain. '*What*, Charlie?'

'You know he's in love with you, don't you?'

'Who? What are you talking about?'

'That guy who came to the door just a minute ago.'

'*James?* No, he isn't. He's a brilliant surgeon, he's not in love with me. He's not like that. And no, he's not gay, OK – he's just too . . . He lives in his mind. There's a lot you don't know, all right? You're making the most obvious assumptions when all sorts of things have happened. We've been through something together, that's all. You don't know about it.'

'He's in love with you.'

'He *isn't*, Charlie.'

'I'm a man – I know,' he insisted – and Leila's face went pale and seeing this Charlie felt a pain more enormous than anything he had ever experienced before. 'If you want to catch up with him you'll probably be able to,' he said. 'I assume he's gone back to the station.'

Her eyes met his for a second, but he could see they did not even register his existence; they were like coloured glass. She did not bother to say anything either but ran out into the corridor and down the stairs as fast as she could.

Charlie heard the outer door bang shut and then he sat down on the sofa and put his head in his hands.

Leila ran out on to the street. Everywhere she looked were people covered in paint and mud, blowing whistles, dancing, laughing and shouting. Two women in matching green feather headdresses walked down the pavement catcalled by the men and boys they passed. A man on stilts made his way down the centre, leaning down to children who either giggled or cried at the sight of him. Moko Jumbie, Leila remembered: a protecting god, able to foresee evil. An enormous speaker sat on the front step of the building opposite. The music pounded out of it, vibrating in her jaw; her teeth. She did not know what kind of music it was. From the other end of the road came the sound of a steel band. Everywhere there was a smell of frying onions and sweet alcohol, of sweat and marijuana and spices she didn't know.

How would it be possible to find anyone in this? she thought. Kate's road was a way through, a designated back route from Bayswater to Westbourne Grove and the main Carnival processions. There was a constant flow in either direction, though most people were heading towards Westbourne Grove. At the end of the road, while a series of floats passed, a crowd had begun to accumulate and wait. Over their heads, Leila could make out the fantastic headdresses; the feathers; the multicoloured butterfly wings and sequinned hats of the dancers high up on the floats. There was a woman with a snake around her neck, her bikini top barely covering her breasts. Her skin was a deep caramel colour, shiny with oil. Behind her gyrated a man in a pair of bull's horns, and following them were men and women in bright green leaves, their headdresses made up of creepers and flowers and birds. And along with all this, much louder now, the steel band rang and clanged out, with its heat and its nostalgia borrowed from far away.

And then there by the letterbox in his crumpled shirt was James. There he was, where he must have been all along, just another person waiting in the crowd.

There James stood, she thought, his arms at his sides, poised in a moment of his own independent existence, which went on and on after all, whether it was observed or not – just as hers did, just as Kate's did, or Charlie's or Gavin's. It was only her mother who had disappeared.

James moved to one side to make room for a man with a child on his shoulders. She felt overwhelmed with tenderness for him. Was it possible Charlie was right? Was it possible he was feeling love for her as he stood there at the end of the road? Had he even come here to tell her he loved her? The possibility of this sent a surge of excitement through her body.

But then what if Charlie was wrong?

A woman crashed into her hip. She had a bucket and a cloth in her hand.

'Dutty mud?' She raised the cloth and wiped it down Leila's arm. 'Dutty mud for *Carnivaaaaal*,' she shouted, spinning off, hopping on one leg and blowing her whistle. Leila stared at her arm, at the mud dripping down it and over her hand.

But Charlie would not be wrong, she thought. She knew this. He saw things clearly. But that was ridiculous! How could she say it? Why, after all that had happened, did she trust this so unreservedly? He had not seen himself clearly, she thought, angrily. But then she had not seen herself clearly either.

Somehow they had both wandered around lost, restless, homeless, like two characters in a fairy tale that had wandered into a wood.

It was only then she realised that when he told her about James she had run out of the flat without saying anything to him. Not a single word.

Another float went past the end of the road. The crowd had begun to dance now and cheer; they had become an audience.

Why had Charlie come? she thought, beginning to feel agitated again. She put her hand on the railing beside her. He could so easily have called. They could have started the . . . proceedings on the phone. Why turn up in person?

Three girls plastered in mud pushed past. A man swigged from a bottle of whisky.

She felt dizzy again. What do we mean when we say we love someone? Kate had asked her. She looked at James.

'If you want to catch up with him you'll probably be able to,' she heard – and from nowhere tears came into her eyes; tears fell down her cheeks. Why? Why *tears*? She resented them! She scrubbed them off roughly. Anger burnt in her chest. Hurt filled her. Why had he . . . but then she herself had . . . but *he* had been the one who . . .

It all faded. She smiled, remembering something that had happened on the night they met. It had been cold and Charlie had offered her his leather jacket.

It was one tiny moment in the story of a life: a young man holding out a jacket and a girl staring back, awestruck for a heartbeat in some way she scarcely understood, until he winked at her and then they found themselves laughing together. Laughing. And when he started the car, music blasting, five others piling in, she had put the jacket on and squeezed in alongside them, too happy, too terrified to speak.

Leila let go of the railing. She turned and ran back.

And just as she did so, though there was no outward reason, no loud bang or flash of light, James looked round. He saw her immediately: the pale blue figure zig-zagging against the crowd. It's not her, he told himself – but this was just a mental reflex and he knew it. He had felt the reality of her presence as if he had been reading a book and he had glanced up from it to find her staring at him. She had felt this way to him since their first drink in the park.

His heart began to race; his fists clenched. She had come out after him! She knew! She knew how he felt and she had come out after him!

But she was not running towards him, she was running away.

He felt lightheaded – as if he was as drunk and stoned and wild as the crowd around him. The steel band continued to play and the crowd cheered and danced, clapping their hands over their heads, stamping, blowing their whistles as if to announce something incredible was about to happen.

There was no question that she had seen him, he thought. No question. Why had she come out and seen him and then gone back again? Why had this strange thing happened, this riddle?

But the answer came simply: *Because she doesn't love you.* And he knew it was true. Then James's face took on an expression of deep concentration, of enquiry. It's a real pain, he thought, it's not just a metaphor. He put his hand over his heart. How strange that it's a real pain. Leila not knowing had preserved him from precisely this.

The floats moved on at last and the crowd pushed out into Westbourne Grove, most flowing on towards Portobello, some towards Paddington.

He was very thirsty. On the roadside was a stall selling cold beer. He felt in his pocket for change and the man passed him the bottle over a few other heads. Along the side of the stall there were openers on strings and he clipped one over the end of the bottle and pressed and as the lid came off, he noticed that for the first time in eight months his hands were not shaking. Not the left or the right.

He held up the bottle and studied the liquid: it was steady. *Why?* But there seemed no point in asking. He shook his head as if a child had told him a joke.

Then he put his hand in his pocket and took out the book he had been so determined to give to Leila. Darwin's letters. You and your little blue ribbon, he thought. He laughed sadly at himself. It was not the right present for a girl. It had never been the right present for a girl. He let it fall from his fingers and right away it was kicked obliviously by one, then another then another set of dancing feet until it skidded into the gutter at the side of the road.

The sun was strong above him. The afternoon was going to be hot. He drank and quenched his thirst and behind him the crowd swelled and then James went out with it, letting himself be carried along.